ACCUSED

A True Story

ACCUSED

The World Will Rob Her...
God Will Restore Her

Will an innocent life be destroyed by a rogue prosecutor seeking the lime-light?

Renee Rose Relf

Tate Publishing & *Enterprises*

Published by Tate Publishing & Enterprises, LLC
127 E. Trade Center Terrace | Mustang, Oklahoma 73064 USA
1.888.361.9473 | www.tatepublishing.com

Tate Publishing is committed to excellence in the publishing industry. The company reflects the philosophy established by the founders, based on Psalm 68:11,
"The Lord gave the word and great was the company of those who published it."

Cover design by Kandi Evans
Interior design by Nathan Harmony

Published in the United States of America

ISBN: 978-1-60696-429-3
1. True Crime: General
2. Religion: Christian Life: Inspirational
09.02.27

Some of the incidents in this book are based on actual events and people in my life.

In instances where the identity of individuals was of concern, I have used pseudonyms to protect the privacy of the individuals in question.

Some sequences and details of events have been changed.

Acknowledgements

Thank you Lord for this wonderful opportunity to share your strength, love, grace, and hope with the world. You and you alone deserve all of the glory, honor, and praise for this book.

A heart filled with love for my loving and devoted husband—my best friend and soul mate. You patiently and lovingly navigated me from beginning to end on this project. I couldn't have done this without you. God gave me beauty for ashes. I never thought anything could be as beautiful as our love. ILUFM!

For my sister, Aly, I'm glad that God picked you to be my sister and that I got to pick you as my best friend! You carried quite a load through this trial and never complained. I love you.

A faithful thank you to my pastors, Grant Thigpen and Dwight Powell of New Hope Ministries, for preaching the infallible, inerrant Word of God and teaching me how to stand in faith on God's perfect promises. A special thank you to the teachers at the New Hope School of Ministries—you prepared me for spiritual warfare and for that I am eternally grateful.

To my Biblical Feasts teacher, Patricia Hilliard, thank you for the opportunity to learn the wonders that God has trusted you to share. You have been a tremendous blessing in my life.

A heartfelt thank you to Stacie Jennings and Vision Communications for seeing that my work had not touched all of the lives that God had intended. Thank you, Stacie, for your careful eye and your godly wisdom.

To my mother and father and my brothers and sisters, thank you for your love and support through the trials of my life. Thank you for your prayers and faith that with God nothing is impossible and for standing beside me and loving me through my darkest hour. Words cannot express my love and appreciation.

To all of the wonderful characters that God has blessed my life with, you know who you are!

This book is dedicated to my daughters—God's greatest and most precious gift. Your love inspires me to press onward and upward everyday. Never lose your God-given desire to accomplish great things.

I love you! Mom.

Do not be overcome by evil, but overcome evil with good.

Romans 12:21 (NIV)

Prologue

Paradise—it is so easy to recognize. The aquamarine water, the rhythm of the waves, and the palm trees swaying in the breeze are all part of what makes Naples, Florida, "paradise."

You can join the list of rich and famous that call Naples home, along with current and former CEOs, successful entrepreneurs, and anyone else with the right net worth. You too can buy a home nestled in one of the award-winning gated communities. And whether you fly to paradise a few times a year, enjoy the Naples "winter," or permanently settle into paradise for your retirement, you will enjoy the magnificent sunsets over the Gulf of Mexico, playing golf on the country's finest greens, and fishing the pristine backwater.

Evil—it is much more difficult to identify. It shows itself in our lives in the most unexpected ways and at the most unexpected times. Perhaps scariest of all, evil rises up in some of the most unexpected people: those you trust the most.

My parents instilled solid Christian values in all six of their children. They taught us to be independent, to be of good character, and to develop the fruits of the Spirit in our lives—joy, peace, patience, kindness, and love. They inspired us to work hard and to be trusted and loyal employees. Upon leaving home, I worked my way up the corporate ladder and received awards from the business and philanthropic communities.

I had much to be proud of in my career and a bright future ahead for my business and my family.

And then, the enemy, the accuser, set his sights to destroy a life.

To be falsely accused of a crime; to endure the full weight of the criminal justice system bearing down on you; to have to explain to your children, your husband, and your family that you did nothing wrong; to endure the humiliation of being arrested, booked, and processed, and then to have the local media waiting with cameras and microphones; to fear that you could be separated from your children, your husband, and your entire life for years.

Such an experience means nothing until you go through it yourself.

And I did.

This is the story of how business dealings led to false criminal accusations and how my faith delivered me from the evil I faced.

The power of the criminal justice system, as personified by an overzealous, self-righteous prosecutor, combined with the power of the media, which think nothing of destroying the hard-won reputations of hard-working, decent citizens, is unimaginably strong.

Fortunately, there is a greater power in my life, which guided and protected me through this excruciating period.

One

"They are going to arrest you both."

Our attorney, Wesley Driscoll, spoke those fateful words as he and his partners entered the conference room in their office in Miami where we had been waiting anxiously for his arrival. Everybody in Naples, Florida, where we lived, understood that a special prosecutor from Miami had been assigned to investigate bribery and influence peddling by real estate developers in our community. The special prosecutor, Martin Strickland, had already arrested two county commissioners, along with Phillip Durkee, a prominent real estate developer and the father of my business partner, Peter Durkee. Strickland would soon be reprimanded by the Florida Supreme Court for attempting to influence a judge—who was, in fact, his former girlfriend—in a murder case. He was a middle-aged man in a hurry, seeking to reestablish a reputation for himself as a crusader for justice. And he wanted to make his reputation by destroying ours.

Present at the meeting on this balmy October day in 2001 were Peter and myself, along with our new legal team. In addition to Wesley were Adam Woerner, the firm's top partner who typically handled high profile and RICO cases, and Matthew Stonesifer, an attorney and the business operations partner for the firm. Peter and I stared at each other, digesting the shocking news. What was this misguided loose cannon of a prosecutor doing? Would he really take the risk of ruining our lives without any evidence of a crime? The answer was obviously yes.

The thought of being arrested! The very idea pierced my heart. My mind raced at hyper speed. I had never committed a single criminal act. I didn't even break the speed limit! (Well, not by much, anyway). I was a wife, a mother, and a hard-working professional in the field of real estate development. After many years of faithful service, my boss, Peter Durkee, had recently made me an equity partner in Durkee Development Group, a developer of golf course communities in Naples. Now I was being accused of being a partner in crime, a corrupt individual, and an influence peddler who had sought to bring illegal pressure on government authorities with respect to a golf course development called Coliseum Golf.

My life had just spun totally out of control.

To his credit, Wesley was both strong and compassionate as he explained what was about to happen. "The prosecutor," he began, "will allow you to turn yourselves in tomorrow at 1:00 p.m. That way, we can avoid having all the media show up at your office."

I had no idea what Peter was thinking, but more thoughts than I could process began to run through my mind. How was I going to break this horrible news to my children? Lauren, at nineteen, needed to be able to defend her mother's honor. At that age, she should have been beginning her own adult life. How was she going to feel when she saw her mother going through such a terrible experience?

My younger child, Taylor, was only seven. How could she possibly grasp that her mother was going to be arrested for racketeering, conspiracy, and money laundering? How could she understand it when I, as an adult, couldn't begin to believe what was happening?

Until the ill-fated Coliseum Golf deal had come along four years earlier, my life had been very simple. Certainly, the Coliseum deal had been a complete financial and public relations disaster for everyone involved. However, there is a big difference between a business deal that fails and a criminal enterprise. What happened was entirely legal—it just wasn't successful from a business point of view. But the prosecutor, Strickland, must have viewed Coliseum Golf as his opportunity to propel himself into the limelight. Now, the statute of limitations—the deadline for making arrests related to the case—would expire in only twenty-four hours. If he was going to arrest me, it had to be by the end of the next day, and he had made the decision to put me in handcuffs and charge me with crimes I had not committed.

It had already been a horrible year. In February, our firm's reputation had taken a hit when Jack Wood, a man who had seemed like a gushing well of money—and our deliverer—a few years earlier, was arrested for running a $150 million Ponzi scheme. Then came the terrorist attacks on September 11, followed by their economic fallout: a free-fall in the stock market and a drop-off in sales in our latest development as potential homebuyers reeled from portfolio losses. Now, exactly thirty days after the September 11 tragedies, we would be arrested. Not the kind of thing that inspires confidence in our residents and contractors.

I couldn't speak. I couldn't breathe. The tears came faster and faster, and I felt as if I were going to faint. *Pull yourself together, Rose,* my inner voice cried out. Beside me, Peter remained equally silent.

"Listen," Wesley said compassionately, "I know you're both feeling helpless and a bit out of control. The best thing you can do is go home and get some rest. Do you have a local attorney who can stand with you during the arraignment?"

Arraignment? Suddenly it dawned on me—if I were going to be arrested, then I would also be arraigned. I'd have to stand in front of a judge, plead not guilty to charges of racketeering and corruption, and then be processed in jail like a common criminal. Again, my mind reeled.

I tried to pull myself together. *Think, Rose, think. Who's a good lawyer, someone I can trust?* My first thought was of Conrad Edmond, a young litigator who had proved his legal mettle defending our business interests in many tough situations over the years.

I was finally able to stop crying long enough to speak. "I think Conrad Edmond should be able to," I said. "He works for Evans and Dorne."

"That sounds fine," Wesley said. "We can call him and—"

Then another thought hit me. That firm was in enough trouble without having us as a client in this case. Andrew Shanahan, our real estate attorney, was also a partner at the law firm of Evans and Dorne.

Because Andrew was on the list of people to be arraigned tomorrow and agents of the Florida Department of Law Enforcement (FDLE) had searched his office, the firm's only interest was in vigorously fighting to defend Andrew's honor and the firm's reputation.

"Wait a minute," I exclaimed. "Conrad may not be the right person. The prosecutor is also arresting our real estate attorney, Andrew Shanahan, and he's one of Conrad's law partners." Evans and Dorne probably wanted to put us at arm's length; having one of its attorneys arraigned with us tomorrow was bad enough.

Wesley nodded. "I see your point," he said, frowning. "You're right; Conrad's not the right choice."

Adam Woerner, Wesley's top criminal defense attorney and the man single-handedly responsible for the current freedom of individuals involved in several of Miami's high-profile cases, spoke up for the first time.

"Can you believe the prosecutor is going after an attorney?" Adam asked indignantly.

I had to laugh. It was one thing to arrest a woman who had no criminal past. But to charge an attorney with a crime—that was clearly unthinkable!

"Rose, give Conrad a call," Adam continued, still indignant about the treatment of a brother attorney. "See if he knows someone with another firm who can stand with you. It's simple. He'll just walk with you up to the judge when you state your name and how you plead."

"Innocent," I blurted out.

Wesley placed his hand on my shoulder. "Of course you are," he said. "All of our clients are innocent."

The room erupted with laughter, but I didn't join in. There were too many haunting thoughts still swirling around in my head. Again I wondered, what do you tell your children at a time like this? Yes, of course my kids would understand I was innocent, but what horrible things would lay ahead for them, and for me? What would tomorrow at school be like for Taylor? How would her second-grade classmates react to seeing a picture of her mother on the front page of the newspaper, arrested for these terrible crimes? How would my husband deal with all of this? Who would tell my parents?

Wesley's voice interrupted my thoughts. "Before you both head back to Naples," he said, "we need to go over our retainer agreement. Our fee to accept the case is two hundred thousand dollars."

I blanched. Where was I going to come up with that kind of money?

Wesley, not unaware of the pained expression on my face, continued. "We will also need a fifty thousand dollar deposit that we will begin billing against," he said. "Our normal hourly fee is five hundred dollars per hour." Pointing at Adam, Wesley went on, "What we're going to do is have my partner Adam handle the case for Peter. Adam is phenomenal. If this thing goes to trial, which I doubt, you can decide then if you want to use me."

I nodded slowly, digesting all of this information.

Wesley continued. "The prosecutor had a problem with my firm representing both of you," he said, "so we'd like to suggest that Adam's brother Jason represent Rose. There is no reason for her arrest, and she will be the first one to have the charges dropped against her or get a plea deal. The prosecutor is just covering all of his bases because the statute of limitations is running out tomorrow."

"Jason is great," Adam said. "His writing skills and legal motions are unmatched in the criminal arena. Even after Rose is out of this, Peter, you and I can still use Jason. If this is okay with you, Rose, we'll plan a meeting with Jason next week. His fees are a lot more reasonable, too!"

The room again filled with laughter, and even I was able to muster a smile at that one.

"Jason will call you tomorrow to review his fee agreement," Adam said. "Your bond has been set at ten thousand dollars. We suggest you call a bail bondsman and ask him to meet you at your home tonight to take care of the details."

I shook my head in disbelief as my mind tried to process these facts. "Come on, Rosie," Peter said, rescuing me from my thoughts. "Let's go home."

Adam offered me a consoling hug and said, "Don't worry. This is all crap. The prosecutor has a bad reputation in Miami. They've just sent him to Naples to get rid of him for a while. We'll put him back in his cage in no time!"

"Thanks, Adam," I said, feeling numb. "Thanks, Wesley."

And with that, the meeting was over. The next challenge: facing my family and explaining this to my children. My nightmare had only begun.

Two

As Peter and I drove back to Naples, the silence in the car was as long as Alligator Alley, which stretched for eighty uninterrupted miles across the Florida Everglades from Miami to Naples, where we lived next door to one another. We were both feeling introspective at that moment. Both of us sat in the car wondering what had just happened and thinking how ridiculous the whole thing was. Peter finally broke the uncomfortable silence.

"Don't worry," he told me in his elegant Irish accent, which seemed especially reassuring right now. "We'll get through this. These charges are ridiculous. They'll never stick."

I wanted to believe him, but I was terrified, not just of a possible conviction, but of the ordeal that lay ahead.

"About tomorrow," Peter added. "This is just another test of character, and you know we've got more than our share of that."

I was about to respond when my cell phone rang. It was Frank Rupp, our chief financial officer, calling from my office. He sounded terrified.

"There are four FDLE agents at our office!" he exclaimed. "They have a search warrant, and they've forced all the employees out of the building. What's going on?"

I put my hand over the cell phone. "Peter," I said anxiously. "It's Frank Rupp. The agents have stormed our building. Call Conrad on your phone to see if he can go to our office right now!"

I turned back to Frank, trying to sound more in control of my emotions than I really was. "Frank, Peter is calling Conrad Edmond right now," I said. "You stay with the agents until he gets there. Watch what they're doing."

"Don't worry," Frank said, sounding reassured by my apparent confidence and self-control. "I got it covered," he added. "What's going on?"

I sighed. "Well," I said, "they've decided to arrest me, too."

"What?" he yelled. "I don't believe this!"

"Neither do I," I said. "Listen. Keep the troops calm—everything is going to be all right. Just pray."

"I will," Frank promised. "Hey, you know we love you and Peter, and we're all standing here, ready to fight."

"Frank, you're the best," I said. "Send everyone home. Call me when Conrad Edmond arrives."

"Okay," he said. "Drive safe."

I hung up the cell phone and shook my head. "Peter," I said, "I don't understand why they've decided to use force. We copied all they asked for and delivered it to their special office."

Peter stared blankly at the road as it stretched out before us. "They're trying to sensationalize this for the media," he explained. "It's going to be ugly tomorrow. You know how *The Collier Enquirer* loves dirt on developers. You'd better call home and let your family know what's happening."

"I don't know if I can contain myself," I said as I punched in the number for my sister, Aly, who was our marketing director. I could envision her standing in the parking lot with the rest of our bewildered staff while agents ransacked the office. She answered her cell phone on the first ring.

"Hi, Aly," I said cautiously.

"What the heck is going on?" she shouted in response. "Agents with guns have just escorted us out of the office building! Are you all right?"

"Yes, I'm okay," I told her, my voice shaking, and then my tears started again. I couldn't breathe. How could I drive the car?

"Hold on, Rose," Aly was saying. "Conrad Edmond is here. Do you want to talk to him?"

"I can't even talk to you!" I said, trying and failing to halt the flow of tears. "Just tell him to review the subpoena, and you try to keep the office running."

Aly started in with her inquisition voice. "How was Peter's meeting with Wesley Driscoll?"

I swallowed hard. "Well," I said, trying to sound brave, "it looks like I'm going to need an attorney, too."

"What!" she exclaimed, her shock registering over the phone.

"They've decided to arrest me, too," I said. "Can you believe that?"

"No!" she shouted. "Oh, my God! What did you have to do with any of those commissioners?"

Aly was referring to the county commissioners whom we allegedly had sought to influence illegally for favorable treatment on Coliseum Golf.

I shook my head sadly. "Nothing," I told her. I had met one of them, Eugene Gannon, only at a few meetings, and I had never even met the other three accused of racketeering and conspiracy. "I wouldn't know those commissioners if I tripped over one. But remember what Mom always said, 'Guilty by association.' That's what they're saying I am."

Aly was speechless.

"Listen," I continued, "I don't think I can bear to tell Mom and Dad. This is going to devastate them—their baby girl is about to be arrested for conspiracy to commit RICO!"

"What does that mean?" Aly asked.

"I'm not sure," I admitted. "We'll know more later. They wanted to arrest me for something, and the statute of limitations expires tomorrow. So it looks like they had to call it racketeering in order to have a reason to arrest me."

Aly responded, but I could barely focus on what she was saying, I was so overwhelmed by the reality I faced. As I understood the situation at that moment, I saw that the prosecutors had a real problem. They wanted to file charges against the commissioners for unlawful compensation, that is, taking bribes. But the problem was that the statute of limitations for the case—the very last moment by which prosecutors could file charges—ran out in less than twenty-four hours. So they needed an ostensibly legal way to circumvent the statute of limitations. Their solution was to call the whole thing racketeering and conspiracy. For complicated legal reasons, when prosecutors allege racketeering and conspiracy, the statute of limitations no longer applies. It didn't seem especially constitutional, but that was the way it was.

Congress passed RICO, Racketeer Influenced and Corrupt Organizations Act, in 1970. At the time, Congress's goal was to eliminate the ill effects of organized crime. To put it bluntly, RICO was intended to destroy the mafia. The law deemed a "criminal enterprise" any organization that committed a number of distinct criminal acts. However, in the thirty-plus years since its enactment, RICO had become a powerful tool for prosecutors, who essentially could charge any business or enterprise with conspiring to commit multiple crimes. Racketeering appeared to be one of the main charges against me.

"This is outrageous," Aly was saying. "This is just unbelievable and surreal. It doesn't make any sense."

I nodded. "I know, I have the exact feeling. It's so unbelievable. Mr. Toad's wild ride is about to begin! Please call Mom and Dad and break this to them the best you can. I'll be back in Naples in about an hour. I'll call you then. Hey, Aly, thanks for being strong."

"What are sisters for?" she asked. "I love you."

"I love you, too. Don't worry about anything. God will protect me from all this madness."

"I know," she said. "Drive carefully."

As I hung up the phone, Peter finally erupted. "Oh, for God's sake, Rose," he exclaimed. "When are you going to stop holding onto God? If he were real, you wouldn't be facing this whole mess!"

Peter and I had been on opposite sides of the faith debate for as long as I could remember. Actually, it wasn't really a debate. If he didn't want to believe, that was his business—and, as far as I was concerned, his loss too.

"Peter," I said calmly, "because of my faith in him, I can face what's going to happen tomorrow."

Peter rolled his eyes. "Whatever. I'd better call home. You should, too."

He was right. I reached for my cell phone again and punched in my husband's number. "Hi, Zack, it's Rose."

"Hey," he said. "How's Peter holding up?"

Peter? Why is he asking about Peter instead of me? True, Zack and I had been having serious marital problems for some time, but couldn't he have had the decency to ask how his wife was doing before he asked about anyone else?

"As well as can be expected," I replied, trying to keep the hurt and disappointment out of my voice. "The bigger question is, how am I holding up?"

"You?" Zack asked, surprised but sarcastic. "Is driving Alligator Alley scaring you?"

I shook my head. "No, it's not the Alley," I said. "The prosecutor has decided to arrest me, too. Are the girls there?"

That got Zack's attention. "Wait a minute!" he exclaimed. "What are they arresting you for?"

"Oh, nothing, really," I said, responding to his sarcasm. "Just conspiracy to commit RICO, whatever that means," I told him.

I could hear his sharp intake of breath.

"I want to tell Lauren and Taylor myself when I get home," I added. "I'll be there in about an hour."

"Do you realize what this means?" Zack asked, stunned.

"No, I can't process anything right now. I feel sick."

"Well, what are we supposed to do?" he asked, dismay evident in his tone.

"Call a bail bondsman," I said, not believing I was referring to such a person with regard to myself. "My bond has been set at ten thousand dollars, and we'll have to use the house as security. Peter is using Bob's Bail Bonds. Call them up and set up a time to get this done tonight. I don't want to spend any more time in jail tomorrow than I have to."

I shook my head in disbelief again. I couldn't believe I was going to jail.

"This sucks," Zack commented blithely. "Our house? You had better not skip town! Ha ha ha."

I rolled my eyes. "I'll see you when I get home," I said.

"How did Zack take the news?" Peter asked.

"Well, he must be in shock," I said. "He didn't ask too many questions. He just hoped I wouldn't skip out on my bail. He'd hate to lose the house!"

"Your marriage is already on the rocks, Rose," Peter said, stating the obvious. "This is either going to turn it around or end it for good."

"Peter," I said sadly, "I can't even think about that now. I'm worried about Lauren and Taylor. Taylor is just a little girl. How can I explain this terrible mistake to her?"

Peter gave me a confident look. "You'll find a way," he said.

Minutes seemed like hours until we reached the end of Alligator Alley on our way back to Naples. My entire life, my business, and my reputation—they were all about to change forever. I was crying hard again, to the point of hyperventilating. *Why is this happening to me?* I asked myself silently. *What kind of test is God putting me through?*

Exit 111 was just ahead. *Pull yourself together,* I told myself. *Walking in the house hysterical will not make the girls feel like everything is going to be okay. Deep breath. There. I think I have control, at least for now.*

We reached my house. "Let's break the news to our families," I told Peter. "Then we'll get back together around nine tonight."

Peter nodded good-bye. He got out of the car and headed to his house next door.

As I stood alone at the door, I cried out, "Lord, I really need you now. The lives of my babies are about to be shaken to the very core. Give me strength. Give me hope."

Three

At that moment, Taylor opened the door and shrieked, "Mommy, you're home! I love you, Mommy!"

Her little arms wrapped around my neck. "Why are you crying, Mommy, are you hurt?"

"No, Taylor," I said, trying to regain control over my emotions. "Mommy is okay, and I have a story that I need to tell you. Do you want to hear it now?"

Taylor broke into a broad grin. "Oh yes, I love stories, Mommy!" she exclaimed as we entered the house and went into the living room.

"Sit on my lap," I said. Taylor placed her two little hands on my cheeks, and as tears welled in my eyes, she looked deeply into them. She said, "Mommy, don't you cry. I love you."

"I know, baby, I know," I told her, trying unsuccessfully to hold back my tears. "Are you ready for the story now?"

"Yep!" Taylor exclaimed confidently.

I tried to think of a way to explain this horrible situation in a way that would make sense to her seven-year-old mind. "You know," I began, "sometimes when Mommy finds a drink spilled, I'll say, 'Taylor, did you do this?'"

Taylor was watching me intently, trying to figure out where this was going. This was clearly not a story like any she had ever heard before.

I continued, "And you say, 'No, Mommy,' but all of the things surrounding the spill—the cup, your toys, the water on the floor—it all makes it look like you did it. And Mommy will send you to your room for a time-out, because I think you are telling a fib."

Taylor, to her credit, got a sense of where I was going. "Yep," she said, looking serious, "even though I didn't do it."

I nodded. "Right!" I exclaimed. "And then Daddy or Lauren comes into the room and admits that they spilled it, and Mommy feels so bad because I blamed you and you didn't do it."

Taylor nodded, never taking her eyes off mine, fascinated by this story of justice, and clearly intrigued as to why I was telling it just now.

"Then Mommy has to come to Taylor," I continued, "and say, 'I'm sorry for blaming you for something you didn't do.' And you say, 'I told you so!' And Mommy feels so bad that she blamed you for something that you didn't do."

Taylor grinned at her vindication from the imaginary accusation.

"Well," I said, taking in a deep breath, "something just like that is happening to Mommy. A man thinks I did something that I didn't do, and tomorrow I have to go to a courthouse and tell a judge I didn't do anything wrong. You'll see Mommy's picture and Peter's picture on the news and in the newspaper. Because Mommy didn't do anything wrong, that man will have to say he is sorry to Mommy."

Taylor looked pensive. "It's okay, Mommy. I'll protect you from that bad man."

What an amazing child, I thought. "Give Mommy a big bear hug; it's time for bed."

Zack was standing in the doorway. "Rose, the bondsman is here," he said flatly.

I sighed. "I'll be right there, Zack," I said. "Will you tuck Taylor into bed?"

I gave Taylor a hug and a kiss and headed for the kitchen.

The bail bondsman looked like a typical Deep South redneck: tight blue jeans, a T-shirt that stretched across his expanding potbelly, and a proudly displayed tattoo on his right forearm.

"Hi, Rose," he said in a friendly way. "I'm Robert. I know you've had a pretty tough day, and I'd like to explain a little bit about what's going to happen tomorrow."

I nodded, wanting him to get it over with as quickly as possible. I invited him to sit down in the formal dining room. I felt that if I kept him out of our family area, this horrific violation of my reputation somehow would not infiltrate my home. I offered him a Coke, but he didn't want one, so I got myself one and joined him at the dining table.

When we were settled, Robert continued, "The judge will call your name. You will stand, and then the judge will ask you to approach the bench. Do you have an attorney?"

I nodded. "Yes, I have a 'stand-in' until my real attorney is available."

"What is your attorney's name?" Robert asked.

"Jason Woerner," I said.

Robert nodded again. "He'll need to copy us on any travel arrangements, hearings, and the trial. Anyway, the bailiff will swear you in, ask your name, and ask you how you plead."

"Innocent, of course," I insisted.

Robert nodded and smiled warmly. He was nice, I had to admit. My initial judgment of him as a typical redneck gave way to a sense that I had someone decent on my side in this mess.

"Then you'll be escorted by a female officer," he said. "She will pat you down. You will need to be mentally prepared for this, Rose. This is not going to be pleasant."

The thought of going through the booking process, so familiar from a million TV cop dramas, suddenly nauseated me.

"I think I'm going to be sick," I said. "Will you excuse me?"

Before Robert could answer, I ran to the bathroom and heaved my guts into the toilet bowl, thinking of my sweet baby Taylor saying, "It's okay, Mommy." When I had finished vomiting, I told myself to pull it together. I looked into the mirror and told myself, *You can do this. You are strong, determined, and full of faith.* I remembered Romans 8:31, which says, "If God be for me, who can stand against me?"

I was about to find out.

"Are you okay?" Robert asked when I returned. "I know this is very difficult. We will make this as painless as possible. As I was saying, after they pat you down—"

I interrupted him. "Excuse me, what do you mean, 'pat me down'?"

"They'll have you take off any loose clothing, put your hands on the wall, and spread your legs," Robert said as diplomatically as possible.

"Like on TV?" I said, and I could feel the bile rising again.

Robert nodded. "Yep, just like on TV," he said as sympathetically as possible. "Make sure you don't wear any jewelry or belts. Nothing in your hair. It will only slow down your processing, and you'll have to claim the items after you have been released from the cell. All of the media will be there, so you want the quickest exit possible, that is, unless you want to be on the cover of the newspaper tomorrow."

"No, I'll pass on that," I said, trembling at the thought of it. *Couldn't this nightmare happen in private? Why does my photo have to be splashed across the front page of the newspaper?*

"Can you tell me exactly what 'processed' means?" I asked, trying to shift my thinking to some other aspect of the ordeal.

"Sure," Robert said. "First they'll fingerprint you, and then they'll take your mug shot. After that, they'll fill out the arrest record for you. The important thing is to stay calm, and we'll have you out in about an hour or two at the most."

I sighed. I just could not believe this nightmare was happening to me.

"Okay, now if you'll just sign this paper," Robert said, taking a document out of his briefcase, "I will file a lien on your home to secure your bond. If you travel outside of Naples, you need to call my office. Basically, we need to be aware of your whereabouts at all times. Clear?"

I nodded. "Clear," I said.

"We'll see you tomorrow. Try to get some sleep. You'll want to look good for your pictures he added with a mischievous smile.

I didn't know whether to laugh or cry. "Good night," I said. "Thanks for coming out here tonight; I really appreciate it."

"No problem. I'm headed next door to process Peter's paperwork next. Have a good night."

After Robert departed, I found Zack, who was in the living room watching TV. "Zack," I said, "can you get your cousin Skip on the phone? He's a police officer. Maybe he can tell me more about what's going to happen tomorrow."

Skip was my only connection in law enforcement. We saw him occasionally at family birthday parties, holidays, and similar events. He was a career police officer and had served some time with the Drug Enforcement Agency. He is not a talkative person, and his general demeanor is that everyone is guilty of something; he just hasn't figured it out yet.

Zack looked pained to be taken away from his La-Z-Boy recliner, but he was good enough to get Skip on the phone.

"Hi, Skip," I said, when Zack passed me the phone. "I guess Zack told you how my day has gone so far. Can you tell me why they're charging me with RICO?"

"Basically," Skip began, "anytime a cop has charges that under normal circumstances won't stick, because of statute of limitations or something like that, they throw it into this RICO charge. It's crap, but it's a way for them to buy time and hopefully get you to make a deal. You know, testify against the big guys to save yourself. Listen, I'll call my buddies at the jail. We'll make sure they treat you right tomorrow."

"Thanks, Skip, I really appreciate it," I said as my tears started to flow again. I glanced at Zack, who was watching me with a strange look, as if I were a character in a TV police drama and not his wife. "I'm sorry," I told Skip. "I can't stop crying, this is so crazy. Racketeering? That's mob stuff—prostitution, drugs. Dear God, I'm as far away from any of that as the man in the moon."

Before Skip could answer, I heard Zack calling out that Peter and his wife, Zelenka, wanted to see us next door at their house.

"Skip, I gotta go. Thanks again for your support and the call to the jail. Maybe I'll get the red carpet treatment."

"Keep your chin up," Skip said, "and get some sleep."

"Right," I said.

Zack and I headed next door. As we walked across their lanai, I saw Peter standing in his living room, looking distraught. *What more could have happened to him*? I wondered.

Peter pointed to their formal living room for us to be seated. I guess Peter had the same feeling I did: keep this horror out of the family area at all cost.

"Apparently, Rose," Peter said, "Zack and Zelenka feel that you and I are having an affair."

"What?" I shouted in disbelief. "This is ridiculous! Where is this coming from?"

"I got a call from your office," Zelenka explained in her heavy Russian accent. "A woman said she was sure that there was more to your partnership than just business."

I was stunned. "And Zelenka, you believe that?" I asked angrily.

"I don't know what to believe," Zelenka said.

"What about you, Zack?" I turned to my husband. "What do you believe?"

Zack shrugged. It didn't look as if it mattered much to him either way.

"I don't know," he said, his tone noncommittal. "You guys do spend a lot of time together."

I shook my head, as if somehow I could make this whole nightmare go away. "We're business partners!" I exclaimed. "We have two real estate communities and run two golf courses, and we've got a third community under construction!" What did they expect, that we'd run our business by walkie-talkie? "Listen carefully," I continued. "Number one, my faith and commitment to God would never allow me to be unfaithful. Number two, well, Peter, you may have been hurt enough today, but you're not my type."

Peter laughed, which helped break the tension to a small degree for everyone else, but not for me.

Angrily, I turned to Peter's wife and my husband. "Zelenka, Zack, I am disappointed in you both, that you would believe strangers. You don't even know who called you! This is more than I can take today. Being arrested for a crime that I didn't commit is one thing. Being accused by my husband and my partner's wife of committing adultery. Let me just say this . . . " I was getting angrier by the second. "I have never and will never be unfaithful to my husband. Never. Good night!" I shouted as I jumped up from the chair to head home.

Now Peter seemed as incensed about the whole thing as I was. "Rose, hold on a minute," he began. "What you and I need to do right now is make sure that Zack and Zelenka are satisfied that we're telling the truth. We need their support tomorrow. All the press needs is more trash to print about us. Are you two satisfied that Rose and I are being truthful?"

I was just disgusted. "Do you want to subject me to a polygraph?" I asked Zack and Zelenka. "I'd certainly pass with flying colors. Maybe you could split the cost with the prosecutor!"

Zack shook his head. "Rose," he said, "now is not the time for your sarcasm."

"Sarcasm?" I practically shrieked. "I was dead serious!"

"Enough," Zack said wearily.

"I'm going to take a shower now," I said, trying to calm down from this latest outrage. "What is the plan for tomorrow?"

"Why don't you come over here around nine?" Peter said. "We can make some personal calls to our bankers, financial partners, and close friends," he added. "I'd rather they hear it from us before they pick up the newspaper. Try to get some rest. You look like crap."

"Thanks, Peter," I said bitterly. "Hit me one more time when I'm down. Good night."

Standing for what seemed like hours in the shower, trying to absorb the day's events did not seem to provide any clarity or peace. Prayer was my only escape. *Thank you, Lord, that although I walk through the valley of the shadow of death, I will fear no evil for you are with me.* Total exhaustion finally forced me into sleep. Nightmares of the day haunted me all night. I fell in and out of sleep, clock watching at 2:00 a.m., 3:00 a.m., and 4:00 a.m. When would this endless night be over?

Four

I was still in bed, tossing and turning, when the phone rang around 7:30. It was Aly.

"Did I wake you?" she asked.

"It's been impossible to sleep," I said, shaking my head to try to clear it. "I'm going to take Taylor to school and spend a few minutes with her teacher. You know how mean children can be."

"Mom, Dad, and I are going to go with you to the arraignment," Aly said. "I think that since you and I look so much alike, we should dress identically today, so as to confuse the press."

That idea provided me with my first moment of relief since this whole ordeal had begun. "Aly, that is a great idea. What are you thinking about wearing?"

"How about a white shirt, khaki pants, and a blue blazer?" she asked.

I grinned. "Great!" I exclaimed. "That's one less thing I've got to decide on today. Too bad my hair is shorter than yours."

"How about a wig?" she asked.

I laughed aloud. Finally.

Living right next door to Peter had its pluses and minuses. Peter would walk in while we were having dinner, pull up a chair, grab a fork, and begin sharing from anyone's plate and start talking about anything to do with the business—whatever was on his mind. This was a good thing, because sometimes business decisions moved quickly and we didn't have to wait for "business hours" to discuss matters. The downside: there was no time off from work; it truly was 24/7, and everyone in my house knew everything about my business. Children deserve better than that. On the other hand, after the arrest, it was very convenient to be able to walk next door when we needed support for our families or to stand outside and talk when we feared that our phones were bugged. This morning, with so little sleep, I was grateful only to have to walk next door.

"Good morning, Zelenka, Peter," I began, thinking about the bizarre accusation of the night before. "Have you started the calls yet?"

Peter shook his head. "No, I wanted you to be here, too. Where should we start?"

"I think that since we owe thirty million dollars to Investors Federal, they may appreciate a personal call," I said. "How's this for a start?" I pretended I was dialing the lender's number. "Good morning. Listen, Peter and I want you to know that the development is doing great, sales and closings are on target. But you might want to get the paper today. We're being arrested on RICO charges. Don't worry, though, it's all crap. It'll blow over in no time. While I've got you, could we have an advance? Our upfront legal fees are over two hundred thousand dollars!"

Peter returned a smile. "It looks like you've recovered your sense of humor," he said.

"Yeah, I figured it's the only way we're going to make it through this mess."

I then thought about Richard Zuker, one of our primary investors, and something of a bottom-feeder when it came to making deals.

"Zuker is going to have a cow," I began. "With his twenty-five percent finance charge on the equity in the deal, maybe we should just hand him the keys and wish him good luck."

Peter laughed, but then he looked serious. "Rosie, it's at times like these when we find out who our true friends are. When you're being blackballed by the government and the press is hot on your tail, you'd be surprised by how many of our 'friends' will hide in the hills. You know the whole guilt by association thing."

I shook my head. "I'm not sure if I can take much more personal disappointment today," I said.

"You'd better prepare yourself," Peter said. "Today is guaranteed to be chock full of crap."

"You're so eloquent, Peter," I said wryly.

"Maybe we should ask Zuker for the upfront fees to the lawyers," he said.

"Can't hurt to ask," I said. "All he can say is 'No.' You call him."

Peter dialed his number. "Hi, Richard," Peter began. "It's Peter and Rose. How's it going?" Peter hit the speakerphone button so I could hear Richard's response.

"Lousy," Richard said. "The luxury boat business is falling off a cliff, the stock market is killing me, and you people haven't had a closing since the World Trade Center attack. What else could go wrong?"

Peter and I exchanged glances. "Well, brace yourself," Peter said. "Rose and I are going to be arrested today at 1:00 p.m."

"What!" Richard exclaimed. "That's really gonna hurt sales." Not much sensitivity to our personal plights, but that was Richard for you.

"What the heck are we going to do?" he continued. "Maybe you two should look for somebody to take me out ASAP."

"That may be more difficult after today," Peter said. "Not too many people will lend money to accused felons, Richard. Look we really need your support here. All the press needs is a reason to start bashing Durkee Development Group Communities, and we'll sink like a rock. The best thing for you to do is to write a letter to the residents. Tell them that you're the financial partner, and their investment is safe. I'm sure some residents will freak out, thinking that if we go to jail, who will run the golf course and club? We've prepared a letter that describes our management team and how capable they are of running all three clubs if we died or, God forbid, ended up in jail."

There was a long pause as Richard digested the news. "This is horrible," Richard finally said. "One more business venture that's killing me."

Again, his sensitivity to our predicament was underwhelming. This was clearly the wrong moment to broach the subject of his covering our legal fees.

"Listen, guys, I've got to give this some thought. I'll call you tomorrow, okay?"

"Thanks, Richard," Peter said and hung up.

Peter and I sat in silence for a while, thinking about the call to Richard. "Wow, Peter, did you feel the love?" I asked.

"See?" Peter said, pouring himself another cup of coffee. "That's just what I was telling you. You'll see that most people will only care about how it affects them and not give a second thought about how we must be feeling. I'll call him tomorrow and ask him to lend us the retainer. He'll want us to be concentrating on business, not on attorney fees."

"I hope so."

Peter checked his watch. "We've got to head down to the courthouse in about an hour."

"I'm going to see what I can do with my face," I said. "It looks like I'm carrying luggage under my eyes."

Peter laughed. "We'll all drive down in the Suburban," he said.

Back at my house, Zack was waiting for me in the kitchen.

"How are you feeling, Rose?" he asked.

"Well," I replied as honestly as I could, "as good as can be expected."

"I'm sorry about last night," Zack said. "I got sucked into the rumor mill with Zelenka. I know you better than to think you would be fooling around—with Peter. Ha ha ha."

I ignored the inference that I might have been fooling around with anybody else. I didn't see what was so funny about the whole thing, to be honest. My head was already swirling with anxiety about the day. I did not want to engage in defending myself at home for another "crime" that I did not commit. My silence must have made Zack uncomfortable.

"I'm going to get ready now; you should, too," I said, leaving the kitchen.

"Yes, ma'am, you're in charge," he called after me, sarcastic as ever.

"I'm not biting this morning," I called back at him. "I've got more important battles to fight today."

Thank God for walk-in closets. Just what I need this morning, more baggage to take with me to the courthouse. Shouldn't your husband be standing by your side at a time like this*? It looks like I'm on my own again. He'll go just for show.* That's all we'd really had for the past five years—a show, not a real marriage. Thank God for my family, my children. Businesses, marriage, freedom—are they all they're really cracked up to be? Today, they really seemed overrated.

"Rose, are you almost ready?" Zack called out impatiently.

"I'll be out in a few minutes," I replied.

"Aly and your parents are here," he said, joining me at the bedroom closet. "Are they riding with us?"

"No," I said, choosing my outfit for the day to match Aly's. "They'll follow us down."

"Okay, then let's roll," Zack said excitedly.

"You make this sound like fun," I said. "I feel nauseous. Maybe we should bring a bucket in the car in case I puke."

"You'll be fine," Zack said dismissively. "Come on. Who are you calling at a time like this?" Zack snapped.

"Hold on a minute, Lauren." I covered the receiver of the phone so that she wouldn't hear my anger. "Zack, I am on the phone with Lauren to let her know what to expect... I'm sure that this will make the five o'clock news.

"I'm sorry, Lauren, we are on our way to the courthouse now. Don't worry about me. I've got God on my side." Saying those words gave me the peace that I needed at that moment.

"Mom, I love you, and I know this is all a huge mistake. Like you always tell me, Mom, 'this too shall pass.' I love you; call me when you're free." Lauren tried to make me smile. I did. I closed my cell phone and joined Zack for what would be the ride of a lifetime.

Five

As the four of us—Peter, Zelenka, Zack, and I—walked up the stairs of the Collier County Courthouse, the area was filled with TV news cameramen, reporters, and photographers. Caught in a sea of lights, some of them trained steadily on us, some flashing demonically, I tried to be stoic and look straight ahead, but I felt my guts churning. "Oh, my God, how did they all know this was happening?" I whispered to Peter.

"Just walk fast," Peter responded. "Don't speak to anyone, Rose. Just get inside the building.

As we made our way up the stairs to the second floor courtroom, more reporters, more cameras, and more microphones were shoved in our faces.

"I'm going to be sick," I said, ducking into the restroom. Zelenka came in behind me, and I was relieved that no mention was made of the previous night's heated exchange between the four of us. I splashed cold water on my face and realized I was trembling uncontrollably.

"Snap out of it, Rose," Zelenka said as she grabbed both my shoulders and shook me. "You need to pull yourself together. Do you want all of Naples to see you like this? No? Then breathe deeply, put on some lipstick, and hold your head up high. Remember, you are not guilty of any crime. Pretend you're a movie star on your way to a Hollywood premiere. Head high, smile!"

Somehow that made the difference. "Let's go," Zelenka said. "The sooner you can blast past the herd of reporters, the better."

I left the ladies' room and found myself again amid the snapping of the cameras, the reporters' microphones shoved in my face, the fast-flying questions. *Get through that door, get through that door—maybe the press will be prohibited from having cameras in the courtroom.*

No such luck. Just as I broke through the first set of reporters, I saw yet another group slinking around inside the courtroom, waiting for us to take our seats so they could get the best shots for tonight's TV news. They had such long telephoto lenses that I was certain they could see the hair in my nose if they got the right angle.

Of all people, it was my husband who came to my rescue. "I'll block you, Rose," he said.

"What?" I asked, not comprehending what he was talking about.

"As they try to get a good shot of you," he said, "I'll lean up in back to block their shot."

"Thanks, Zack," I said, touched by the gesture.

Somehow, they managed to get some tight shots anyway, and now Zack would be infamous, too.

Suddenly I heard a deep voice boom, "All rise!"

Oh, I think I'm going to puke—breathe, breathe, I told myself. The deep voice continued, "The Honorable Judge Faye Barrett presiding."

I felt shaky on my feet and extremely relieved when I heard the judge say, "Please be seated."

The prosecutor, the notorious Martin Strickland, was pacing the courtroom, eyeing his prey, sporting a tie with a pattern of handcuffs, of all things, and offering a smirk to all of the reporters. He was a showman, ready to give Naples some real Miami-style justice.

"Your Honor," Strickland began, "the defendants Delaney, Wood, Shubert, Shanahan, Durkee, and Visconti are here for their arraignment. The charging document clearly outlines the charges against each of them."

The judge studied Strickland dispassionately. "Thank you," she began, and she turned to face us. "I'm going to call each of you, swear you in, and read the charges filed against you. You will then enter your plea and be processed. Before we do that, let's figure out the schedule for the next hearing. Gentlemen, how do November and December look?"

"Your Honor," Strickland replied, "since most of the attorneys are

Jewish, Christmas week would be wide open." He laughed out loud, but no one in the courtroom dared join him.

"Thank you for your flexibility, Mr. Strickland," the judge replied evenly, "but I take that time to be with my family."

"Of course, Your Honor, of course," Strickland said solicitously, his first foray into courtroom humor having gone down in flames. And then the judge began to call up the defendants.

I was the third one called. When I heard my name, my knees went weak, and as I stood up, the sound of all the cameras snapping literally made me dizzy. *It's okay, Rose,* I told myself, *just look at the judge.*

"State your full name," the judge said.

"Rose Visconti," I replied in a shaky voice.

"Your age?"

"Forty-one," I said, wondering if that was really necessary.

"You're being charged with conspiracy to commit racketeering. How do you plead?"

"Innocent," I said as firmly as I could.

"Thank you," the judge said to me. "Bailiff, please escort Mrs. Visconti for processing."

The side door of the courtroom opened, and there stood a woman known to all as "Large Marge." She was in charge of the frisking process. To the sound of clicking cameras, the bailiff escorted me out of the courtroom and into the care of Large Marge.

Thank God my bondsman had prepared me for this moment. The courtroom door slammed behind me.

"Put your hands up to the wall and spread your feet shoulder distance apart," Marge said calmly. My arrest might have been a big deal to me, but to Marge, I was just another prisoner. No big deal.

I certainly wasn't about to argue with her. She put on latex gloves with a frightening snap and began pressing into my body—first my inner thighs, then my sides.

"Are you wearing an underwire bra?" she asked.

"Yes," I said.

"I'm going to have to press my hands all the way around that, okay?"

I shrugged. "Sure, what could be worse?"

She finished frisking me and then said, "Let's go, and stay to your far left. There are cameras along the hallway that need to record you."

I dubbed the corridor that connected the courthouse to the jail "The Green Mile" because it seemed to go on forever. Finally we reached a group of police officers that were pals of Zack's cousin Skip. They must have recognized me, because they gave me a warm welcome, asking, "Are you here for a tour?"

I grinned. The comic relief was most welcome. "Well, I guess you could say that."

"No, she's here for booking," Marge said humorlessly. One officer looked as surprised as I did. I guess Skip hadn't gotten through to all of them.

"I'll take it from here," one of the cops said.

"Thanks," I said. "Have a blessed day," I told Marge, who just winced, turned, and departed.

I was led into a small waiting room with linoleum floors, a metal folding chair, and a folding table. I later learned that this was the interrogation room.

"Mrs. Visconti," the police officer told me, "it's time for your mug shot."

"Do you have a mirror?" I asked, trying to take the tension out of the situation for me.

"Please, ma'am," the officer said, somewhat embarrassed, "just step up to that black line."

I was ready with my big smile.

"Ma'am," he said, "no smiling in your mug shot."

I couldn't help smiling, I was so nervous.

"I have big teeth," I said as I heard the camera click. Since I would have to live with that photo being printed a thousand times on the front page of *The Collier Enquirer*, I was determined to muster the best smile I could under the circumstances.

Fingerprinting was not the TV show version of rolling fingers on ink and paper. Now it was like an X-ray, no muss, and no fuss. After the processing was completed, the officer said, "Have a seat right here. We just need to review your bail bond and get some information."

The interrogation room where I started was now occupied, presumably with one of my fellow defendants, so I was escorted to a holding cell.

"As soon as your bond is posted, we'll let you know. Sit tight."

The door slammed shut. I couldn't believe I was alone in a jail cell. The cell was cold. The stainless steel bench was unwelcoming. As I sat and absorbed my surroundings, I noticed the icy metal toilet/sink combination jutting from the wall. How could anyone use this? Other holding cells had a perfect view of my cell; I would wet myself before I would use that toilet. Raging shouts of drunken prisoners flirting with anyone passing by rang out across the uncarpeted halls. *What is taking so long?* I wondered.

At that moment, a police officer walked by. "Excuse me, sir," I said, "can you update my status?"

"What is your bondsman's name?"

"Robert," I told him.

"No, what company is he with?"

"Oh, my God, I can't remember," I said, embarrassed. "I'm not sure he ever told me the company's name."

The officer started to name a few, but none of them sounded familiar. What a terrible feeling it was not to be able to recollect the sole link I had to freedom.

"You'll just have to be patient," he said.

"Do you have any magazines?" I asked.

He stared at me in disbelief. "Are you kidding, lady? This is jail, not a beauty salon!"

And off he went. Suddenly the reality of my situation caught up with me. *I'm in jail!* I had been accused of being part of a criminal enterprise—a huge conspiracy in the mind of the Collier County government that had been created to defraud the citizens of the just services of the county commissioners.

"Trust me," I heard a voice say. "Though you can't see me, trust me. The road may be steep, but you can trust me. Let me lead, trust me."

My God was calling out to me in my time of need. He did hear my prayer and was there to comfort me. I sang "Trust Me" by Crystal Lewis aloud and found the peace of God flowing over me. *I can make it through this trial,* I told myself. I imagined how Jesus felt when he was being falsely accused. This was my faith promise; this was my faith growth time that only personal trials can produce.

Six

Minutes seemed like hours. Finally, the police officer came by and said the words I had been waiting anxiously to hear: "You're free to go, ma'am. Just need you to go claim your personal effects."

I headed out of the cell, grateful to God and my bail bondsman, whatever company he represented. Just then, the mirrored sliding doors of the holding area opened wide and the flashes of what seemed like a hundred cameras went off like the Fourth of July. They had been waiting in line for that perfect shot for the six o'clock news and the front page of the next day's newspaper. Zack and Aly rushed in to shield me from the horror, Aly flashing a smile to distract them as best she could.

"Hurry, the car is running—it's just outside," Aly told me. "Come quick."

We fled the building as quickly as possible toward the waiting car. Zack swung the door closed behind me, jumped into the driver's seat, Aly into the passenger seat and we sped off. My ordeal was over, at least for now.

"Well, how was it on the inside?" Zack asked, trying hard to lighten the mood.

"I'm glad to be out!" I exclaimed, and now, relieved that the arraignment was over, I sent words tumbling out of my mouth. "It was a very humbling experience. I've never had a speeding ticket, much less a mug shot and fingerprinting. You just don't realize how precious your freedom is until you've lost it. I'm now a number in the criminal justice system.

"Let's go home and catch the news," I continued, my strength somehow returning. "I can't wait to see how they present the story. Did you realize that I'm the only female in the entire mess? Maybe they'll make me the brains of the operation. No, I'd rather be the beauty." The words continued pouring out of me—I was so thankful to be free.

"That should be easy," Zack said, "looking at the lineup of characters."

"Thanks for the vote of confidence." I said to him, rolling my eyes.

"You're too sensitive," he said, not taking his eyes off the road. "Lighten up!"

Yeah, right, I thought. *Lighten up? He isn't the one who has been to jail!*

"After you did your deal in front of the judge," Zack continued, "Craig Delaney was up next. Did you hear that he pled guilty?"

I was shocked. Craig, a former county manager, had left that job to become the president of our real estate development firm. "Are you kidding?" I asked. "Guilty of what?"

"He gave a statement to the press," Zack explained. "Evidently, he said there was an appearance of impropriety when he gave pay raises to top county officials prior to coming to work for you and Peter. He also said he couldn't afford the legal costs or the emotional drain that fighting would cost his family. You know what attorneys say, 'You're innocent until proven indigent.' I guess he doesn't want to know what indigent feels like."

Under other circumstances, we might have laughed. But not today.

Zack continued. "Craig also said that since he was a public official, his attorney only gave him a fifty-fifty success rate on beating the charges."

I shook my head. "That stinks," I commented. "Who recommended his attorney?"

"I don't know," Zack said.

"Craig didn't commit any crime," I said. "He's got more integrity than anyone I know."

This case should be a wake-up call for everyone in the county, I thought. *This prosecutor Strickland, with the unbridled power of a one-man grand jury, has essentially told us all, "You are guilty until you can prove yourself innocent." Well, let the games begin. I don't think this is how our forefathers envisioned justice.*

"You know, Rose," Zack was saying, "maybe by pleading he can put this behind him."

"What do you mean, Zack?" I replied, surprised. "Behind him? This is just the beginning. The *Collier Enquirer* has attacked Craig in the paper as county manager for ten years. Don't think for a minute that they won't have a field day with this one. I can just see the headlines in tomorrow's paper—'Boy Wonder Hits Bottom.'"

Poor Craig, I thought. *Who knew when he resigned as county manager five years ago to come to work as president of our company that he would be in the very jail that he built, being fingerprinted as a common criminal.*

"Zack," I said, "we need to swing by the office on the way home. I'd like to see what kind of mess the FDLE agents left behind."

Zack glanced at me. "Are you sure you're up for that?" he asked.

"Yeah, I need to see that all I've worked for isn't really lost, that this has all been a very bad dream."

"I wish it was," Zack said as he headed the car toward my office. "Rose, I tried really hard to confuse the reporters and photographers as we exited the jail, but I don't know if it worked. We'll have to watch the news at six to see for sure."

My heart began to race as we turned the corner into The Preserve, the 575-acre luxury golf course community where our office building was located. We had worked so hard for so long and now everything we had struggled to build seemed to be shattered in one afternoon.

"Durkee Development Group" was in huge letters on the front of the building. Zack's first suggestion was to take down the name "Durkee," because we didn't need to call attention to ourselves at this point.

"I think Peter's suffering enough right now," I said. "Removing his last name from our building may be another blow to his ego. If he feels that his name is a problem, then we'll take it down."

As we entered the lobby, I was relieved to see that the building did not look like it had just been the host site for an episode of *Cops*. My sense of relief quickly vanished as I opened my office door and realized the boxes that I had prepared for the special prosecutor were gone. File drawers had been left open, and some very important files clearly were missing. As I scanned my office further, I panicked. My computer was gone. My personal files and my QuickBooks files were on there. How could I pay my bills?

I turned around so quickly that I ran into Zack, who was standing directly behind me. "Whoa, where are you going?" Zack inquired.

"They've taken my computer!" I exclaimed. "All of our personal accounts are on there. I have no idea what our bank balances were, what check numbers are out—"

Zack interrupted. "I told you that putting that stuff on the computer was a bad idea," he snapped.

I pressed by him, panicked, to see if the agents had taken our network computer. When I opened the closet that housed the network, all I found was an empty room. All of the equipment had been removed. Not only had they robbed me of my personal effects, they literally had crippled our office, as everyone's computer used the network to operate. There would be no business at Durkee Development Group, at least not until we could get our computers back. This was a disaster.

Just then, Frank Rupp, our CFO, entered the building, followed closely by my sister, Aly. He had been at the courthouse as a show of support for Peter and me and had agreed to meet me at the office to recount the search and seizure.

"Hey, Rose," Rupp said, a pile of disks in his hand. "I had that dweeb of an agent make a backup copy of our hard drive of the network so we wouldn't be dead in the water."

What a relief, I thought. *At least we can still do business. If anyone will still do business with us, that is.*

"Now all we have to do," he continued, "is buy a new network computer and get everything reloaded as soon as possible. It will probably be a day or two before we are back to normal."

Rupp must have realized, as those words left his lips, that nothing would ever be back to normal again. Our lives, our company, our reputations, would never be restored. We had to accept the fact that our lives, from this moment on, were going to be different, very different.

I knew that the staff had to be terrified. The owners of their company charged with a RICO conspiracy—it was unimaginable. We had never had enough money to run the company without a struggle. Maybe in some ways this was the best thing that could have happened. The company's motto was "Dreams Realized." I knew I could not quit. I knew I couldn't back down from what we as a company stood for and believed in. I believed in big dreams. We started this company with three people, and now we had three hundred employees who all wanted *their* dreams realized! This was our family's business. We would not let this prosecutor from Miami rob us of our dream or the dreams of our staff members.

I turned to my sister, who was standing next to me, and said, "Aly, I'm ready to fight. This man has falsely accused me of participating in a crime, of bribing county officials for votes on our real estate projects. If all the hassles we got from the county were special treatment, I'd hate to see what their business as usual is. This is un-American!"

I felt my strength returning. "Listen, let's get the marketing firm on the phone. We need a standard statement that all employees can recite. We also need to calm the fears of the residents and the builders of all three communities."

My sister studied me. "Rose, can you handle this?" she asked.

I shrugged. "I'm tired and hungry, and I need some time with Lauren and Taylor. They've got to be worried."

"No problem," Aly said firmly. "I'll call the marketing firm right now."

"Thanks for being so supportive, Aly. I couldn't have done it without you."

"I love you," she told me. "Try not to worry about this; you have great attorneys."

"Not worrying would be impossible," I admitted. "But I'm ready to go home. I'll call you later."

I said my good-byes to everyone, and Zack and I headed back to the house. The first part of the ordeal was over. The worst was yet to come.

That evening, I turned on the television news, with seven-year-old Taylor on my lap. "Good evening, I'm Karina Kroh," the chirpy news anchor began. "Tonight's feature story—nine prominent business people and two more county commissioners are arrested in what the special prosecutor calls the worst case of institutionalized corruption he has ever seen."

And there we were, heading into the courtroom.

Taylor's eyes went wide. "Mommy, that's you and Peter on TV!" she exclaimed.

"I know, honey," I said, my insides churning, unable to take my eyes off the screen. "Remember the story I told you yesterday?"

Taylor stared at an image of Strickland at his triumphant press conference. "Yeah," she said, and she pointed at the screen. "Did that man hurt you?"

"Only my feelings and my future," I admitted.

"What's a future, Mommy?"

"Good question!" I said. *A very good question indeed.*

We watched in silence as my partners and I were arraigned on charges of RICO and conspiracy to commit racketeering, our ordeal made available to anyone in the region with a TV set. I had never understood the phrase "being put through the wringer," until now. Zack was kind enough to see Taylor to bed so I could take a hot shower and get the smell of the jail experience off my skin. As I stood with the water cascading over my head, I wondered how all of this could have happened.

By most people's standards, I had it all: I was a wife, a mother, and a prominent businesswoman. In just five years, what had started with three people working in a construction trailer had turned into a successful real estate development company employing more than three hundred people. Our offices were situated in prestigious golf community complex located in what is known as the crown jewel of Florida's Gulf Coast—Naples.

I had worked hard for everything I had, earning the respect of my peers and members of my community along the way. I was proud of my accomplishments and thrived on the positive recognition that came with each new venture. But now one man—Martin Strickland—was threatening to take it all away.

Seven

Zack and I met thirteen years earlier, while we were both on the job at Universal Studios Orlando. I was the project accountant for the development of the studios, and he worked as a project manager for the Earthquake ride and show. It was lust at first sight: he came striding across the job site in his black jeans, six feet two inches tall, four years younger than I was, an Italian dream... brown eyes, curly brown hair, buff body, and not afraid to spar a little with me. Brave man! *This could be fun,* I thought... and it was.

We enjoyed the nightlife that working at Universal Studios provided. The development team was a small and very tightly knit group. After our typical seventeen-hour workdays, we all went together to sports bars to unwind. We played cards at our house on weekends with the team, ordering in dinner. I guess in retrospect, we didn't have much of a dating experience alone. Zack seemed to have found the "strong woman of his dreams," and I found a very handsome young man who wanted to marry an older single mother.

Once he completed the Earthquake ride and show, Zack was going to be transferred back to Ohio. Since we had fallen madly in love, or so I thought, he quit his job and decided to look for new opportunities in Orlando. But once Universal opened, Orlando suffered a severe construction slump. A recruiter contacted Zack with an opportunity in Naples, a beautiful gulf coast community only four hours away from Orlando. Love takes you many places, and Naples was a sunshine-filled paradise. Eight-year-old Lauren and I packed our bags, and we moved to Naples that September. Zack and I were married the following month, just nine months after we met.

I began a job search immediately. I hated leaving Universal Studios, the most fun job I have ever had, and with the holidays upon us I knew most places would not be in the hiring mode. Perhaps that is why, when Zack and I were invited to attend a Sunday service at a church with a funny sounding name, I agreed to go. *Might as well. There's not much I can do about finding a job right now,* I reasoned as we turned into the church grounds.

Having been raised Catholic, everything about New Hope Ministries seemed strange to me. Instead of holding its services in a traditional sanctuary filled with polished wooden pews flanked by stain glass windows, this congregation met in a room that seemed more like an auditorium, complete with folding chairs and a stage sporting microphones, choir risers, and band instruments.

"Let's not sit too close to the front in case we need to get out of here," I told Zack as I located three aisle seats near the back door, taking care to position Lauren between us.

Just then a big, well-dressed man in his early fifties greeted Zack. "Hello, brother, I'm glad to see you," he said. But before Zack could reach out to shake his hand, the friendly stranger put both arms around my slender husband and virtually swallowed him in a hug. He kept one arm around Zack as he extended his hand to me, saying, "How are you doing today?"

I mustered a smile and replied, "Fine, thank you" as he bent down to greet Lauren, giving her no less the genuine attention he had given to Zack and me. And then he disappeared into the crowd of people rapidly filling the auditorium.

Before I could say anything to Zack about the man I presumed was the church's "greeter," a young man stepped up to one of the microphones as the choir and band took the stage. "Good morning! Are you ready to stand up and praise the Lord?" he asked in a loud voice; the crowd answered by erupting into applause.

For the next twenty minutes I felt as if I were attending a concert instead of a church service. I even found myself clapping along with everyone else at one point but quickly folded my hands in front of me in an effort to keep from feeling irreverent. We were, after all, in church. The final song was a hymn I remembered from my childhood, and when the pastor stepped behind the podium and asked us to be seated a sense of peace settled around me.

It wasn't until everyone in front of us had taken his or her seat that we could actually see the pastor from our back row vantage point. At the same moment, a wide-eyed Zack and I turned and looked at each other. "Oh my gosh," I mouthed silently to my husband. "It's *him*!" I couldn't believe it. Our "greeter" was the pastor of New Hope Ministries! I quickly opened the church bulletin that had been handed to me as we entered the building, and sure enough there was his smiling face. Beneath the photo I read, "Pastor Grant Thigpen."

I had seen preachers like him on television, but I had never heard one in person. Instead of reading a written message, he had us open our Bibles as he taught directly from the Word of God. What I found most interesting about Pastor Grant was when he talked about God it was like he was talking about someone he knew personally. He explained that, through Jesus Christ, we could all have a personal and meaningful relationship with our Heavenly Father.

I wasn't sure what it was that this group of people had, but whatever it was, I wanted it. Zack also felt comfortable at the church and we continued to attend Sunday after Sunday.

Thanksgiving passed, as did Christmas, with no prospects for a job that was even close to the salary I was making at Universal Studios. But along with my newfound faith in God had come the assurance that he would take care of me.

I went to a Junior Achievement bowling event with Zack, carrying the slender hope that there might be some sort of work prospect there. I met the CFO of Zack's company, and after exchanging discussions about our background, I hoped that I had impressed him with my outgoing personality and work experience. "If you know of anyone looking for a financial analyst," I said, "keep me in mind." March was now upon us—seven months without a job. Out of desperation, I accepted a job at a manufacturing company in Fort Myers, about forty-five minutes north of our home. I hadn't done manufacturing rework accounting since my days at Martin Marietta fifteen years earlier, and the worst thing was that the pay was about the same as I had earned then. Rework accounting, keeping track of failed parts repaired and put back on the manufacturing line, is about as exciting as its name implies. There I sat, analyzing grimy folders filled with paperwork that had been handled by the grease monkeys on the line. What a nightmare. I was going backwards in my career. I had goals and dreams, and suddenly they all felt shattered.

That forty-five-minute drive each morning gave me lots of time to pray for a miracle. After three weeks at the plant, that miracle call arrived. A recruiter had learned about me from the CFO I'd met at Junior Achievement—God truly does work in mysterious ways. Our first call was early March; I quickly fixed up my résumé and the following Sunday I asked one of the prayer partners at church to pray that I would have favor. My Universal Studios land development and accounting experience was about to save me!

"You have an interview with a real estate developer in Bonita Springs," the recruiter told me when he called Monday morning. "You're the only candidate being presented by a placement firm. They're interviewing two or three other people, so you really need to shine. Wear your best knock-'em-dead suit and keep your edge. The company is owned by two young guys who are around thirty or thirty-five. Use everything you have, Rose!"

I smiled; he was undoubtedly thinking about the fee he would earn if I got the job. "Okay," I said. "I'll make you proud. I know you have to earn a living."

It was difficult to sleep that night as my mind ricocheted between excitement and fear. It felt as if I had just dozed off to sleep when the alarm clock blared. I jumped into my closet to choose my battle attire. Naturally, I chose a red outfit, full of power and personality. I wanted to stand out among all the other candidates. As I drove north on I-75, the advertising signs for my prospective employer's "Nottingham Country Club" began to pop up. But when I arrived, just before 9:00 a.m., I wasn't greeted by any kind of country club at all. Instead, I saw five hundred acres of laser-leveled dirt. But to me, it was the land of opportunity. Others may have seen it as a virtual dust bowl, but my experiences at Universal taught me to see beyond the dirt—to see the "dreams realized."

A golf clubhouse peeked out of the vast nothingness. Three single white trailers constituted the rest of the construction. *Great,* I thought, from *a grease-filled cubicle to an office on wheels!* I had spent my last year at Universal in "trailer world," so I was no stranger to the experience. Little did I know that the next four years of my professional life would be in those three trailers.

Okay, Rose, I told myself, *it's show time.* As I entered the development trailer, a woman about forty years old with bright red hair greeted me.

"Yeah?" she asked in an accent straight from the Bronx. "How can I help you?" A cigarette burned on her desk. Her ashtray told the story of a chain smoker.

"I'm here for an interview with Earl," I said.

"Right. Have a seat and I'll let him know you're here—what's your name again?"

"Rose Visconti," I replied. Just then we were interrupted by a male voice shrieking over the intercom on the credenza behind her desk, "Fern!"

"Oh, for God's sake," she said as she spun in her command central chair. "What?" she replied with all the New York attitude she could muster. The voice began barking orders at her, calls that she needed to make ASAP. Fern rolled her eyes and took a drag of her cigarette as she pretended to be taking copious notes from her caller. She ended the call with some gestures that were appropriate only on the construction site.

Fern spun back around. Reaching out with her long artificial red nails, she grabbed the phone and buzzed Earl. "Your interview is here," she said, not even mentioning my name.

"Thanks, send her over," I heard Earl say.

Fern used her lethal nails as direction signals. "Just go to the next trailer, that's accounting," she said.

"Thanks, nice meeting you," I said.

"Whatever," Fern replied, already having forgotten me.

In the thirty seconds it took me to walk from one trailer to the other, I wondered if I could deal with Ms. New York. Just then, a young man came blazing around the corner, nearly knocking me down. He greeted me with a big "Helll-o, how can I help you?"

"I'm here to see Earl," I said.

"What company are you with?"

"This one, I hope," I replied as engagingly as possible. "I'm interviewing for the assistant controller position."

"I'm Harold Densmore, the president of the company. Good luck."

I suddenly felt very uncomfortable as he gave me the proverbial once-over. I guess the red suit was working.

"If you pass muster with Earl, I'll meet with you later," he said.

"You can count on it," I said confidently. *That was a good start,* I told myself.

As I opened the door to the accounting department, I saw a kind of inner sanctum with a window and a bell on the door. A sign said, "Accounting Employees Only." *Not very welcoming,* I thought as I pressed the bar gently. A woman pushed back in her chair from her cubicle and glared at me. The gesture was a shrug, as if to say, "What do *you* want?"

"Hello, my name is Rose. I'm here to meet with Earl."

"Hey, Earl, your appointment is here," she yelled, without moving in her rolling chair. *Where did they find these people?* I wondered.

"Come on in," a voice bellowed from behind the door.

Dear God, what am I getting myself into? However, Earl, the controller, and I actually had a great chat, and he invited me to meet the owner. *I've done it*, I thought, *I've made the first cut.*

"Fern, Earl here. Can you see if Harold and Peter have a minute to meet one of the candidates?"

"They're here," Fern snapped back at him over the intercom. "Do you want me to ask them, or could you get off your butt and walk over here yourself?"

"You have to get used to Fern," Earl said with a smile. "She thinks she's still in New York."

As we passed by Fern again, she gave me a roll of the eyes as she lit the final cigarette of the pack. *Was that a full pack since eight this morning?*

"Harold Densmore, Peter Durkee, this is Rose Visconti."

Peter was Irish, and his strong accent was clear in his welcome. For the next thirty minutes, they interrogated me about my background. They even asked if I was married—I couldn't believe that anyone would ask me that.

"Yes, I am married," I told him calmly, "and I have an eight-year-old daughter and I am a Christian." I figured I would save him a lecture from the controller by offering the details. Peter entered the conversation by saying, "We should hire her. She's the best-looking one we've seen so far."

Harold's head dropped into his hands and Earl turned scarlet.

I smiled, but I thought, *What a cretin.*

"You won't regret it, Mr. Durkee," I said.

"Call me Peter, please," he said, turning on the charm. "My father is Mr. Durkee, and I'm sure he won't regret it, either"

My first day on the job was April Fool's Day. I now wonder if there was a message buried deep in that coincidence. About three months later, my boss, Earl, left the company and Harold and Peter promoted me as the controller for the company. My miracle career had arrived—God was blessing me abundantly.

My professional growth was more than equaled by my spiritual growth. I couldn't wait for Sunday to arrive each week so we could be in church again. I had become accustomed to Pastor Grant's preaching style and actually looked forward to hearing his voice grow louder and louder as he drove home biblical truths. Along with my Bible, I carried a notebook into each service and made ample notes, which I poured over during the week.

But the best part was I was enjoying a relationship with God that I had never dreamed existed. Each time I read one of his promises in the Bible, I knew that promise was for me personally, direct from my loving Heavenly Father.

The next four years with Harold and Peter were fascinating. They had previously worked for Peter's father in his real estate development company, and Nottingham Country Club was their big chance to fly solo. Since the mid 1980s, Naples had become a mecca of planned gated communities that included single family and multi-dwelling homes. These communities offered a vibrant lifestyle supported by amenities like golf, tennis, fitness, and an active social life. Nottingham was Harold and Peter's ticket to finally see their dream development come true ... if they could survive each other.

Harold was the operations guy and Peter was definitely the sales guy; they were polar opposites in every other way. Even the ways they approached the project differed: to Harold, Nottingham was his big chance to make a name for himself as a developer. He stuck to the rules and wasn't big on taking chances that might risk the project's success. Peter, on the other hand, saw Nottingham as just another development in a series of developments. His style, to put it mildly, was more freewheeling.

Peter was much more interested in building relationships, both with his employees and the new residents, than Harold was. He found it difficult to say no to people, which caused a mountain of construction problems for Harold. As leader of the sales group, Peter would offer the sun, the moon, and the stars to buyers, even sparing the profit margin. Harold, leading the construction team, would find himself in the middle of many jams with both employees and customers when Peter promised something that cost the company profit. The two never agreed on employee relations, and they had radically different concepts of loyalty. Peter had a deep sense of loyalty to his family and friends. Even if they did a mediocre job, Peter's sense of honor would prohibit him from firing them. Harold, at the other extreme, would fire his sister without cause. The tension between the two men eventually peaked at biblical proportions, leaving the staff to choose which side of the battlefield they were on. I found myself serving as peacemaker between them most of the time.

Harold married about a year after I started working for the company. A year after that, Harold and his wife, Becky, announced they were going to have a baby. There must have been something in the water cooler at the office, because shortly after Harold's grand announcement, I was sharing the same joyful news! We both gave birth to beautiful girls. Harold's wife delivered in June, and I gave birth to Taylor in July. The four of us had so much in common that my personal relationship with Harold became much stronger than my bond with Peter.

Nottingham development was approaching completion, but those four years had taken their toll on the partnership of Harold and Peter. Harold went on to develop another project, and Peter decided to help his father in a neighboring development, Turtle Cove. This was Peter's entry to the "Prima Home" building business: a high-end luxury development in the middle of a field. It was slow to get off the ground, as luxury homebuyers were not exactly knocking down his door to build homes.

Harold assumed that I would be joining him at his new development at Fort Myers, but Taylor was only three months old. I couldn't bear to leave her or to make a two-hour commute and be a mom. I had done that drill before, and I was not going to do it again. I decided to work from home, farming out my accounting services to anyone who needed them. Prior to that point, my personality was more like Harold's in that I was very rules-based. Now, though, I was finding that Peter's kinder, gentler way was not so bad.

Zack and I had built a home next door to Peter's, so our families became very close as well. Harold clearly believed that I had chosen

Peter over him, and we hardly saw Harold and Becky after that. I thought it was sad that I had to choose between the two of them, as I liked and respected them both so much.

After about a year in the Prima Homes business, Peter began to sense some financial strain and asked me to look at the books. He had enjoyed quick success at Turtle Cove, growing to a staff of thirteen and selling a dozen homes in the first year. Father, as Peter referred to him, had him build two model homes in the new section of Turtle Cove, which was open farmland. But they weren't selling, and neither had the big model that housed his office. I spent about a week reviewing the books and called Peter into my office.

"You're upside down right now to the tune of about $250,000," I told him. "You need to downsize immediately to one worker—you. The model homes need to be sold as soon as possible—the carry cost is over $16,000 a month."

"Holy smokes," Peter exclaimed, a hand going involuntarily to his forehead. "Where am I going to get that kind of money?"

"Peter, this is not the time to bury your head in the sand. I've laid out a recovery program of sorts. There hasn't been a new sale in over six months, and your sales staff needs to go. You have no homes under construction, so your superintendents need to go. You have no need to keep a secretary or accountant. You can be the secretary. I'll help you with the books to close the business, but you've got to do it."

Peter was still slack-jawed at the unexpected bad news. I plowed on. "You also need to consider a new career," I told him.

Peter pondered my advice. "Father has a lead on some property," he said. "He also has a resident here who used to be in real estate. This guy retired here at age forty and is now a hedge fund manager. Father says he has him interested in financing the project. If this all works out, I'll be back in the development business."

All well and good, I thought. *But that's for another day.*

"Peter, in the meantime, you've got to call the staff together and give them the news."

"Will you do it for me, Rose?" he asked. "You know I don't like conflict."

"Sure, why not? I'll be the wicked witch. After all, it's not about them. If they want to work free, they can all stay. Otherwise, there's no money to pay them. Sad but true. And I'll call your investor and let him know that he won't be seeing any interest payment until this beast of a house sells."

Peter looked at me gratefully. "Rosie, what would I do without you?"

"Peter, I don't know, and you probably shouldn't think about that right now."

Peter sat up in his chair. "I promise," he told me, "that if you stick around and help me clean up this mess, if this new development works out, you'll be back in business, too."

I grinned. "Thanks, Peter," I said. "You know I'm always here for you, too."

Two months after the mass housecleaning, there were no real bites on the big house, and the other two sold at a loss. I wondered how long Peter could wait this thing out; the stress must have been killing him. And that's when the news came that would shake our lives to the core.

"Rosie, you won't believe it," Peter told me excitedly. "Father just called. I've got a meeting with Jack Wood."

"Who's that?" I asked. I had never heard the name before, and I now wish I had never heard it in the first place!

"He's that young investor resident here that Father has been meeting with about financing the project in Naples."

"When do you meet?" I asked.

"Today at lunch, at the club," Peter said.

"I know you'll charm him to pieces," I said. "He'll be lucky to have you as a business partner. There's no better land developer than you, Peter!"

Peter grinned. "Thanks for the pep talk, I'm ready for action."

"Go knock his socks off!" I exclaimed.

It was nice to see the old Peter returning. A failing business was enough to keep anyone down, but Peter was cut from some strong cloth; he looked at everything as an opportunity. He had done everything from roadwork and gold mining in far away places to being a homebuilder, and now … *Oh Lord; please let this be the angel from heaven that you've sent to Peter. Let this Jack Wood be the one who puts Peter back in business.*

As Peter went off to meet with Jack Wood, neither one of us could ever have imagined what this man was going to put both of us through.

Eight

Here's the story about Jack Wood that I later pieced together:

He had moved from Michigan to Naples to "retire" and trade his own personal millions, or at least that was the story he spread around. With his second wife and toddler daughter, he rented an upscale home in posh downtown Naples. After just a few weeks in paradise, Jack set up shop in an executive office building named International Executive. As he said, he needed a place to work, and his home on the beach was proving a distraction. Jack began to socialize with the other tenants of the building—networking, you could call it. The owner of the building, Jonathan LaForge, a wealthy Republican hotshot in town, was very interested in his new tenant's portfolio performance.

Jack told Jonathan, "I only trade my own funds, and I'm up over fifty percent already this year!"

Greed, the greatest advertising and marketing strategy in the world, did its job. Who wouldn't want to begin doubling his investment?

"Hey, Jack," Jonathan said, "why don't I give you $25,000, and you see what you can do for me?"

Wood scratched his head.

"I don't know, Jonathan," he said. "I really like doing my own thing. That way the loss or gain is my own. No customer complaints."

Jack must have been smirking when he said that. The line was cast, the hook was set, and it was time to reel in the big one!

"Come on, Jack," Jonathan persisted, "I promise not to complain about a fifty percent return."

"Oh, all right, but just for you," Jack said. "Don't go telling all your friends. I'm retired, remember?"

The International Executive building was chock-full of wealthy entrepreneurs. Tenants included ESPN founder Nicholas Shubert, a semi-retired advertising executive from New York who just for fun liked to do marketing for high-end clients like Jonathan. The building was also home to a number of real estate sales people, mortgage brokers, and a cigar aficionado. *A plethora of potential investors*, Jack must have thought to himself. *If I can get one client, how hard could it be to get a few more?* He knew he could capture a management fee that could help him build his personal dream of fabulous wealth.

On the first of the month, another check for $25,000 arrived from Jonathan. The check was marked "additional investment." This continued each month without any conversation between the two men. Jack created a makeshift Excel spreadsheet on which he could report the phenomenal returns to Jonathan.

"Hey, Jonathan," he finally said, "I know this is a little less than a professional financial investment statement, but I thought you would like to see how your investment is doing." Jonathan let out a loud "Yee-haw!" at the numbers as he was returning to his office. Just then, Nicholas Shubert entered the building.

"What are you all smiles about, Jonathan?" Nicholas asked in his sports announcer's voice.

Lurking behind the open door of his office, Jack Wood was eavesdropping on their conversation.

"Oh, nothing," Jonathan grinned, "we've just got a Mr. Midas over here who's breaking Wall Street records. And I'm lucky enough to have gotten in on the ground floor."

"Mr. Midas?" Nicholas asked, intrigued. "I'd like to meet him. I've got some deals that could use a golden touch."

"Follow me," said Jonathan. "We'll see if he's in his suite."

Jack leaped from behind the door, scrambled across his office, and jumped into his black leather desk chair.

"Jack, are you in?" Jonathan's voice boomed down the long marble hall.

"Yeah, come on in," he said, trying to sound deeply engrossed in his work.

Jonathan and Nicholas entered the luxurious suite. "Jack Wood," Jonathan began, "meet your neighbor Nicholas Shubert. Nicholas founded ESPN on a credit card years ago and sold it out for a bundle. He's 'retired' just like you, Jack!" The men chuckled.

"I didn't work this hard when I had a job," Nicholas replied, grinning.

Jack nodded and laughed in agreement.

"Jack," Jonathan said, "I was telling Nicholas about your fund and its performance."

"Fund?" Jack replied, looking surprised and almost pained by the word. "Hey, I'm just playing around in the market with my own money. This guy started sending me checks, and now it's a fund!"

"Isn't Naples great?" Jonathan asked. "Everything grows here, especially your investments."

"Nice to meet you, Jack," Nicholas said, "But I've got a golf tournament to organize. I'll see you around."

That piqued Jack's curiosity. "Golf tournament?" Jack asked. "Which one?"

"MediaGolf Challenge," Shubert explained. "My new company, MediaGolf, is the title sponsor for the Senior PGA stop in Naples. We've had the tournament stop in Naples for about three years; it brings many tourists to the area. I'm going to present it to the county commissioners this week to see if the county will contribute tourist tax dollars to promote our little paradise. Wish me luck—those county bureaucrats don't have much vision."

After the two men left, Jack leaned back in his chair. "Vision," he said out loud. "My vision since I was thirteen was to be a millionaire. And I just hit the jackpot—in Naples!"

Jack's daydream was interrupted by a loud "Excuse me?" He spun around.

"Hi, I'm Jeremy Pernell. I'm your next door neighbor here." Pernell's large hand reached across to grasp Jack's. "What's your shtick?" Jeremy asked.

"Shtick?" Jack replied, nonplussed.

"Your business," Jeremy said. "What do you do?"

"I'm a hedge fund manager," Jack said confidently.

"What kind of returns are you getting?"

"I'm averaging about fifty percent," Jack said modestly.

"Holy smokes, sign me up!"

"No problem," said Jack. "We have a minimum entry investment of $25K." He looked directly into Jeremy's eyes to see if he was a real player.

"I'll have a check for you tomorrow, partner," Jeremy exclaimed, turning the corner to exit as quickly as he had entered the office. Jack leaned back in his chair, spun around, and smiled. "This is easier than I ever imagined—they're throwing cash at me!"

Now that Jack had a "fund" per se, he needed a legal entity and some paperwork to make himself official. Jack headed to Office Max, bought a "lawyer in a box" kit, and decided to form a limited partnership. Next, he thought, "What should we name this fund? It is all about me right?" Jack thought to himself... "That's it, I'll call it Wood Investment Fund."

Jack busily produced applications, forms, and a chart that graphically demonstrated his fund's phenomenal growth performance under his masterful guidance. And the fund began to grow, one office neighbor introducing another. A few even suggested that Jack should pay a commission for referrals.

Now that the fund was growing by hundreds of thousands of dollars each month, Jack needed to build his reputation in town. His first move was to purchase a luxury home in the elite Turtle Cove, a Durkee development in North Naples. His first million-dollar home! Jack, his wife, Tara, and little Tamara were thrilled with their new home and with their new car, too. The old Mercedes was no calling card for Mr. Midas. How about a Jaguar XJ?

"Now I'm starting to look like a successful hedge fund manager,"

Jack told himself. "Big house, nice car. Let's see, how about a wardrobe enhancement? Life in paradise is great!"

Jonathan LaForge, who always looked like a million bucks, set up Jack with his personal tailor, and within weeks, Jack was outfitted with new suits and shoes of the softest Italian leather. Jonathan began inviting him to fundraising dinners, and Jack quickly ingratiated himself to other deep-pocketed Republicans. Suddenly, his Wood Investment Fund was growing by the millions, fed by the city's seemingly endless stock of ex-CEOs ready to invest with Mr. Midas.

"Nothing is going to stop me from being a millionaire," Jack thought. "I am eclipsing the standards in Naples. Not bad for a refugee from a Jeep plant in Michigan."

Jack continued to grow the fund by adding commodity, futures, and precious metal "traders" close to his executive offices. He began to tout his new secret trading program, which he called, with characteristic flair, "the Raptor." Malik Kasal, a twenty-five-year-old Ph.D. graduate in mathematics, had developed this trading program for Wood and frequently visited Naples to test the results.

The fund was growing rapidly, and so was its staff. Jack needed more space and decided that moving all of his ventures under one roof might provide synergy to the success of Wood's fund. So Jack leased space in the North Naples Professional Suites, which had plenty of room for the real estate development team he intended to create. Everybody knew there was a lot of money to be made in real estate in Florida. Wood wanted his share.

Nine

It didn't take long for the good news to arrive.

Jack Wood was about to invest his money with us and keep us afloat financially. We were almost desperate for an investor of his magnitude at that moment. He seemed like an angel straight from heaven.

"He's in!" Peter screamed as he ran through the office. "This guy is amazing. He showed me the results of his hedge fund. He's getting a return of fifty percent a year in the market. Everything this guy touches turns to gold, and he just touched me!"

I was delirious with joy. "I'm so happy, Peter," I said. "This is great. What's next?"

"Father has planned a meeting with the landowner next week with Jack and me. Can you pull together a cash flow pro forma this week so that we've got something to offer?"

"Of course, as long as you have all the numbers."

"Rosie, we're back in business!" Peter danced around the office for what seemed like forever, giggling, smiling, and dreaming. Finally, he had found a partner with loads of cash—a developer's dreams realized.

The model home that had been for sale for over a year now became our offices. What a wonderful change from trailer world.

Peter returned from a meeting with Jack, as excited as I had ever seen him.

"We've got ourselves a deal," Peter hollered as he entered the office. "Get ready, Rosie, we're off to the races! We're probably going to have to pull a few all-nighters. We've got to get a pro forma together for Jack so that he can start offering a Class B partnership to some of his investors."

That caught my attention.

"Class B?" I asked. "Then who's Class A?"

Peter grinned. "Oh, you always want to know all the details. Can't we just enjoy the fact that we're back in the game?"

"Sure I enjoy being back in the game, but don't you want to be sure the deal works financially first?" I asked.

My lot in life, I thought, was to protect Peter from all of the financial hazards in his business life. I had never met anyone who trusted everyone he met the way Peter did. Peter believed that all humanity was honest, trustworthy, and loyal. I was constantly—and vainly—trying to convince him that, unfortunately, he was one of a kind and that many folks in the real estate and development business were far from trustworthy business partners. After all, what did we know about this Wood character? Sure, he has a nice house in Turtle Cove, appears to have money, but what was his M.O.? Why would a guy who retired to Naples with a hedge fund want to get involved in a giant real estate endeavor? We'd find out soon enough.

Jack Wood certainly seemed like a savior when he arrived. At least he did to Peter.

"Jankowski's in, too!" Peter exclaimed, referring to landowner Charles Jankowski, a seventy-five-year-old tomato farmer who had been in the produce business since his childhood in Pittsburgh. The big growers squeezed him out of the tomato business in Naples, and his land was in bankruptcy proceedings. Jankowski would contribute land to the partnership as soon as he could get it out of bankruptcy court. Jankowski's land and Wood's money meant that we could go forward with the development of The Preserve Country Club, a 575-acre, twenty-seven-hole gated golf course community.

There was only one small glitch to the program. Because Jankowski was in bankruptcy, it would cost about $10 million to get the land free and clear. Jack structured a loan to get the deal done in about a month. The speed didn't come without a price—24.9 percent. This wasn't in our original profit projections. But at least The Preserve was a viable project.

When I finally met him, I had to admit that Jack Wood didn't look at all like I had pictured him. He had on shorts, a golf shirt, and Birkenstocks, with a big fat unlit cigar in his mouth. He was short and slight, about five feet seven, not much taller than I was. His hair was so short on top that he resembled a porcupine—too youthful a hairdo for a forty-year-old.

It soon turned out that Jack had overestimated his ability to find a secondary equity partner. Jack invested in many small businesses in Naples and one of them was a mortgage company owned by Jeremy Pernell, one of his early Naples hedge fund clients. Jack eventually had to call on Jeremy to find a venture capital company and get it excited about our great real estate project in Naples. Jeremy agreed to take on the task, but he wanted in on the deal—a two-percent fee on any money he found. Jack agreed and Jeremy was off like a dog on a hunt.

He succeeded in convincing Heartland Bank and Trust to lend us $22 million to develop the project. We began construction in February, believing Jeremy's estimate that we would close the loan in thirty days. We had completed seven months of construction and fulfilled endless requests from the bank for reports, verification of assets, and similar documents. Yet we felt as though we were no closer to funding than we were in February. Although the bank had agreed in February to the loan, the first disbursement did not come until August. Jack was getting nervous—after all, he did not want to finance the entire project. With the returns he was experiencing in his fund, he wanted to keep his money there. And he couldn't afford to continue financing the construction project at The Preserve.

The bank wanted a strong equity partner to guarantee any expenditure above their $22 million loan. Jack agreed to be that partner. The bank was very impressed with Jack's fund performance, and with the success of the many other businesses he had started since moving to Naples just three years earlier. From the bank's perspective, Jack was truly investing in the community. And from our perspective, things were looking good. We had the land, we had the financing, and we had a highly respectable, successful investor on our team in Jack Wood, a man we could rely on if things got messy again.

Or so we thought.

Ten

Peter buzzed my office. "Rose, Jack and I would like to meet with you. Do you have a minute?"

"That's about all I do have," I said.

"Well, swing by my office. Jack is already here." I wondered what new Nancy Drew/Hardy Boys mystery needed to be resolved. *First Heaven, maybe he's franchising, and Hell is opening soon.*

Jack Wood now had his hands in more things than a Sunday potluck dinner—cigar bar, Internet games, hedge fund, mortgage company, real estate. *What's next*, I wondered as I raced down the hall to meet the boys.

"Gentlemen," I said, "and I use that term loosely, how are you both today?"

"Have a seat," Peter said as Jack motioned me to sit in his lap.

"You're a pig!" I exclaimed to Jack. "How does your wife stand you?"

While Jack laughed like a hyena, Peter tried to change the tone.

"Listen, Rose," he began, "You stood beside me through some really hard times. You worked for almost a year without being paid so that I could get back on my feet. You work like a dog now and, well, Jack and I were talking about giving you a piece of the pie, making you a partner, non-voting, of course."

I grinned. "Of course. How could any female penetrate the glass ceiling around here?"

Peter smiled back at me. "Ten percent. I know it's not much, but if we hit the pro forma profits, you could be a millionaire."

"It's not about the money, Peter, you know that," I said.

Peter nodded. "I know," he said. "I just don't want you to ever leave, and if another developer found out about you, you might just get sick of our antics and take off. Then what would I do?"

"Rose," Jack interjected, "my intentions are not so noble. I figured I could sexually harass you if you were a partner and not an employee. Heck, that's worth at least five percent of my share!"

Once again, Jack unleashed his hyena laugh, holding his tiny stomach and slapping his knees. He caught his breath, stood up, slapped me on the back, and said, "See you later, partner."

"In your dreams, Jack."

"You're in my dreams all right," Jack said. He laughed again and headed back to his office.

"What a jerk," I said.

"Hey, Rosie, it's better than a kick in the butt."

"I guess that's up for debate, Peter. This guy thinks he just bought a license to harass me, to be rude and crude."

"I don't think so, Rose, he was just kidding."

"We'll see, Peter. He's like a chameleon. He reveals more and more of his true colors as time passes."

"Rose," Peter said, getting down to business. "Jack and I need you to focus on The Preserve. Father called yesterday with another deal. One of the county commissioners, Eugene Gannon, who's a longtime friend of Father's, has a guy who Father said founded ESPN on a credit card. Apparently, he's developed a once-in-a-lifetime coliseum golf concept, and they need a developer. Anyway, as this company grows, we're going to need projects to keep everyone employed. I think you gave me that lesson a long time ago."

We both smiled. Peter's near-failure had happened less than a year ago. It seemed like a distant memory, ancient history. Life was moving very fast.

I learned the background to this part of the story through *The Collier Enquirer* and the prosecutor's accusations surrounding the case.

Commissioner Eugene Gannon had a long-term relationship with Nicholas Shubert, the ESPN founder. Shubert had pitched the county to contribute $500,000 a year in tourist tax dollars to run his Senior

PGA Tournaments in Naples. He suggested that the advertising for the tournament in Naples would bring new tourists here to the golf capital of the world, filling our hotels, restaurants, and beaches. For three years, the county committed those funds to the Senior PGA Tournament. Shubert convinced Gannon that the most difficult part of the Senior PGA Tournament was that each year he had to find a new venue.

All the courses to date had been in private gated communities that were willing to host the event for the exposure they would receive on national TV, which would help sell homes in their developments. But as more and more people moved into the developments, they did not want to have the inconvenience of the tournament. Their course is closed to residents for a week, and the public is allowed into the community. It just didn't sit well with our Naples residents after the first year or two.

So Shubert developed the idea for a coliseum devoted purely to golf that would be the permanent home for the Senior Tour, and maybe even the Ryder Cup. He envisioned a twelve thousand-seat grandstand wrapped around the eighteenth green of a tournament course, just like the Colosseum in Rome. He needed Gannon to find him a developer. After all, as chairman of the County Commission, he would know every prominent developer in town.

"Phillip Durkee is the best real estate developer in town," Eugene Gannon offered. "Other developers thought he was crazy when he began developing North Naples. What everyone considered the end of town was south of Phillip's developments by fifteen miles. I know him. He is a visionary. He has produced six square miles of the most beautiful high-end communities in North Naples. He's our guy—I'll call him to see if he'll meet with us to hear your idea."

Eugene agreed to call Phillip in the morning.

Almost everyone in Naples who knew Peter's father, Phillip Durkee, referred to him as "the Pope." The Pope agreed to a meeting with Gannon and Shubert, as the concept of a golf coliseum sounded intriguing to him. Although he was too busy with his own development to take on any more projects, this might be another opportunity for his son, who was doing so well with The Preserve. Our development company would be his suggestion for the coliseum deal too. Phillip, nearing seventy, was getting too old to keep up the multiple-development pace. Although he was in good shape physically, he had worked hard all of his life and felt it was time to reap the benefits of his success. He had found, though, that if he fed these opportunities to Peter, his road building company would get the infrastructure work and he could collect a management fee. Everybody's happy.

When Phillip entered the room to meet with Eugene Gannon and Nicholas Shubert, Shubert eyed him and thought, *Well, he's as old as a pope is; maybe that's how he got the nickname.* Phillip wore very thick reading glasses that he would slide up and down his nose, mostly for effect. He would peer over the top of them when he wanted to make a point. If he was finished with you in a meeting, he would look straight through the lenses that enlarged his eyes to three times their normal size and widen his eyes for effect, as if to say, "You may leave now." He always had his No. 2 pencil and his yellow legal pad in hand, ready for the next deal.

As Shubert began to unveil his dream, the Pope listened intently and began to outline the operation in his head. Consummate dealmaker that he was, he recommended a limited partnership.

"I typically offer fifty percent to the limited partner," the Pope began. "That would be Shubert and Gannon. And fifty percent to the developer. I am not available as the developer, but my son Peter and his partner Jack Wood would be perfect."

Shubert wondered how Gannon was suddenly a limited partner. This was his deal, not Gannon's. All he really wanted, though, was compensation for his idea as intellectual property and, of course, recognition as father of the concept of Coliseum Golf.

A few days later, the Pope gathered all four men around his conference table to create the deal. It was easy to see that Shubert, who was a real modern-day P.T. Barnum, mesmerized Jack Wood. Peter was far less enamored with him. He knew intuitively that a pure golf venue would never make any money. You had to sell real estate. Gannon was the self-styled peacekeeper, the Henry Kissinger of the pair.

Still, the project was put into gear. Peter quickly began assembling the land and working up multiple land plans for the property. He created a plan for homes around Shubert's coliseum golf course so that it would be a win-win situation for all the egos involved. The assembled land totaled fifteen hundred acres by the time Peter was finished. Wood agreed to be the financier for the startup costs, and Peter was effective in his negotiations with the landowners for little or no money down.

Although the project had plenty of land, there was a big problem: all the property was landlocked, without a single road providing access. Installations of roads serving the immediate area were part of the county's twenty-year plan, but we didn't have twenty years to wait. Peter's fallback was to access the property through The Preserve, which was just south of the coliseum tract. *That will go over like a lead balloon with The Preserve members*, I thought. I could just see twenty-five thousand cars streaming through the "Community of the Year" to get to a golf tournament. Peter always needed an exit strategy, and this provided one for him that he might never need to use. It did make the land more valuable for us than for any other developer in town, and land with no access was cheap.

The four men began to meet regularly, trying to agree on a concept and a partnership structure that would resemble the Pope's original work, while I continued moving The Preserve through its development life. Peter finally insisted that I sit in on one of their meetings so that I could witness Shubert's pompous behavior and, using numbers, demonstrate to Shubert that it was the real estate that made the money, not the golf. I was so busy with The Preserve and all of its bank requirements, construction schedules, and the like that my attention span in these meetings was short.

Shubert thought my job was to be his secretary and coffee provider. After all, what other purpose would a woman in business serve? At least, at age sixty, he had an excuse for his frame of reference on women in the workplace. Jack Wood was just ignorant, and Eugene Gannon was a country boy from Arkansas who didn't know any better. But it was Peter, in many ways, who tried my patience the most. He had lived in Central America for six years and liked the philosophy of the all-powerful Latin male. He would tell our female employees that they should be home, barefoot, and pregnant. After all, that was what God intended for women, not for them to be hanging out in the man's world!

Before any internal partnership deal was finalized and contracts on the land signed, Shubert, in his P.T. Barnum mode, got an old pal of his from *Sports Illustrated* to run a story in the magazine. With excitement mounting, Shubert called a press conference in October, just six months after introducing the concept to Jack and Peter.

"We don't even have all the contracts on all the parcels," Peter complained.

"Details," Jack retorted. "You need to get more passionate about this deal. Does your heart burn for Coliseum Golf, Peter, Rose?"

"Well, Jack," I said, smiling. "I'd say Coliseum Golf gives me heartburn. Does that count?"

Jack frowned. "You're always a downer, Rose," he said. "Don't you feel the thrill, the excitement of having a one-of-a-kind golf coliseum, a place where the Ryder Cup will one day be held? Where's your sense of adventure, Rose?"

"Hey, Jack," I retorted, "where's your sense, period? You'll blow the land deals that Peter has been working on if you two marketeers have the cart before the horse."

"Shubert has had only two things to focus on," Jack replied. "One is on his only hope—keeping the man with the money happy. That would be me, of course. And the other is seeing his dream coliseum built. All this other political and home building hoo-ha is wasting precious time. We've got to build the excitement now.

"We've got the LG Group, a big South Korean electronics conglomerate, teed up to host this year's Senior PGA tournament at Royal Tern. We've got to assure them that the tournament has a permanent home in Naples, or LG's out. Naples is the golf capital of the world, and the president of the LG Group is foaming at the mouth with excitement. Our exposure will firm up any financing issues we have. Come on, guys, let's get some vision here!"

Jack concluded his pep talk and exited in a puff of smoke.

I had my own vision. It was to see The Preserve, our real deal, reach successful completion. We had our own set of challenges, including permits, sales, and marketing, ahead of us. This Coliseum Golf was a real distraction for me. I had bank draws to do, and sales reports for the partners. I had vision all right, and it was 20/20 on The Preserve. Jack Wood and Nicholas Shubert were like little boys playing in a sandbox. I had a mission with a real goal and an overwhelming workload.

Nicholas scheduled a press conference, much to Peter's dismay, and by marketing standards, it was a huge success. Coliseum Golf was front-page news for a week solid. Nicholas was so pumped that he was no longer taking suggestions from anyone. Although Eugene Gannon attended the press conference as chairman of the Collier County Board of Commissioners, he did not disclose that he had a prospective ten percent interest in the deal. Eugene must have assumed that with no partnership agreement signed, anything could happen, so he could disclose when a solid deal was made. He was there simply to confirm the continued support of the county and the tourist tax dollars for the tournament. These tournaments had put Naples on the golf tourist destination map.

The boys continued their weekly brain-freeze sessions, where the egos would fight for their individual dreams. Finally, Peter brought a beautiful full-color land plan with eighteen lots surrounded by water and priced at $1 million each and fifty-four holes of golf: one eighteen-hole course for members only, one for the tournament, and the other for nonresident members. Nicholas Shubert roared like a discontented lion, not willing to "bastardize" his concept with real estate. Eugene Gannon continued to try to make peace between Peter and Nicholas, with minimal success. But it looked as if each of them could see his own dreams realized. Coliseum Golf for Shubert and island lots for Peter.

Jack was going to walk away with forty-five percent of the projected profits of $100 million, so he was happy, too.

Our real estate attorney, Andrew Shanahan, was working on a limited partnership agreement with the help of his Milwaukee office, since Jack Wood had decided to sell shares in the limited partnership to raise development funds. That pushed the offering documents into territory controlled by the Securities and Exchange Commission—land onto which we never should have strayed.

"Peter, Andrew Shanahan just called and said it's time to decide if we are serious on the Livingston Road Property," I said. "That's going to take four million dollars. Do you have a plan?"

Peter's answer was filled with discontent with Shubert.

"Yeah," he said. "My plan is that the land has no legal access. We're the only buyers in town. If that damn Shubert would have kept his big mouth shut, I could have gotten the land for half the price. Once he held his press conference and that parcel was on TV, I lost all my negotiating power. That SOB. I think we should let the contract expire, get our $100,000 deposit back, and when we've got a deal internally, renegotiate the deal with a landowner."

"What about the land?" Jack asked as he entered the room with his oversized unlit cigar, which had become his trademark.

"Well," Peter began, "we either need four million dollars to go hard on the contract or let it expire. Nobody's going to buy the property—it's landlocked. It'll take three to five million dollars to build Livingston Road to the south end. No developer in town would take that risk. It may cost us a little later on, but better safe than sorry."

Jack scowled. "Safe, my foot," he said. "I'll write the check right now. We can't afford to take a chance that Shubert gets another developer and that land."

"Jack, four million dollars is a lot of scratch," Peter argued. "And unless you're prepared to close on the entire deal in ninety days, that's another eleven million dollars."

Jack rolled his eyes. "Peter, Peter, Peter," he began. "Shubert and

I are going to New York next week; we'll get the Wall Street boys all excited. Naples, golf, ESPN founder, *Sports Illustrated.* It doesn't get any sexier than that. We should be able to raise $100 million easy. So your little fifteen-million-dollar land deal is a drop in the bucket. Get the vision, Peter. You and Rose really bring me down. You worry too much. We've got to get you into the trader mentality. When you make a bad trade, you walk away. No looking back."

That sort of talk cut no ice with Peter. "Listen, Jack," Peter said, "that's your world. Mine is my reputation as a developer in Naples. My word is my bond. I can't start walking away from contracts like a stock trade gone bad. I'll never be taken seriously by a seller again. Plus, this real estate business is my life. The Preserve project is sink or swim for me. I can't afford to lose focus on what we have for the sake of Shubert's dream."

Jack was not dismayed in the least. "Peter, what is your dream for this company?" he asked. Before Peter could answer, Jack offered his own dream. "From the very beginning, I wanted to take our development company public, Initial Public Offering, really make big returns. I'm not some local Podunk real estate developer. If that's what you and Rose want to be, maybe you need to find a replacement partner for me. Originally, we had the Coliseum Golf land contract in Wood Investments' name. I was going to sell the land to Coliseum Golf Ltd. for fifty percent more than I paid, to cover all of these up-front risks, but now that I think about it, that's just plain greedy of me. We need to share all of the upside with Shubert and Gannon."

As Peter sat in silence, Jack continued, "Have Andrew transfer all of the land contracts to our development company. We'll keep it out of the investment company altogether. If we can book enough of these assets through the development company, it will help our IPO."

Peter looked pained. "Jack," he began, "I don't think this is a good idea. Try to understand; the land has no legal access!"

"Do it—now!" Jack shouted. "I've gotta roll. I'm going to write the check for four million dollars today. Get the details from Andrew." And off he went.

I came into the room to find Peter rubbing his forehead.

"What's Mr. Big up to now?" I inquired.

"Oh," Peter sighed, "he's feeling the effects of the Shubert sales pitch overdose. We're going hard on the Livingston Road Planned Unit Development. He doesn't understand our business any better than we do his. He called you and me a couple of Podunk real estate developers. For God's sake, it's May and we don't even have a partnership agreement finalized, and Jack's buying $15 million in land."

"Hey, Peter," I said, trying to cheer him up. "Look on the bright side. If Shubert's idea tanks on Wall Street, Mr. Big just bought our next real estate project!"

Peter brightened. "I guess you're right," he said. "What's the downside?"

That, of course, proved to be a prophetic question.

I changed the subject to our new company president, Craig Delaney. "I'm really thankful that we hired Craig," I said. "He has a way of dealing with Shubert; no nonsense, all business. Plus, with all of his previous experience as county manager, it should make permitting and dealing with all those bureaucrats a breeze. Craig had a lot of public recognition. I don't think being president of a Podunk real estate company would have been enough for him."

Peter smiled. "You don't think we're just a couple of yahoos trying to eke out a living in the Everglades?"

"You're gonna have to work on your Southern accent, boy," I said. "The Irishman is still coming through."

"Maybe we can teach Craig to be a little bit more entrepreneurial," Peter said. "He's got so much bureaucrat in him I'm not sure it's possible."

"Well, look at it this way," I said. "He offers a balance to your shoot-from-the-hip type of planning. Our company motto should be 'Ready, Fire, Aim!' "

Eleven

"Rose, it's Jack," the all-too-familiar voice boomed through my cell phone a week later. As I was about to discover, the pressure of his cash outflows must have awakened demons in him that had been lying dormant.

"Can you come to my office right away?" he asked, sounding remarkably serious.

"Sure, do I need to bring anything with me?"

"Nope, just you."

As I entered Jack's office, he pointed to the chair across his desk. "Please sit down," he said. This was a change. Usually he patted his lap.

"Rose," Jack began solemnly, "God has spoken to me about you. I don't know if you're aware, but I was a deacon in my church back in Michigan. Rose, do you believe in demons?"

I stared at him. *What the heck is this about?*

"I don't know what you mean, really," I responded nervously. "I was raised Catholic."

Jack nodded rapidly. "Well, demons are the spirit beings that Satan uses to tempt people and mess up their lives by telling them to do bad things. I know this, Rose, because I have heard them talking to me before. But I have talked back to them, and I am stronger than they are, so now they pretty much leave me alone. Anyway, God spoke to me about you. You are very special to him and to the spiritual growth of our company. He wants me to pray for you so that demons will not be able to tempt you. Is that okay?"

Fear raced through my body as Jack stood up and walked behind me putting his hands on my shoulders. He began talking to his unseen demons in a way that was obviously familiar to him, but completely unfamiliar to me. I prayed silently for spiritual protection from my God. I feared that Jack was putting a curse on me, some satanic ritual. He had been demonstrating Jekyll and Hyde personalities lately. I wasn't sure what was going on. I just wanted to get out of his office and fast!

When Jack finished, I raced into Peter's office. "Peter, you won't believe what just happened," I shouted. "Jack called me into his office and said God spoke to him about me. Then he started talking to demons and telling them to leave me alone. Is he nuts?"

Peter looked annoyed that I could have been so bothered about this. "Oh, for God's sake, Rose, I told you this religious stuff is a bunch of hocus-pocus. Now you've witnessed it firsthand."

"Peter, my faith in God is real! That business in Jack's office was just scary!"

Peter shrugged. "Maybe he just wants to get into your pants, like Jimmy Swaggart did with that prostitute. I'm sure he was 'praying' over her, too. Hey, I'm an atheist, and I pray when I have sex! 'Oh, God!'" He grinned wickedly at me.

I was annoyed. "Peter, you're going straight to hell! I swear, I've got to stand clear of you. Lightning might strike at any moment!"

Peter rolled his eyes. "Rose, I wouldn't be alone with Jack if I were you. He may use your faith for his plot to take over the world."

He was still laughing at me as I went back to my office. *Well, I'm not giving up on him*, I thought. God put me in his life for a reason, and I'm sure it wasn't for his entertainment. Peter needed a dose of trials if he was going to find God. Obviously, several business reversals were not enough to bring him to his knees. What was God trying to reveal to Peter? Or to me?

As the new president of Wood Durkee Development Group and Coliseum Golf, Craig Delaney chaired our weekly meetings and attempted to keep Shubert and Peter from physically assaulting each other. Jack would occasionally grace the group with his presence, but only to announce trading signals, put and call options, long and short hedges. He'd sit there monitoring the market on his PDA, which was like a Blackberry but the Radio Shack version.

Craig called a meeting of the group to order. "Agenda item number three," he announced. "Eugene Gannon's resignation. Who wants to head up this discussion?"

"I will," Peter announced. "Listen, Eugene, you're a liability to us as a commissioner. You can't vote on any items that we present to the county on Coliseum Golf or on The Preserve, for that matter. On The Preserve project, we have some items that will require a super majority. We can't get that if you abstain."

Eugene looked betrayed. "Peter, every commissioner has a job outside of his or her position on the board. How is this any different?"

Peter tried to remain patient. "I'll tell you, Eugene, one more time. We need all commissioners voting. If one is out and you abstain, we're screwed. It's not optional, Eugene. Resign from the commission or—"

Jack interrupted Peter. "Eugene, listen, besides all of the permitting and voting issues, I'm sure there's gonna be some public outcry that a seated commissioner is in on a one-hundred-million-dollar real estate deal with no money down."

"I hear you, Jack," Eugene said. "But I've cleared all of these issues with the county attorney. There may be what I'll call an Arkansas cow dung storm when we make the initial announcement that I have a ten percent interest, but voters have short memories. This too shall pass."

Now Craig weighed in. "Eugene, I have to agree with Jack and Peter. Having been county manager for ten years, I've seen a lot of things come and go. Nobody is going to like this deal of yours."

Nicholas Shubert had become tired of the distraction that Eugene was causing his dream project. He interrupted, "Can we move on to the real business, gentlemen?"

"Which item is that on the agenda, Nicholas?" Craig snapped.

"Intellectual property," Shubert retorted. He glanced at me, wondering why I was at this very important meeting. "Listen, gentlemen, I don't know how or why Eugene has ten percent, except Peter's father thought it was equitable. For me, I just want my $150K for use of my coliseum concept and a fair salary for marketing and sales for five years. Oh, and of course, an extra two to three percent commission on any real estate I sell, Peter."

He continued, "This partnership deal seems to be slowing the project to a crawl. We've been at this for a year, off and on. Maybe I need to find another developer that would just build the coliseum for me and get away from this real estate business altogether."

Peter rolled his eyes and murmured, "Pompous old geezer" just loud enough for me to hear.

"I've been talking with Golf Concepts; they are at the forefront of developing and managing top golf facilities nationwide." Nicholas continued. "They seem to believe in the pure coliseum dream."

Shubert's threat hung over the group.

Jack slapped both hands on the boardroom table as he rose up from his chair. "Listen, folks," he announced, "I don't have time for this petty crap. Get the marketing going. I have almost five million dollars in this deal. Make sure that Andrew Shanahan gets the partnership, intellectual property, and offering documents done by the end of May. He's got two weeks, or he's fired! There are plenty of real estate attorneys who would love to bill $100K to do this job." He glared at each of us and shouted, "Now move!" Then he stalked out, slamming the door behind him.

The jerk factor around here is growing exponentially, I told myself. How important was it to me, the only woman in this testosterone haze, to show my mental muscle? How is it that men can pound their fists and slam doors, and it's macho? But, if a woman behaves that way she's a ... How did I get so lucky to be surrounded by all this machismo?

I worked so hard. I just wanted a little respect and recognition. Not the bone of a ten percent non-voting partnership or a big title. I wanted personal acknowledgment that my efforts, my contributions, my blood, sweat, and tears mattered.

"Rose," Peter said, interrupting my thoughts. "Wear that red dress of yours tomorrow. The bank inspectors are coming for a site visit, and that's some sight!"

"Yep, that's Rose's job," Shubert interjected. "You're a sexatary—our secret weapon! Although she's getting a little old, isn't she? I'm sure there are younger versions of her around here" he smirked as I bit my tongue until it bled.

I could tell Craig was embarrassed to be a part of his gender at that moment. He winked at me and shook his head in disgust. "Let's get back on track with this meeting, please," he said.

"Hey, Rose, can you get me a cold soda?" Shubert asked.

What would Jesus do? I asked myself. I knew.

"Diet or regular, Mr. Shubert?" I asked politely. "Anybody else need a cold drink while I'm serving?" *Did anyone hear the sarcasm in my voice?* I wondered.

Following the meeting, our attorney, Andrew, got the Jack Wood message loud and clear about the deadline for the documents. On May 27, 1997, the deal was cast, ready for the principals' signatures. I wasn't one of those principals, and if I felt excluded then, I would come to bless the day my signature was not on that deal acknowledgment.

Once the papers were signed, Craig made the official Coliseum Golf announcement to the world. Our PR firm busily pulled all of the facts together—who owned what, where it would be built—and the business section of *Collier Enquirer* ran a big story. Life changed forever after that: twenty-four hours of fame, followed by five years of pain and loss.

Eugene Gannon's prediction of an Arkansas cow dung storm turned out to be an understatement. Every environmentalist and random do-gooder in the area wrote a letter of outrage to the editor or the city. A commissioner using his office for influence? And those pompous developers? How arrogant to have a commissioner so blatantly in your back pockets as you seek development rights. Did you think the citizens of Collier County would allow this behavior?

It took more than a year for Peter Durkee, Jack Wood, Eugene

Gannon, and Nicholas Schubert to reach their partnership deal, but less than thirty days following our press debut for Jack to announce that our real estate development company would scrap its involvement in the Coliseum Golf deal. We had The Preserve and our reputations to protect, and the public outrage over Eugene's free stake in the deal was just too heated to put out. Jack released a press statement to the *Collier Enquirer* in July calling his $4-million investment a "bad trade." That little gem of a press release brought him a flood of phone calls from his investors, many of whom lived in Naples, wondering where he'd been focusing his attention and whose money he had actually invested in this "bad trade." Was the money his own, or had the clients in his magical hedge fund unwittingly invested in Coliseum Golf—and lost?

Jack said his large overseas investors required him to cut loose from all real estate deals until the smoke from Coliseum Golf cleared. What did that mean? Heartland Bank and Trust, the lender for The Preserve project, reminded Jack that the date for his equity guarantee of $8 million was quickly approaching. It was August 10, and the bank was releasing the only remaining funds from our loan. The September draw would be Jack's responsibility.

With construction costs for that period estimated at a million dollars, Jack suddenly instituted new withdrawal rules: ask by the fifteenth of the month and add thirty days. This meant I had to submit the September 10 construction draw to Jack immediately in order to make the funding cutoff. Jack became harder and harder for us to reach. Feeling a little Coliseum Golf heartburn himself, he needed someone to blame in order to placate his investors. That became us, the real estate development company.

Instead of personal visits or phone calls, e-mail now became Jack's preferred method of communication, composing many of his stinging, blame-filled messages in the middle of the night. Despite my recent encounter with Jack and his story about demons, not to mention the fact that I thought he was a pretty big jerk, there was still a part of me that wanted to reach out to him. I did what I could to respond to his venomous e-mails in love; after all, isn't that what Jesus would do? But my efforts to "extend the olive branch" were fruitless. He walled off the hallway between Wood Investment and the Wood Durkee Development offices as a physical act of separation; he had already cut us off emotionally. I guess if he didn't have to see his project begin its hellish descent, he could live with himself, or could he?

I began to sense some multiple personality dysfunctions in Jack's e-mails. One would praise me for my hard work and faithfulness to God and my commitment to The Preserve. The next would admonish me for permit delays and would criticize me for quoting Scripture in my messages to him. He was truly under pressure, but weren't we all? I kept thinking of 2 Corinthians 4:8: "We are hard pressed on every side, but not crushed; perplexed, but not in despair."

For our part, Peter and I wanted Jack to understand that we were on his side, not against him, but we needed him to honor his commitment to The Preserve.

Jack had now been involved in a series of business ventures in Naples, including a golf course community, a cigar bar, a sports café, an Internet game company, and a polling research firm, the last two in partnership with Nicholas Shubert. I estimated that he had invested more than $15 million in new businesses during the past year, hoping for one of them to strike gold or planning to bundle them up for his dream IPO (Initial Public Offering). IPO's can be risky investments, especially if they are all Jacks 'high growth' companies that he's founded with his friends. I don't know how he'll pull off issuing shares to the public for the first time. None of these companies have any history, making it very difficult to analyze the value of the company. I guess Jack will have to put his big city slicker spin on this one!

His startup dollars didn't come cheap. The Preserve's borrowing rate was 24.9 percent, just under the limit set by usury laws. "We could afford it," Jack explained, "because Wood Investment Fund has steady annual gains exceeding fifty percent after fees that amounted to thirty percent of the yearly total return." Wood had reported no losing years and only five down months in its eighty-eight-month history. The fund was pulling in more than $100 million in total with most of the dollars arriving from Naples retirees—people among whom time hangs heavy and word-of-mouth travels fast.

As August 10—the deadline for the cash infusion—drew near, I began prodding Jack about the cash we needed to continue construction at The Preserve. Jack had promised to have a million dollars wired from his bank in London to Heartland Bank and Trust. I made sure he had all the information he needed to make the transaction go smoothly. If we couldn't pay that million dollars' worth of bills, we would be sunk.

Either Jack would not respond at all, or he would forward my nagging e-mails for funding to Tara, his wife and the fund's CFO. Tara would always act surprised by the request, requiring me to prove that my original request had been submitted under the timing of Jack's new rules.

On August 9, I began to panic. Would I have to tell the contractors, who had been working double-time schedules to meet our production plans, that the funds to pay them had not arrived? I printed all the checks, signed them, and readied the clerks to print the required lien releases for each contractor. Why worry them, if I kept things moving along, business as usual? That way they would not have to suffer the ulcer that was starting to eat away my stomach. I was paid to carry that burden, not them. Jack's wire would come through—it had to. We had already taken a lot of abuse over the Coliseum Golf deal in the press, and our bankers were breathing down our necks for the required land and permit approvals that were already months overdue. Everyday life felt like an overtaxed boiler waiting to explode.

Meanwhile, another hurdle we had to clear was an amendment to our zoning permit, which had to be approved by the Collier County commissioners. The original zoning permits for The Preserve allowed us to use two hundred of the five hundred seventy-five acres for the purpose of building six hundred eighty homes, an eighteen-hole golf course, and a grocery store surrounded by offices and shops. We submitted an amendment requesting to rezone the remaining three hundred seventy-five acres from agricultural to residential. We proposed to add five hundred twenty more homes and another nine holes of golf. Since this change would reduce the overall home density of The Preserve, adding green space to the community, we figured this would be a no-brainer for the board. And with former County Manager Craig Delaney as our company's president presenting the request to his former employers, we appeared to be heading down the home stretch. This amendment approval was critical to the success of The Preserve.

At the meeting, Craig addressed the commission beautifully, thrilled to be on the other side of the table for the first time in his career, presenting instead of approving. Craig was an eloquent speaker, his oratorical style and ability to choose the right words honed by ten years of public speaking as county manager.

"Commissioners," he began, "as you know, Wood Durkee Development Group is a responsible developer in Collier County. Our goal—my personal goal as president of this company and former manager of this county—is to assure that we continue to enhance the beauty of Collier County through responsible development. The Durkees have demonstrated time and time again, with Turtle Cove, Turtle Bay, Sandpiper Lakes, and Nottingham Country Club, that they are committed to preserving the beauty of Naples.'

"Mr. Delaney," one of the commissioners, Evan Hanover, interrupted, "who exactly is Wood Durkee Development Group? Who are the principals of this company?"

"Peter Durkee and Jack Wood, Mr. Hanover," Craig said.

It was then that Eugene Gannon excused himself from the meeting, leaving the four remaining commissioners. Hanover and the other commissioners continued to question Craig about roads, traffic, and water and sewer services. A rezoning required a unanimous vote, and we got it. After a few hours of a bureaucratic nightmare, the Collier County Board of Commissioners had voted four to zero, with Gannon absent, to approve our request. We were saved!

"We did it!" Craig told me jubilantly. "Call the bank, Rose, and tell them we finally broke up the zoning logjam and are ready to start Phase Two."

The county's approval of the zoning change freed up our Phase Two loan. Jack Wood was hopeful that the good news would give the bank some confidence on the project and he asked to use Phase Two money for Phase One costs. Jack always tried to avoid putting any of his high-earning fund dollars into our project. Of course, the bank declined Jack's request, stating that they preferred partner funds being invested in the project.

I was pleased that the zoning issue had been resolved but I was still nervous about Jack's wire transfer to our account. The vendors would be in my office in twenty-four hours to pick up the checks that I had already printed. I dialed our contact, Sean Rice, at Heartland Bank and Trust.

"Hi, Sean, Rose again," I said. "I hate to be a pain, but can you check to see if that wire of Wood's has arrived yet?"

"Sure, hold on, anything can happen in five minutes around here."

I waited impatiently for good news, but none was forthcoming.

"None," he said apologetically. "You still have an empty tank. I'll call you when it arrives, okay?"

I tried to suppress my fear. "I'll try to wait, but it's hard."

"I know," Sean said, "but I promise to check every half hour."

I brightened as I realized that Sean was on my side. He wanted that money to be there every bit as much as I did. After all, he had recommended this loan to the bank, using Jack's financial strength as guarantor to close the deal. How bad would he look if his financial guarantor just duped him on a million-dollar wire?

Jack hadn't answered any of my voice messages, so it was time to e-mail him again.

> To: Jack Wood
> cc: Tara, Tom, Peter
> Re: Wire

> I've called the bank. No wire yet. Please verify with your bank that the wire requested has been processed or e-mail me a confirmation from Barclays. Our bank cannot track your wire without that information.
>
> Thanks—Rose

I guess Jack was online at that moment, because suddenly I heard a "bing" from my computer. *Thank God,* I thought, *it's from Jack.* The message read:

> Rose: Called Barclay's in the UK. Seems it's teatime there—no wires today—hold tight. Should be there tomorrow. Jack

I stared at the screen in disbelief.

"Tomorrow!" I said out loud. "He's never faced the working men who want their money, not excuses. Teatime just ain't going to cut it with them. The contractors have their own trades and workers to pay."

Pray, Rose, pray, I told myself. *Stand in faith. Believe that God will provide. He has brought you this far—he won't abandon you now.*

I tried to busy myself with other things, but I could focus only on the missing money. After what seemed like an eternity, Peter was standing in my doorway.

"Hey, Rosie, it's time to go home," he said.

I looked at him with what I hoped was not stark terror. "Peter," I began, "what if Jack's wire really is late? How are we going to keep the troops moving? This is just what our competition is waiting for—to catch word that we can't pay our vendors. All the stories they've been reading in the paper already have them spooked. I spend more time on the phone calming people down, telling them that everything is okay at The Preserve, than I do moving the project forward. If Jack's wire is late, it will just destroy us—me, my credibility with the trades, everything. You know, Peter, that if these trades don't get paid, they'll pull off our job so fast our heads will spin. There are seventeen other communities competing with us to open first. They would love to see us fumble the ball now."

Somehow my torrent of words and fear stopped long enough for Peter to respond.

"Nothing we can do about it tonight," Peter said patiently. "Now get home, make dinner, and love your kids."

He was right. There was nothing we could do. "Okay, Peter," I said, "I'll see you in the morning.

Twelve

I found it difficult to concentrate on anything but the wire transfer as I muddled through dinner preparations. I was anything but good company for my family that night. What was I going to tell the trades—the people who did the actual, physical work of building our communities—if the money was late? They didn't care about our financial situation. They only wanted to be paid for their labor. And who could blame them?

We couldn't afford any more bad press. All our eggs, or at least Peter's and mine, were in one basket—The Preserve. After dinner as I sat on the edge of the tub keeping Taylor company, I was still working, of course. I began to prioritize payments if Jack's money didn't come in, mentally determining which trades we needed the most. The road building company that Peter's father owned was owed the most. They had been working double time to get the road to the clubhouse finished. Maybe Peter should call his father tonight and prepare him for the worst-case scenario tomorrow.

My thoughts were interrupted by little Taylor's sweet voice. "Mommy, will you read me a story?" she asked.

I was grateful for the interruption. "Sure, honey," I said. "Let's dry you off. You've been in the tub so long you look like a raisin."

"I was just waiting for you to stop working, Mommy," Taylor explained. "Do you ever stop?"

I sighed. The last thing I wanted was for this business to interfere with my family.

"Yes, honey, I'm sorry. Mommy has a big problem at work, but I shouldn't bring it home. Listen, I need some special Taylor time to make me all better. How about a big bear hug around my neck?"

Taylor jumped out of the water and threw her little arms around my neck. Her long curly blond hair, green eyes, and double-dimples smile wiped all my troubles away.

After we finished in the bathroom, we climbed onto her bed. "Will you lie down with me?" Taylor asked.

"Sure, honey," I said, yawning. As soon as I put down my head, I was fast asleep.

"Rose, time to get up," Zack was saying. "You fell asleep with Taylor last night. I didn't want to disturb you so I left you here."

"Thanks, Zack," I said, rubbing a kink in my neck. "What time is it?"

"Seven," Zack said.

Suddenly all the terror about the missing million dollars returned to me. "I better get moving," I said, already on edge.

"What's on your agenda today?" asked Zack, oblivious to my anxiety.

"Well, Zack," I began, trying not to get impatient with him, "we're holding our breath for Wood's wire transfer to arrive. Otherwise, I've got to call the vendors and tell them to wait a day or two."

For once Zack understood my tension. "That's no good!" he exclaimed. "Who's your biggest trade?"

"The road building contractor."

"Just call the Pope," Zack said. "You're better off getting to him before some crew leader does. I'm sure he'll understand."

I nodded. "Thanks, good idea. I think I'll let Peter make that call."

As I drove to the office that morning, I found myself praying out loud: "I am claiming victory in prayer over this day today."

While I waited in a long line of cars for the traffic light to change, I pulled out my now well-worn book in which I kept my notes from Pastor Grant's sermons. Flipping to the entry I had made the previous Sunday, I read Romans 8:31: "What then, shall we say in response to this? If God is for us, who can be against us?"

I began to have a clearer understanding about what James was talking about at the beginning of his letter to the Jews: "Consider it pure joy, my brothers and sisters, whenever you face trials of many kinds, because you know that the testing of your faith develops perseverance. Perseverance must finish its work so that you may be mature and complete, not lacking anything" (James 1:2).

The verses echoed through my mind. I was facing trials, all right, and the only thing I had to hold was my faith, my belief that God would see me through this dark time. My immature faith was being stretched.

It was 8:30 when I reached the office. I thought I would call the bank first to see if Sean was in. He was notorious, though, for keeping banker's hours. "Come on, Sean," I implored. But he wasn't there. "Dang it, voice-mail again," I muttered, and I left him two urgent messages. I figured that would be enough from me before nine.

I waited anxiously for Peter to arrive. As soon as he entered the office, I pounced.

"Peter, I'm glad you're finally here," I said. "We need to call your dad. He may have to carry us if Jack's wire doesn't arrive."

"Good morning to you, too!" Peter replied, surprised by my already high level of anxiety. "You're already on high speed, and it's only 8:30. Slow down and answer a few questions before I call my old man. What do we owe on the road construction?"

"Seven hundred thousand dollars this period," I replied.

Suddenly Peter looked alarmed. That was clearly more than he expected. "Holy smokes," he said, his anxiety level suddenly matching mine. "I don't know if he can carry that. What does Jack say about his wire?"

"Here's his latest e-mail," I said, and I read the part about teatime in London.

"Well, hopefully today your troubles will be for naught," Peter said.

I nodded. "I'm claiming that victory."

Peter laughed. "Oh, don't go preaching again this early," he said.

"You better get with it, Peter, or you may be too late,"

Now Peter's grin widened. "Oh, Rose," he said, "you'll put in a good word for me with the big guy. I'll be just fine."

Peter left my office as my phone rang. It was Sean. I held my breath, hoping for good news.

"Hey, Rose, Sean here," he began. "Don't get too excited hearing my voice; no news on the wire. I just wanted to keep you informed."

I slumped a little. "Thanks, Sean," I replied. "I'll get on Wood right away. The more time I have before the English bank stops sending wires, the better."

No more e-mail for Jack, I decided. *I'm calling his cell phone*. Fortunately, he picked up.

"Jack," I said, relieved to get him. I tried to sound pleasant and calm, but I wondered how much of my anxiety was leaking through. "Good morning, how's it going?"

"Okay," he replied cautiously. Obviously, he could hear my deep concern. "What's up?"

"Well, the wire. We've got a million-dollar payout at 3:00 p.m., and if the money isn't in, all hell is going to break loose."

Jack paused before he replied. "I'll call Seany Pooh," he said, "and get back to you."

I was relieved, although something inside told me I shouldn't be that relieved.

"Thanks, Jack," I said. "Call me as soon as possible."

I fretted for what seemed like an eternity but was probably more like four or five minutes. My computer chimed to notify me of a new e-mail. *Oh, please*, I thought, *let it be the wire confirmation.*

Jack wrote in his e-mail, "Spoke to Seany, he's cool. Go ahead and release the checks. He'll cover the overdraft until my wire arrives. Jack."

How the heck did he do that? I wondered. *Well, I'm not going to sign a check and overdraw our account by one million dollars. We'll have old Jack do that.*

E-mail time again. "Jack," I wrote, "I prepared the $1M transfer check from HBT to our operating account for your signature; need you in ASAP to sign so that we can make deposit."

Chimes rang out of my computer again as Jack's response came almost immediately.

"In the office now. Bring the check for my signature."

I was relieved, but I shook my head as I walked over to Jack's office. *How did he convince Sean to cover a $1 million overdraft?* I wondered. *Must be nice to be that rich—you have answers when everybody else just has questions.* I felt relief that we could cut the checks, but something told me that we weren't quite out of the woods.

"Hi, Jack," I said as pleasantly as I could as I entered his office. All the worry, all the sleeplessness—had he really resolved everything with a thirty-second phone call to Sean?

"How did you pull off the $1 million overdraft with HBT?" I asked.

"I went to see Sean," Jack said, looking as imperturbable as usual. "He wasn't comfortable making that size decision, so I went to see Dale."

That struck me as odd.

"Isn't he in the hospital?" I asked. Dale Burbank, Sean's boss at the bank, had been in a car accident that almost killed him.

Jack shrugged as if it wasn't that big a deal. "Yeah," he said. "His back is broken. He's in pretty bad shape, but the morphine seems to be working just fine." Jack grinned. "I got him to okay the overdraft based on my wire from Barclays being delayed."

I stared at him. "Jack," I began, "that's crazy. The guy didn't—he couldn't begin to comprehend what you were asking."

Jack laughed. "Well, all that matters is Sean holding a piece of paper signed by Dale that covers me. And all your worries are solved, at least today's!"

I shook my head leaving the office. This was insane. Still, I wrote and distributed the checks as planned, and progress at The Preserve continued. I hoped we didn't have any more of those teatime delays. I didn't think my heart or stomach could take that kind of stress every month.

I settled back at my desk to turn to projects that had taken a back seat to finding that million dollars when the phone rang.

"Rose, it's Sean," my banker sputtered. "What the heck is going on?"

"What do you mean?" I asked cautiously.

"Your checks have overdrawn your account by a million bucks—and that wire is still not here."

"Jack told me you were covering the overdraft. I'll read you his e-mail."

I could hear Sean sighing over the phone. "Oh, crap," he said. "I thought he was joking when he asked me to do that."

"Well, he says he cleared it with Dale Burbank," I said, my anxiety returning.

"Dale is so sedated that he doesn't even know where he is," Sean said, disgusted. "This really stinks. I've got auditors coming in next week!"

I had heard enough. "Listen, Sean," I said, "you'd better call Jack yourself. He will respond better if you talk to him. I'll just get in the way at this point. I'll e-mail him and let him know that he 'misunderstood' your willingness to cover a million-dollar overdraft."

"Great," Sean said. "I'll wait a few minutes, and then call him."

Sean called Jack and told me later that Jack had a very matter-of-fact attitude about the whole thing. Sean explained to Jack that his job at the bank would be on the line if Jack didn't get that million dollars into the account or sign documents to make the overdraft a short-term loan to Jack until his wire arrived. They arranged to meet at 1:00 p.m. at Sean's office, at which time Jack would sign the loan documents guaranteeing the $1 million in the event that the wire transfer still hadn't come through. Sean said he got pretty annoyed when Jack told him, "Hey, Seany, just relax, man!" Sean replied that he'd relax when Jack signed the loan documents or had that money in the account.

The wire never came through, so Jack dutifully went down and signed the loan guarantee. I thought that was the end of it, but an entire week passed, and still no cash infusion. Oddly enough, Jack didn't seem too concerned about a missing million dollars. *What could be up?* I wondered. We were still in the hole for the money, and the bank was breathing down my neck.

On the seventh day after the wire was due, I called Jack.

"Jack, what the heck is going on?" I asked.

"I tell you what," Jack said, sounding bothered but not overly distraught. "You guys are going to have to work something out. The best I can do is about $200,000. How about the Pope—what can he do?"

This was getting weird. "Hold on a minute," I said. "Where is the wire?"

"That's another story," Jack said. "You better get Peter and the Pope together for a meeting. I'm available this afternoon or tomorrow." And with that he hung up.

What is happening? Just as I picked up the phone to call Peter, Sean was on the line.

"Listen, Rose," Sean said in an "all business" tone of voice. "Call your partners and tell them that the bank is calling all of the personal guarantees on loan. That means Wood, Durkee, and Durkee Senior need to cover this gigantic overdraft or the loan is in default."

He hung up. I caught my breath and called Peter. "Peter, Sean just called. He said the bank is calling all the guarantors to fix this overdraft today. He's really ticked off that Jack would take advantage of Dale while he's in the hospital and drugged to the point of not knowing his own name. Sean is now responsible for this mess, and he says his job is on the line."

"Who are the guarantors?"

"You, your dad, and Wood," I explained. "And the bank isn't pleased with Wood's performance, so it looks like you and your dad."

"How did Father end up as a guarantor on our loan?" Peter asked, confused.

"I guess the bank wanted an older, more reliable guarantor than the two of you. It looks like they were the smart ones on this deal."

Peter sighed. "I'll call him," he said. "He is not going to be very happy about this at all."

And he wasn't. The Pope immediately called a meeting including Craig, Peter, Jack, and me to get an understanding of what had led to this funding train wreck. Everybody assembled in the Pope's office that afternoon, and nobody looked very happy.

"Gentlemen," the Pope began, opening the meeting as he peered over his glasses, "and lady," he said, acknowledging my presence. "What the Sam Hill is going on here?"

Jack cleared his throat. “The pressure of Coliseum Golf,” he began. “The $4 million loss. It’s got my investors crawling all over me. Plus, I don’t ever remember agreeing to fund $8 million. I was the one who refused Peter’s offer to give up all interest in The Preserve and do it for management fees only in the beginning, if I would fund it. I could have done so at the time, but after thinking about it overnight, I came back and refused. I told him that it was not going to happen that way and that we would do it together and find the financing to keep it fifty-fifty.”

The rest of us were exchanging glances. Jack’s comments did not hold together well enough to make clear what he was trying to say.

“Part of why I did that,” Jack continued, “was because I felt God prompted me to do it, though it was not my kind of investment, and specifically that God wanted me to do it for Peter. If I had not felt that, I would not have gone into business with him. I’ve been kind of angry at God about that lately. I did this project on his prompting, and God, you got me into this and the coliseum deal, and it’s been nothing but pain and suffering for me.”

I just stared at Jack, wondering how he had the audacity to blame God for his financial missteps. The man clearly had no shame.

“I told you that dreadful day I agreed to meet you for lunch, Phillip,” Jack continued, “that I was liquid, thank you very much, and that I did not want to be in real estate anymore. At times, I’m sorry that day ever happened. Sorry I ever moved to Turtle Cove and sorry that I ever got involved in real estate.” Jack finally stopped talking and waited for a response.

I was tired of Jack’s finger-pointing and general line of crap. Before anyone could say anything, I pulled the “out of balance personal guarantee” of $8 million and slid it across the table to Jack.

“Here is your personal guarantee,” I said. “That is your signature, isn’t it?”

Jack kept his cool. “You must have slipped that paper into a bunch of others at the closing,” he said calmly. “I don’t remember that at all. If I am forced to add more to the project, I will have to expect my participation in the project to increase substantially. I do not desire to increase my position. In fact, I desire to sell it to anyone who will buy it."

Peter and the Pope were equally shocked at Jack—now he was demanding a bigger piece of the deal.

"The range on real estate deals," Jack said, oblivious to the chaos he was creating, "goes from where I am a 'signature guarantor' to eighty percent for a full equity partner with limited liability on the part of the minority partner. I would suggest that you do something quickly, because up until several weeks ago I was under the impression that the loan was a revolver, and frankly, I think we all were. I also assigned the task of making sure the company was properly capitalized to Craig and Rose, and nothing has been done. Lack of planning and proper handling of this matter on the part of the management of this company does not constitute an emergency on my part."

My head was about to explode. "Hold on a minute, Jack," I began, but the Pope interrupted me.

"Rose, wait just a minute," Phillip Durkee said. "Jack, we're not here to assign blame. We're here because all of us have signed personal guaranties on this $22 million loan, and based on your word to the bank about a wire that has not yet arrived, we're in the hole over $1 million. Now, having said that, how are we going to fix it before they call the note, and instead of a $1 million problem we've got a $22 million problem? I can hold off on my payment to my road building company for about a month, but no more than that. Does that give your wire time to cross the Atlantic, Jack?"

Jack remained incredibly calm. "Listen," he began, "I never said anything about a wire on the first. The day was always the fifteenth. I may have other money coming around the first that will allow me to assist in covering the overdraft. I think we're overreacting to the bank's call, though. It's just a little hiccup. Let's just sit tight and see what they do."

"Jack," Peter replied, his voice quivering. "You have to place yourself in my position to appreciate my perception of our present situation. The Preserve is the only true asset I have and my only source of income.

This income feeds my family and pays my first and second mortgages. The debacle in which we find ourselves with Heartland Bank and Trust is putting The Preserve at risk, and the possibility exists that we could lose the project. This is not a hiccup—it's a heart attack! It would be poor judgment on my part not to do everything possible to minimize the risk factors threatening the project. There are immediate and possible future capital calls that can jeopardize our loan and the project.

"On Wednesday," Peter continued, sounding increasingly desperate, "the subcontractors will not be paid and as of today, we have no solid idea when they will be paid. My sense is that Heartland Bank and Trust is not going to give you any slack on your guarantee, Jack. If I were in Heartland Bank and Trust's position, I would just sit patiently for a few more weeks until the note matures in thirty days and foreclose on the property. We cannot play chicken with them. We have everything to lose, and they know that their loan is adequately collateralized. Jack, if you're not willing to live up to your guarantee as our financial partner, we've got to find somebody who is."

Jack did not look at all pleased by Peter's spin on the situation. I wondered if he was going to blame God for this as well.

"It would appear to me," Peter concluded, "that we can accommodate both our needs by negotiating between a third and a half of our position for some cash infusion and another strong guarantor. Jeremy Pernell suggested that we meet with one of his contacts, a company called Golf America, as a potential investor. If we can develop a relationship with them, that may open up a host of new opportunities. But for now, they may be the sole remedy to cure what presently ails us. My strategy is very simple, ladies and gentlemen—survival. We are definitely at risk, and I am willing to forgo future upside potential to strengthen our current position."

That was the best speech I had ever heard Peter make in our entire time together. But Jack wasn't buying it.

"Perhaps I should write a letter detailing my thoughts to Golf America," Jack replied testily, "to tell them they should take the position of being the financial partner for The Preserve. I understand they're positioning themselves for a reverse merger with a company—a shell that had some problems in the past. They have a real opportunity for making big bucks this way. They could be getting fifty-one percent of a going concern, not a startup, that's going to add anywhere from double to six times what they're paying for the value of this company. They would be getting into Naples, and for a company whose concentration is in the golf industry, our location is a huge plus for them, and so are our real estate expertise, experience, and background.

"What you guys need to understand is I have what basically amounts to an ultimatum to get out of The Preserve and high visibility real estate projects after the letter in the *Collier Enquirer* last week saying, 'Developer Jack Wood.' This comes from another fund investor who is very large offshore. I will have to sell all my interest in The Preserve to satisfy my offshore fund investors. I would like to maintain at least some token for all the pain. I hope you understand that I cannot kill any part of my business to maintain a piece of ours, which is an investment and not a priority for me."

What planet was Jack on? Did he forget that it was because of him, his financial statement and his signature, that Heartland Bank and Trust agreed to lend us $22 million and that they were gracious (or stupid) enough to allow him to fund the equity portion after their loan had been fully funded? Most lending institutions required your money up front. *What a jerk,* I thought. I couldn't believe what I was hearing: "I cannot kill any part of my business?" *This is a part of your business, you buffoon!*

"Gentlemen," I said, "I'm not sure how we went from solving a $1 million overdraft to selling Jack's interest, but we've got to brainstorm this issue and come up with cash today."

Jack realized that he had gone too far. "You're right, Rose," he said with an oily charm. "I'm sorry. We were thinking about the big picture, while you were wallowing in the details."

"Whatever, Jack," I said angrily. It took all of the WWJD (What

Would Jesus Do) I had in me not to call him everything from a loser to a slippery, slimy SOB.

"Listen," Jack offered as Peter and his father remained silent. "I've got this investor, Mary Smith. She's got about $1 million in the fund now. She's been after me for a while to get some of her cash into real estate, maybe $200,000. This may be an opportunity that works for both of us. I imagine she'll want about eighteen percent annually. The only problem with her is that she's a bit high maintenance."

"What does that mean?" Peter asked warily.

Jack shrugged as if it weren't that big a deal. "She calls a lot," he said. "She wants to be sure that the money is safe. She's elderly, about sixty or so. You know how those folks are."

The Pope winced at Jack's characterization of sixty as elderly.

"I can deal with phone calls," I said. "You can add them to the fifty or so I get every day from Charles Jankowski, the bank, and every subcontractor who has a question."

"Okay, boys," the Pope said. "That's only $200,000. Where are we going to get the other $800,000?" He wanted his company to get paid.

"I've already spoken to Mr. Jankowski about this," I said. "I figured if the bank called him first he might freak out. He said he'd just sold one of his businesses and has about $750,000 he can lend us. He's been steaming about the 24.9 percent rate since the inception of the project. He wants Jack to lower his rate from 24.9 percent to twelve percent. He wants to make sure the project is completed and profitable for everyone, not just you, Jack."

"I'd rather you people pay me back the money you owe me," Jack said. "I've told you I can get a seventy percent return on the market. I'm losing money with this project every day."

"You will have to suffer those losses," I said, "and the only way Jankowski will put in the $750,000 is if you agree to reduce your rate going forward."

"This is crap," Jack fumed, "but I guess we don't have any other options. It makes me want to work harder to sell out of The Preserve. These little minds are bringing me down."

"Let's get back to this investor of yours, Jack," Peter said, clinging to a shred of hope that his financial life and reputation as a builder and businessman had not already been trashed. "Give us some background on her. How did you meet her?"

"Well," Jack said, feeling that he was back in the driver's seat. "I met her daughter Hannah first. She was here visiting one of my employees, Douglas Endsley, and his wife, Lisa. She went to college with Douglas, I think. Anyway, she's pretty hot!"

When none of the other men at the table expressed an interest in hearing more about her physical attributes, Jack returned to the financial story.

"During her first visit to Naples," he continued, "Douglas sold her on the fund idea, and she opened an account first in her own name. I'd say she had about $50,000 in the account for a while. Then she brought her brother into the fund. I've been making several trips a month to the Bahamas to set up Wood Bahamas, LLC, and I think one time she and her mother were there, too. In fact, they had the same $200,000 they might invest now in our real estate development. Her mother didn't like the idea of their money not being in the States, so she took it back with her on that trip."

"Hey, Jack," Peter said with a smirk, "did you give Hannah any special investment advice in the Bahamas?" Even the threat of financial ruin couldn't keep Peter's mind out of the gutter.

"Yeah, I bopped her a few times during that trip," Jack said, and he burst into his hyena laugh.

"You're a pig, Jack," I told him disgustedly.

Jack grinned happily. "I know, Rose," he said. "I just can't help myself!"

"You're a married man," I said, shaking my head. "Doesn't that matter to you? And what about your Christian beliefs?"

Jack's grin faded and his eyes became dark. "Don't preach to me, Rose," he said.

Jack then regaled Peter with the precise details of his sexual relationship with his investor. The two of them giggled like high school boys until the Pope, who was as disgusted as me, attempted to bring the swine back to order by asking, "Where did Mary get the money, Jack?"

"She got a settlement from her divorce and kept the cash," Jack explained. "She didn't want to overinvest in a fund, and she's been after me for a more solid investment in real estate."

"What do we have to do to get her to lend us the $200,000?" the Pope asked. "Send her some brochures on the project?"

"Sure." Jack said breezily. "Put a package together, and I'll call her when I leave this meeting. I could be in Knoxville tomorrow with loan documents if Andrew can produce them that fast."

"Peter," the Pope said, "get with Andrew. He can use a boilerplate agreement and have them couriered to Jack's office."

"I'll call Jankowski and have him wire the funds into our account," the Pope said. "I will have him call you directly, Jack, about the interest rate. I don't want to be in the middle of this bickering."

The meeting broke up as Jack arranged to fly to Knoxville the next day to meet Mary Smith.

Finally, I believed that the next day we would be able to take a breath—one that would not feel like our last.

That evening, when the house was finally quiet, I opened my Bible to the book of Proverbs and read:

> For the Lord gives wisdom and from his mouth come knowledge and understanding. He holds victory in store for the upright, he is a shield to those whose walk is blameless, for he guards the course of the just and protects the way of his faithful ones
>
> Proverbs 2:6–8

"Lord," I prayed, "thank you for being my shield; for guarding my course and protecting my way."

I was at the office the next day, nervously awaiting the news from

Knoxville. If Jack's smooth talking didn't work with this investor, we were sunk. And then the phone rang.

"I've got the money, Rose," Jack said happily. "It's all cash, so I'm going to drive back with my son to avoid any security issues at the airport. It'll give Jack Jr. and me some quality time with each other on the road."

"If it's cash, Jack," I said, realizing that a new problem was simply taking the place of the old one, "I'm going to need Mary's Social Security number. The reporting requirements for deposits of ten thousand dollars in cash require the source of the cash and the social."

"I don't think that's going to be possible," Jack said carefully. "Evidently, if Mary reports that she's getting interest income, like on our note—$36,000 a year in interest—it would cause some kind of problem for her."

I rolled my eyes. "Jack," I said, trying to keep calm, "there's no way that I can deposit the cash without it. You can use your Social Security number if you want, and then you can deal with the IRS."

"No," Jack said quickly. "Let me think about what to do. I'll call you back."

Just then, Craig Delaney poked his head into my office. "Did I hear you say the money we're borrowing from Jack's investor is all cash?" he asked.

"Yep, that's what he said," I replied. "And I can't take it without source of funds information."

Craig nodded. "Stick to your guns on that, Rose. You don't need any more headaches. I'm sure Jack will work something out with Ms. Smith."

I nodded. "I hope so," I said. "Sean is about to lose his job. I'm sure that Jankowski's deposit helped, but we're still upside down $250,000, and that's not chump change. I hope that Mr. Durkee is willing to hold off on the balance. We're still short $50,000 even after Jack's funds."

The phone rang. "Rose, it's Jack again. Listen. I spoke with the Pope. He's okay with taking the cash. It's clean. Mary just can't afford to lose her disability. The Pope will write The Preserve a check tomorrow after I give him the cash. He's going to meet me at Andrew's office and document the transaction. Problem solved!"

Whatever, I thought. "Drive carefully, and don't stop in any shady neighborhoods on the way home!" I told him.

"See ya soon," he said. "After this trip, I won't be in the office early. Jack Jr. and I are going to push it and see if we can make it home tonight."

The next day, I received via fax a new note signed by the Pope and Jack that showed us borrowing $200K from the road building company. It looked as if Phillip was lending us funds from the road building business and keeping the cash, potentially avoiding income tax on that $200K and saving himself more than $50K. That was between the Pope and the IRS, and I didn't even want to think about it. Our problem, at least for this month, was solved. But what about next month? Would we go through the same thing all over again? Then I realized, we've been jerking around with this overdraft for so long, next month is in just two weeks. Lord help us all!

Thirteen

The Heartland Bank and Trust, our chief source of financing, was so spooked by Jack's mystery wire and the amount of time that this multimillionaire was taking to cure the problem that its principals called a meeting, summoning all of us to their headquarters in Ohio. What better time to introduce our potential new investors from Golf America? Jack had been working with the principals of that company, and there was power in numbers. So we all flew to Ohio to give Heartland Bank and Trust our song and dance following Jack's missing million. They were most interested in Jack's financial condition. They had made this loan based on his financial strength, along with the value of the property. Totally misreading the vibe at the meeting, Jack felt singled out and became more than a little defensive. The bankers wanted him to give them some warm fuzzies, a sense that all was well. Instead, he gave them a case of ice-cold pricklies, a feeling that everything was unraveling fast.

"I repeatedly told all of you—and your attorneys—that I am under secrecy laws," he said to the gathered investors and bankers. "Yet you continue to ask me to reveal my offshore assets and to create documents to give the bank comfort. No document will survive on U.S. soil, as the trustees offshore are under the penalty of jail time for providing any. And I could possibly be held under the same laws, since I do business in those jurisdictions and have a fiduciary responsibility to my investors."

Everyone at the table was puzzled. What the heck was this guy talking about?

"Mr. Wood," the chairman of Heartland Bank and Trust said, "while we appreciate your desire to protect your investors offshore, what we are interested in is your personal funds, the ones you outlined on the financial statement that you gave us when we approved the loan."

He held up Jack's personal financial statement that touted a net worth of more than $100 million.

"We aren't interested in your fund," the chairman continued, "or for that matter any of your other businesses. It appears here on this certified financial statement that you have cash and liquid assets of more than $30 million. We simply need a method of verification. A bank statement would be sufficient."

Jack began to squirm in his chair. He pulled papers from a folder but was unable to produce what the chairman wanted.

"I didn't bring any of my personal records with me," Jack said, his tone more defensive than ever. "I didn't realize that I would be the focus of this meeting."

"Mr. Wood," the chairman replied, trying to conceal his mounting concern, "you are the financial guarantor on this note. Mr. Durkee has no sizable assets, and when we agreed to this loan, you, Mr. Wood, agreed to fund the equity of $8 million. Is there a problem with that now?"

Before Jack could answer and cause further damage to the project and to our relationship with the bank, Peter introduced Walter Thompson from Golf America as our alternative financial investor.

"It seems," Peter began diplomatically, "that Mr. Wood is suffering some investor pressure after losing $4 million on the coliseum deal and feels that he needs to reduce his involvement in our real estate project. Today, we would like the bank to release Mr. Wood as our financial guarantor and accept Golf America in his place."

Walter popped out of his chair like a jack-in-the-box.

"Hello, my name is Walter Thompson" he said, delighted to take the focus off Wood and onto his own potential involvement in the deal. "I'd like to give you an overview of what we're proposing. We'd like to have the bank approve a stock-for-stock transaction, no cash changing hands, and no taxes due. Golf America would get an eighty-one percent interest in The Preserve Development Company. In exchange, we would give stock to Wood Durkee in our IPO, which will be World Golf Clubs. The transaction, the reverse merger, that is, will take place just after Thanksgiving. Wood Durkee Development Group would then have stock worth over $9 million in a publicly traded company. We, as the eighty-one percent shareholder, would take on any of the equity calls for this project. It's really a win-win for everyone."

The bank chairman studied Thompson. "Mr. Thompson," he said, "are you able to invest $2.5 million before year's end into this project? That looks like the cash projections for the balance of the year that Mr. Wood would have been responsible for."

Thompson nodded quickly. "No problem," he said. "We've got a lot of cash. We're backed primarily by German investors. We could give the $9 million in cash to Wood Durkee Development Group, but the tax consequences would kill them. Plus, they'll have a huge up-side once the stock price rises. Of course, I'm not guaranteeing that, but we are valuing the shares at today's prices, which is $2.75. I'm projecting to hit $10 a share right out of the box."

After a few stomach-churning days, we received good news. The bank agreed to take Golf America in exchange for Jack Wood. After all the secrecy issues, they felt more comfortable with a company that operated on U.S. soil. The stock-for-stock transaction did in fact occur close to Thanksgiving, actually the first week of December. Just as Walter Thompson promised, Wood Durkee Development Group received 3,272,725 shares of restricted stock valued at $9 million.

On December 12, just one week later, the SEC filed a lawsuit against Thompson's new shell company. It seems a prior owner was charged with penny-stock fraud manipulation. The stock price fell from $2.25 to seventeen cents a share. That was the fastest personal financial decline I had ever seen.

Now Heartland Bank and Trust was smoking mad! Where was that $2.5 million? We were closing in on Christmas. These had been the most stressful three months of my life—or so I thought.

We attempted to reverse the transaction with Thompson's group under the premise that he knew or should have known that he had a problem with the SEC. He begged us for time to correct the overreaching SEC charges and promised that in short order he would pay off the Heartland Bank and Trust note with cash if he had to. Or, better yet, he said, he'd been working with First Manhattan as a partner in some other deals, and they would take out the bank in a New York minute! His optimism was along the lines of the kid in the old joke that said, "With all of this horse poop around, there must be a pony in here."

Peter Durkee and Charles Jankowski agreed to give Walter until May to solve all of The Preserve's financial problems. The goal was for him to adjust things based on the stock price's dropping to pennies, making us whole in the transaction. If unsuccessful, we'd reverse the transaction and go our separate ways. Our project, however, was now tied up in the byzantine world of the Securities and Exchange Commission. We had just traded Wood's wacky secrecy laws for a dance with the SEC. Heartland Bank and Trust was reeling out of control. They were worse off now than before, or so they thought.

Jack fled the scene of this financial crime. All he cared about was being released from his financial commitment to The Preserve, and he never looked back. He moved his trading operation to a more upscale financial district in Naples, making a clean break from his real estate debacles—and from us. He had more important things to focus on. His dream for the fund now was to top $400 million under investment.

A few months later, though, Jack suddenly resurfaced.

Fourteen

It was about six o'clock one evening a few weeks after the latest banking crisis had somehow passed. As usual, I was the first in the office and the last to leave. That meant I was alone, or at least I thought I was alone. I was finishing some of the cash flow reports when I sensed a presence behind me. As I turned around slowly, there stood Jack Wood in my doorway.

"What are you doing here?" I was trying not to show that he had scared me to pieces. *I've got to rearrange my office furniture so I can work facing the door and see danger approaching,* I told myself.

"I was over in our old offices," Wood explained, "packing up some final personal effects, and I saw your car. Listen, I know that things got crazy with that last draw and everything. I just want you to know that without you, this company would have crumbled. You are so faithful and you stand so strong in your faith. It is that determination, that belief system, that will take you far, Rose."

Well, that was a surprise! "Thanks, Jack," I replied. "I appreciate your kind words."

"So what are you working on now?" he asked nonchalantly.

"We're on to the next project," I said. "I've got to get some pro formas done tonight. We have a meeting with a new investor tomorrow on the Oak Haven project. This investor's actually got the cash."

"Ouch," Jack responded looking pained.

"Sorry," I said. "I guess I still have some open wounds from that whole mystery wire ordeal."

"All I can say, Rose," Jack said, "Is that it's probably for the best that you guys have a partner now who understands your business. It's so different from mine. I've got to keep my finger on the pulse of the market and hang out with the big boys. They're my bread and butter, you know."

Terrific, I thought. *Must be nice to be so important.* "Yeah, well, nice to see you," I said. "But I've really got to get this done tonight."

Wood didn't take the hint. "Well," he began, clearing his throat, "to tell you the truth, Rose, the reason that I came over, was, well, I was praying about the success of my own company and God spoke to me and had me focus on you and the real estate properties. I've been on my knees over at the Oak Haven property for more than an hour, and I had a vision. Evidently, the property just north of Oak Haven was owned by some brothers maybe a hundred years ago or more. That was not clear in my vision. But there is, well, there's like a curse on the property."

A curse? That caught my attention. I raised an eyebrow.

"One of the brothers killed the other," Jack explained. "And I believe that as he was dying, he cursed the land. Anyway, God has led me to you and instructed us to go out and pray over this property, intervene in the spiritual world, per se, and ask the brother for forgiveness and release of the land. If we don't do this, Rose, you will suffer the same traumas that you have on The Preserve. We have a chance to give you and Peter a clean start on this project. Why do you think those two pieces of real estate have been vacant for so long? Coincidence? I don't think so, and when I get these visions, I act! Will you pray with me on the property?"

Has this guy gone Looney Tunes or what? Brothers, killed, a hundred years ago? I realized Jack could see the disbelief on my face, and his expression suggested that maybe my spiritual life had not advanced as far as he thought it had. Maybe I was still a baby Christian, unable to move to the next level of belief. He certainly knew how to push my faith buttons.

"It'll be light for about two more hours," Jack said. "I don't want to take any chances on getting lost in the woods. You're not afraid of me, are you?"

A little bit, to tell the truth. "No, Jack," I said. "I just don't like the idea of your vision, deep in the woods—in the dark."

"Not if we go right now," Jack said excitedly. "I've got the SUV."

I thought about it for a moment. The property was only five miles down the road and maybe a mile from my house. If anything happened, I could walk home—as long as I could find my way out.

So reluctantly, and foolishly, I said, "Yes."

The property looked like ancient woods, very thick with pines and hundred-year-old palm trees. There was a dirt path that appeared to have been used by hunters. *What in the world could be living in these woods? Wild boars? Maybe Jack is getting "sooey" call from his spirit world!* I laughed nervously to myself.

Jack turned the SUV onto that path, and as we approached the gate, a sign clearly stated "No Trespassing." My heart began to pound. *What am I doing? Is this going to end in some crazy voodoo murder? Will some forensic team uncover the truth of my death in ten years?*

Jack was navigating the woods as if he had been there before. *Could this be where he's decided to kill me for all the financial stress I caused him over his guarantee at The Preserve?* A branch hit the windshield, startling me. The path was so narrow that the branches from the seedling trees were scraping the sides of the car, making the most awful sound, like fingernails on a chalkboard. I was totally creeped out. Suddenly, there was no way to tell direction. I began to panic. Jack had done a few turns on the road, and now we were so deep in the woods that I couldn't find the sun. *How can I get out of here? Which direction can I run if something awful happens? I should have been leaving some trail, clues so that somebody could find my body!*

My fearful thoughts were interrupted as we came upon a clearing. There were signs of a recent campfire with trash everywhere. Could this be where Jack was planning to kill me? *Oh, my God, why have you forsaken me?* That was the only thought I could conjure up in terms of prayer.

We crossed the clearing and reentered the narrow path. Then, without warning, Jack slammed on the brakes.

"What the heck?" I asked. Then I realized we had reached the line between the two properties. There was a chicken wire fence between the two and another warning sign that said "Keep Out." I was all for that.

"We're here," Jack said quietly. "I can feel the presence of the brothers."

Man, this is crazy, I thought. *I can't find my way out of here alone. Lord, please protect me from evil!*

Jack killed the engine and got out. He began to pace up and down the property line, mumbling, when suddenly he grabbed the fence and began to shake, almost convulsing. I was frozen with fear. I felt as if I were now involved with some sort of séance with the underworld. As I looked out the window of the locked car, a sudden calm came over Jack. But I wasn't getting out of the car for anything!

"Rose, come here," Jack called to me. "You've got to feel this."

"Feel what?" I replied, not moving. "I'm not liking this at all."

"No, really, there is such peace here now," Jack replied, his tone certain. "I worked out a treaty with the brothers—did you see them?"

"What, are you crazy?" I asked, getting more scared by the minute. "Did I see who?"

"The brothers!" Jack exclaimed, wide-eyed. "Man, they were both right in front of me! The one had an ax in his head from the murder. His brother was still covered in blood and was crying, asking for mercy and forgiveness. It was an accident, a hunting accident. Anyway, I was able to provide the spiritual forgiveness transference that was needed, so that they could pass through to the other side."

I rolled my eyes. This guy was bonkers. "Right, great, can we go now?" I asked, more appalled than afraid.

"You need to feel this peace," Jack said resolutely.

"I can feel it just fine from here," I said, just as firmly. "Now let's go!"

Jack returned to the vehicle. "Okay, okay," he said, somewhat disgusted with me. "I can see you're not ready for this level of spirituality."

"You've got that right," I said. "I don't think I'll ever be ready for this!"

"Don't hold back your potential, Rose," Jack said patronizingly. "You've got the spiritual power in you. You've just got to unleash it."

I knew at this point that any reasonable comment would go unheard; Jack had clearly left the planet. He got back in the SUV, closed his eyes, and sat quietly for a few minutes, meditating. *Man, oh man, get me out of here alive!*

Fortunately, after about five minutes, Jack opened his eyes and appeared normal again. *Just get me out of here, Lord,* I silently prayed.

About halfway back, Jack once again stopped the car abruptly.

"Why are you stopping?" I asked, alarmed.

"I know you want me," Jack said, glancing slyly at me.

"Want you for what?" I asked, uncomprehendingly.

"Don't play with me, Rose. I know you want me." Suddenly I understood his game.

"Have you lost your mind?" I shouted at him. "Start this car now and take me back to the office."

My emotion meter went from fear to rage. I was prepared to defend myself, even if I had to hurt this man.

"You know, Jack," I said, "You profess to be a deacon, a Christian man, for God's sake, you just brought me out here under the pretext that God wanted me to pray with you over this property, and now you sit here asking me if I want you—you are one sick puppy!"

"Look, Rose," Jack said calmly, "God created sex. He expects us to enjoy it."

"Yeah, with your wife," I retorted, "not every woman who walks the earth. You better review those Ten Commandments, buddy. There are a few on adultery and coveting."

"Rose, come on," Jack said dreamily. He leaned toward me, and I held up my fist.

"So help me, Jack," I told him angrily. "The only thing you'll be explaining in a few minutes is how you got two black eyes and a broken nose! Now put this car in drive and get me back to the office."

Jack let out his hyena laugh. "I was just kidding, Rose," he said. "You don't have to get all worked up."

I rolled my eyes. "Whatever," I muttered. "You are a complete jerk and you need some psychological counseling—and soon."

The ride back to the office found me poised to engage in a fistfight and Jack grinning and laughing like a hyena. *Peter is never going to believe this story,* I thought. *The biggest kick he'll get is when he asks me what I was thinking going into the woods with this psycho.*

Once I could see the main road, I released one of my hands from a clenched fist position and held onto the door handle, ready to jump if I had to. As Jack pulled up to the office building, I was already halfway out the door and heading toward my car. I did not want to take a chance that he would follow me into the office.

"Bye, Rose," he called out after me, "have a peaceful night!" Then he punctuated his farewell with his hideous laugh.

I walked straight to my car, locked the doors, hit the gas pedal, and never looked back. I grabbed my cell phone to dial Peter but stopped myself before the call went through. What was I going to say to Peter that would not cause him to further doubt my faith and my beliefs? I could hear him already, saying something like "You people talk out of both sides of your mouths, praising God on Sunday and returning to fleshly behavior the rest of the week. You need to be more like me. I'm no hypocrite. What you see is what you get."

I've got to keep this to myself, I thought. *I don't need to share this story with Zack either. Who knows what he would do? He never liked Jack and blamed him for my long hours and stress at work. It's too weird to believe anyway—spirits in the woods.*

By the time I got home, I had myself under control. I switched into my "mommy mode" and managed to get through dinner and Taylor's bedtime routine with a smile, yet I couldn't get my mind off what had happened earlier in the day. It was people like Jack, with their bizarre behavior, who called Christianity into question for agnostics like Peter.

When I saw that Zack was still in his recliner in front of the television, where he had been since he finished dinner, I knew this was the perfect time for me to get my Bible and continue my study of the Beatitudes. "Let's see," I said out loud as I skimmed the topics listed in my Bible. "A tree and its fruit; this one looks interesting." I settled into my chair and began reading:

Watch out for false prophets. They come to you in sheep's clothing, but inwardly they are ferocious wolves. By their fruit you will recognize them. Do people pick grapes from thornbushes, or figs from thistles? Likewise every good tree bears good fruit. A good tree cannot bear bad fruit, and a bad tree cannot bear good fruit. Every tree that does not bear good fruit is cut down and thrown into the fire. Thus, by their fruit you will recognize them

Matthew 7:15–20

Maybe I was still a baby Christian, but I knew God was speaking to me at that moment through his word. I may have missed it with Jack, but from now on if someone told me he was a Christian I wasn't just going to take his word for it; I was going to be a fruit inspector! Jack Wood was just about out of our business lives anyway, and I was out of his SUV.

Fifteen

While we were fighting our own battles to keep the cash coming in and get our projects built, the county commissioners, including Eugene Gannon, one of the commissioners involved in Coliseum Golf, were fighting battles of their own. After the local newspaper harshly criticized ethics in Collier County government, Gannon and the commissioners created a citizen panel charged with creating a local ethics ordinance that would be even more stringent than state law. Still, the community remained unsettled.

The Women's Political Caucus drew a crowd of more than two hundred people to listen to public officials and media representatives give their points of view on the Gannon matter and on ethics in general.

Then a local environmentalist, Stan Gofman, filed a sworn complaint with the Ethics Commission asking for a further probe of Gannon's involvement in the now-defunct Coliseum Golf, a complaint that seemed to be merely a springboard for retired right-wingers to stir the pot. Two months later another complaint was filed; this one claimed that Commissioner Anita Satterwhite improperly accepted tickets to a Nuveen Tennis Event and did not fully disclose the amount on her gift report. The complaint was followed immediately by an accusation that Commissioners English, Hanover, and Gannon had played in the Naples LG Championship Pro-Am, a golf tournament put together by Nicholas Shubert, when three scheduled players dropped out.

Collier County began to spin out of control. The *Collier Enquirer* made the commissioners sound like the mob. Every move the commissioners made—from the votes they cast to the lunches they enjoyed—was recorded in the paper and scrutinized.

The formal complaints filed against Gannon triggered a state attorney's office investigation. State Attorney Mike Pennino's Florida Department of Law Enforcement (FDLE) agents interviewed each of us and, in exchange for our truthful testimony, granted us immunity. Pennino said that direct, not circumstantial evidence of a quid pro quo would be "indispensable" in proving criminal charges of bribery or unlawful compensation under state law. After a fourteen-month investigation that included a review of 7,500 pages of documents, Pennino said he could not establish direct evidence to show a money-for-votes exchange between Gannon and Coliseum Golf founder Nicholas Shubert. Therefore, the state attorney could not charge Gannon with bribery or unlawful compensation, and he concluded his investigation without filing formal charges.

The headline in the *Collier Enquirer* on October 16, 1998, however, carried a mixed message: Gannon: No Criminal Charges Filed, But Panel Still Looking At Civil Ethics Violations.

Unsatisfied with the state attorney's decision, environmentalist Stan Gofman continued to beat the drum in front of the Florida Commission on Ethics. The ethics panel wound up using many of the files assembled by Pennino's investigators as evidence. After several months of meetings, the commission voted unanimously in favor of a finding of probable cause—the equivalent of a formal charge. If he was found culpable, the Ethics Commission could fine Gannon $10,000 per violation or even have him removed from office. The commission also found that Gannon violated ethics laws by accepting free play in Shubert's pro-am golf tournament. Gannon denied all wrongdoing but had to decide whether to agree to a settlement or fight the charges at a hearing before an administrative law judge. He stated publicly that "facts and the law" were on his side, but the cost of the legal bills could influence his decision.

Six months after Gannon was cleared of criminal charges, Stan

Gofman told the Florida Ethics Commission that Pennino had a conflict of interest because of his financial ties to the Coliseum Golf project.

For thirty-one years, Pennino had been the top elected prosecutor for five southwest Florida counties. Could the fabric of our local and state government be rife with the level of corruption Gofman was claiming? Had the good old boy network finally run its course, allowing our snowbirds, relocated from the big cities up north, to take over the local government and hold our officials to a higher standard of conduct?

Gofman, with nothing but time on his hands, continued to press Florida Governor Jeb Bush to prosecute Gannon. Finally, in May 2000, Gannon faced a civil trial on six ethics charges, including misuse of his public office for his stake in Coliseum Golf.

"I think it's worth spending my money to prove I'm right and you're wrong and you'll be eating crow," Gannon was quoted by the *Collier Enquirer* in response to the upcoming trial.

As Peter and I continued to toil and grow our development company, Jack Wood became just a bad memory. He continued to invest in a myriad of companies, both locally and abroad.

In keeping with his image, Jack had moved the offices of Wood Investment Fund to what served as a financial district for Naples. He hired the interior decorators that had designed the club at The Preserve and had them replicate much of the interior design, a very rich, lavishly decorated Charleston/Savannah theme for his 7,000-square-foot suite. The space brimmed with leather chairs and sofas, cherry wood credenzas and armoires. Expensive artwork hung on every wall. The conference room featured a massive mahogany conference table; potential investors sipped their coffee from Wedgwood china and their cold beverages from Waterford crystal. Jack's office included photos of him shaking hands with former president George H. W. Bush, Barbara Bush, and General Norman Schwarzkopf, among others.

Jack's fund was eclipsing Wall Street's top performers when he came crashing down. I learned of Jack's downfall from people close to the story. Jack stood on the balcony of his top floor office watching the sunset in the Gulf of Mexico just a few hundred yards away. Returning to his desk in the sun's last orange glow, Jack threw his head back against the rich brown leather chair and gazed through the skylight above him—a beautiful gold trimmed glass pyramid ceiling that allowed him to admire the night sky.

The sky, the moon, and the stars are my only limitation, he thought, smiling as he lit his evening cigar.

Wood Investment Fund had become more of a personality cult than a conventional money management firm, and Jack was clearly the object of employee awe. They were all indebted to him for their fancy company cars, homes, and lavish vacations in the Cayman Islands, the Bahamas, and Belize, which he called "business trips."

Jack surrounded himself with family and close friends at the office, with family members holding key positions. His wife, Tara, was the CFO who produced the monthly performance results. Tom, his older brother, was the president of the operation, touted in the company brochure as a former "transportation executive," though he really had been a salesman in waste management. Jack's son from his first marriage, Jack Jr., was vice president and head trader. Jack's son-in-law, Herman Stutz, worked as the company's systems development manager, and the company treasurer, Thelma Shaw, was Tara's cousin from Michigan.

No one had to know that Junior was just a low-level clerk and runner at the Chicago Board of Trade or that Jack's son-in-law had flipped burgers and managed restaurants before Jack began his "on-the-job training." After all, his daughter Amie had to be provided for properly. And if their backgrounds didn't appear particularly distinguished, the trade-off was the security Jack felt being surrounded by loyal family members whom he had rescued from dead-end careers and furnished with enviable lifestyles. None of them was likely to hack into his computers or reveal his secret trading system as long as the gravy kept flowing.

Only two outsiders were close to Jack. One was his personal assistant, Keri Phalen, who protected Jack the way a lioness protects her cubs. All meetings, calls, and even e-mails went through Keri. She treated Jack like some kind of god.

The other was Malik Kasal; the young mathematician who had developed the computer model Jack called the Raptor. Malik designed the Raptor to identify historic patterns in the market that produced outsized swings in either direction, finding the best opportunities for investment the way a bird of prey seeks out only the best opportunities to hunt.

Malik was often troubled when Jack would call him at all hours of the night with questions about the computer program that required, at least in Jack's mind, immediate action. *What the heck are you doing down there, Jack?* Malik wondered.

Jack began to believe his own publicity and behave as if he were invincible. He really began to think that everything he touched turned to gold. As Wood Investment Fund press releases reported the fund topping $400 million, Jack decided that he could trade from anywhere in the world.

The millennium New Year was approaching and Jack could not think of one good reason to ring in 2000 in Naples. He decided to pack up the entire staff and their significant others for a weeklong celebration in the Cayman Islands. Jack rented a private jet for the trip stocked with champagne and caviar, the first leg in a lavish junket to thank the staff for the fund's stellar performance that year.

When the private jet landed, a local representative met the Wood Investment Fund staffers and whisked them away—without Jack. He had a meeting with a banker—a meeting to which he had to take three large suitcases—and he promised he would meet up with the group at the hotel in a few hours.

Those suitcases never made the trip home to Naples. A wire transfer would have been easier and a lot lighter. Was Jack hiding money from his wife or, worse, from the IRS?

After this trip, Malik began to question some of Jack's methods with the Raptor system. He had always called Malik at all hours of the night, but now he was calling with really weird questions. It was time to produce the year-end statements for the fund. This was a task that only Jack did, alone. This would be the final Wood Investment Statement of this millennium, 1999. *What would* 2000 *hold for Wood Investment Fund?* Jack thought to himself.

He emerged from his office to the trading area with a wild look in his eyes.

"The return for this month, the final month of 1999 . . . is 6.66 percent." Jack broke into his hyena laughter.

Everyone stood in horror. They'd all been spooked about the dangers of Y2K and how it could cripple the market; and now a real sign of "the mark of the beast"—666!

What had happened to Jack? His eyes were wild with rage; his cold laughter terrified those present in his office.

The clock struck midnight without the computers around the world crashing. "Thank God," Jack thought as he twirled in his leather chair staring up through his glass ceiling. It was January 2000, a new year. The fund had performed phenomenally.

"It's bonus time—for me!" he said out loud in his office, although there was no one there to hear. The staff had been given an all-expense-paid trip to the Caymans for Christmas. Each of the fund investors received two Waterford crystal champagne glasses engraved "2000" from Jack and Tara. But what about Jack? He'd have to take care of this bonus matter himself.

Jack had read somewhere that the CEOs of Fortune 500 companies were making a cool million-dollar bonus this year. Jack figured that since he had eclipsed all of the Wall Street returns this year, he would give himself a $2 million bonus. "That's right," he told himself as he spun around in his massive leather desk chair, "$2 million!"

He had just completed an interview with *Barron's* financial magazine that would take his fund to a new level. I hope he was wearing a seat belt for this ride!

Sixteen

A local attorney, my very first landlord in Naples and now an old friend, Joseph Temple, contacted me. He asked if I would join him and one of his associates for lunch. He wanted to get some insight on to ask me a few questions about this Wood character for some of his clients.

By that point, I had not seen or even spoken to Jack Wood in what seemed like years. What could I possibly offer to these attorneys?

I met them for lunch the following day, in late January 2000. Joseph and his associate stood as I entered the restaurant. He waved me over to the table. My heart began to pound. *Why would Joseph Temple, an attorney in downtown Naples, want to know anything about Wood, especially from me?*

"Hi, Rose, it's great to see you, it's been a long time," Joseph said as he greeted me with open arms. He introduced one of his law partners, Steven Warrick.

After we ordered lunch, Joseph wasted no time getting to the point.

"Listen," he said, concerned. "I'll cut right to the chase. Steven specializes in securities cases for our firm, and we have several clients who are investors in Wood's investment fund and are a little concerned about some of Wood's methods. Our clients have enjoyed some pretty unbelievable returns, and frankly, we just don't think that they are humanly possible to attain."

"Rose, do you have any money invested in the fund?" Steven queried.

"Yes, I do," I said. "My husband and I have two IRAs with Wood's investment fund. Actually, the statements come from a company called Retirement Accounts Inc. Why do you ask?"

I began to feel my palms sweat. Just last week, Douglas Endsley, Wood's "outside guy," was in the office, and I had given him two checks for $2,000 each to put into our IRAs. Was I about to learn that my IRAs were at risk?

Steven continued, "We're not suggesting that Mr. Wood is doing anything wrong. I'm merely trying to get some insight into his company. Joseph tells me that you were once partners with Wood, is that correct?"

"Yes, well, sort of. Wood was to be our financial partner at The Preserve," I said. "Unfortunately, after the coliseum land deal, where he lost four million dollars, he pulled out of The Preserve. We were left to negotiate with Heartland Bank and Trust and a new partner, who turned out to have some serious problems with the SEC. The Preserve project has been a problem from the start. Peter and I have done another project since The Preserve, and it took half the time and none of the stress."

"Listen, Rose," Steven said, "if you've got any money in that fund that you're not willing to kiss good-bye, get it out now."

I stared at him. *Jack Wood was a strange guy, but a criminal? What would this mean for our company? Have we been in bed with a criminal all this time? Will people think we knew who Wood really was?*

"I believe that things are going to get a little uncomfortable for Mr. Wood very soon, and I think you've suffered enough based on what you've told me today. Get your money into a qualified plan *now*."

I raced back to the office feverishly dialing Peter's cell number; he was not going to believe this!

Great, I told myself as I raced up the stairs of our office building. *Peter's truck is in the parking lot. I hope he's alone, because I don't want to cause a riot.* I opened Peter's office door to find him in his typical office attire, faded shorts and a golf shirt, and his typical position, bare feet up on the desk.

"Brace yourself, Peter," I said. "You're not going to believe this."

Peter sat up straight in his chair. "Where have you been, and what are you so excited about?" he said.

"I got a call yesterday from Joseph Temple—he's an attorney friend of mine. Anyway, he asked if I would meet him and one of his law partners for lunch to chat about none other than our Mr. Wood."

Peter's eyes widened with intrigue, and I repeated what Steven had told me about Wood and Wood's investment fund.

"Oh, for God's sake, Rose," Peter responded. "You have one attorney with a burr in his butt over Wood and you're ready to shut down your account?" It struck me that Peter seemed almost to be defending Wood.

"Look, Peter," I replied, "things have not been great between us and Wood since Coliseum Golf and the whole million-dollar overdraft. It would be no love lost for me to call and close my IRA accounts. How much money do you have in the fund yourself, Peter?"

"I don't have a pot to piss in or a window to throw it out of, but my father, and for that matter my mother, have about a hundred grand in the fund. I may want to call Father and tell him about your little meeting, and then he can decide."

Peter looked at me pensively. "Do you think the guy's a fraud?" he asked.

"I don't know. These attorneys didn't give much detail about their investigation. They asked a lot of questions about how much money he had invested in our companies and if we noticed any unusual behavior. I told them that unusual behavior was all we ever saw."

Peter and I had a good laugh for a moment and then both considered the possibilities.

"You know, Rosie," he mused, "there is one trader at Wood's office that seems like an honest guy. His name is Jimmy Carranza, and I always said that if he ever left, that's when I would get nervous about Wood. I wonder if he is still there."

"Why don't you call Leonard Cicero?" I said, "He's got an office at Wood's investment fund, and he can tell you what Carranza is doing."

The sooner we knew the better. "Call him right now!" I exclaimed. This whole investment fund thing was getting to me. More Wood headaches—it was just too much.

"Okay, Rose, just relax, I'll call Leonard's cell phone, see what's going on in Hell, or is it Heaven this week?"

Peter smirked at me as if this whole thing was an ambulance-chasing attorney after an upstanding citizen. Typical Peter—making light of a critically serious situation.

Peter dialed the number and put the call on his speakerphone so I could hear. "Leonard, it's Pete, I'm with Rose. Hey, is Jimmy Carranza still trading at Wood's investment fund?" Peter and I waited with anticipation for Leonard's response.

"No, he left Wood last month and opened his own firm," Leonard said. "Evidently, Jimmy decided that the way Jack was moving was counter to his trading methods. Why do you ask?"

Peter's heart began to beat faster. He took the call off the speaker. "The wheels may be flying off of the wagon," he told me, and then he punched the speaker button again so I could hear Leonard.

"Thanks, Len. Keep your ears to the ground. Call me if you hear anymore about Carranza."

"Will do, Peter. Later."

"I'd better call Father and let him know what we've heard, and I'm not sure what that is, but we'd better be safe then sorry."

I left Peter's office as he was dialing his father's number; I was definitely feeling more sorry than safe at the moment.

Peter left for New Jersey the next day expecting to settle a suit he had filed against the big venture capital firm that had "stolen" our $200,000 deposit and never performed at The Preserve. Peter had a sense of valor; he needed to protect other small companies like ours from these kinds of snakes. He was pumped, sure that we couldn't lose. Jack was supposed to testify that the firm promised to lend $20 million in development funds for The Preserve and instead took our deposit of earnest money and ran. The night before the trial was to begin, as Peter was preparing for his testimony, he got a call from Leonard Cicero.

"Peter, all hell has broken loose here in Naples," Leonard said. "*Barron's* ran an article about Wood's investment fund that's got the whole town in a frenzy."

"What the hell happened?" Peter was eager to hear all of the gory details.

Leonard summarized the *Barron's* article for Peter in short order. "Hold on a second, I'll read you a paragraph. 'Late last year, *Barron's*, the popular financial weekly, began to investigate a new trading guru. They refer to Wood as the 'King of Naples.' Would you trust your money to this guy?'" Leonard went on to say that the article dug up details about Wood's past. "Evidently, he filed personal bankruptcy and had a brush with the law in Saginaw."

"Oh for God's sake!" Peter exclaimed.

"Well," Leonard replied, "there was like this giant sucking sound. Investors tried to get out of the fund to the tune of over $40 million."

"How did Wood respond?"

"Wood was in the *Collier Enquirer* today," Leonard said, "and I quote 'There is no effect really,' Wood said, 'of the investor's withdrawals. We've never had any problems with redemptions. They'll have them out in the normal period.' He is also quoted as saying, 'You could have fifty percent go out and it would not hurt the fund.' He told the paper he's ordered an audit and hopes to have the results in two days to calm the investors down."

"Good grief," Peter said again as the implications of Jack's negative publicity sank in. "This sucks! I mean, tomorrow Wood takes the stand. If his credibility is an issue with the jury, we're screwed."

Leonard continued. "Evidently, there are two attorneys in town that are beating the drum to get Wood to 'show them the money.' Wood said it's a vulture mentality, circling in for what they hope will be the kill, and then he said, 'They're going to be disappointed.'"

"Leonard, I've got to try and find Wood to see what's going on before the trial tomorrow. Call me back if anything else breaks, okay?"

"Okay, Peter. You call too if you hear anything."

"Deal!" Peter pressed the receiver down just long enough to get a dial tone to call Jack.

"Hey, Pete, is that you?" Jack said as if nothing was wrong.

"What the heck is going on down there?" Peter asked.

"Oh, some egotistical opinionated writer from *Barron's* wanted to make a name for himself and used me and the fund. Don't worry, I'll be there tomorrow bright and early for the trial."

"Okay," Peter said, relieved. "Do you need a ride from the airport?"

"No, Peter, I've got a limo to the courthouse. Don't worry, get some rest."

"Okay, Jack, take it easy. I'll see you tomorrow."

Peter was stunned by Jack's nonchalant attitude, but after thinking about it, Jack always acted inappropriately under pressure. As Peter got in his hotel bed, he reflected on his relationship with Jack and The Preserve debacle. After all, that's what had landed Peter in Hackensack, New Jersey, on a freezing February night. *Jack Wood*, Peter pondered. *What is this guy about?* He drifted off to sleep.

"All rise, the Honorable Judge Black presiding." The court bailiff's voice rang through the old courtroom the next morning at 9:00 a.m.

"Please be seated," the judge instructed. "Let me hear from the plaintiff."

Just then, Peter's cell phone began to vibrate—it was Leonard with a "911." Peter leaned over to his attorney and asked for a short recess following the opening arguments. He ran out of the courtroom as soon as the judge was out of sight, punching in Leonard's number as he ran.

"Len, what's up?" Peter asked.

"The FBI and the SEC just raided Wood's office. The news report said they've charged him with a massive securities fraud—he's cheated investors out of $59 million!"

Peter looked up and saw Jack walking across the street to the courthouse.

"What the heck? Wood just got here! Do you think he knows what's going on there?" Peter asked, confused.

"Oh, yeah!" Len replied. "He provided sworn testimony today admitting the scheme. The SEC complaint was filed yesterday in New York."

Leonard's words pierced Peter's heart.

"Maybe that's why he's here. Listen, Len, I'll call you back." Peter needed to talk to Jack, and fast.

The next day's edition of the *Collier Enquirer* showed investors crying in the parking lot of the office building that once held their dreams. Their retirement plans had ended as the FBI and SEC raided the Wood Investment offices. Agents were filling a large U-Haul with boxes of seized records.

The newspaper quoted Assistant SEC Enforcement Director William Baker saying, "Wood has pledged his cooperation to locate assets. We're seeking the return of all of the money that was not his."

The article added:

> Wood Investment Fund employee Tony Fugate said Wood sent an e-mail message to employees last night. 'He apologized for what was about to happen and let us know there would be a shortfall in funds.' Just ten days ago, *Barron's* financial magazine ran a front cover article on Wood headlined, "Would you trust your money to this guy?" and now, the FBI and IRS agents are raiding his office.

We were in serious trouble.

Seventeen

Of all the financial fakers who have caused trouble in Naples, Jack Wood will be known as the perpetrator of the biggest investment fraud ever to occur.

Wood had fleeced more than three hundred investors in his fraud for more than $150 million.

Did the wealthy and sophisticated residents of Naples feel that they had financial and investment savvy? They must have; how else did they get rich in the first place? Yet they were caught up in a scheme that was too good to be true from the very beginning. There were several suicide attempts by investors who were too old to return to the work force and too embarrassed to face their families.

Wood succeeded because he made people feel lucky to be accepted into his fund. The minimum investment had grown to $1 million, a far cry from the original investors' measly $25,000. Greed drove many Neapolitans to invest as much as $8 million into the fund just weeks before the *Barron's* article questioned Wood's credibility.

Wood hoodwinked his victims with a classic Ponzi scheme—the con game named for the 1920s Boston swindler who promised fantastic investment returns of fifty percent in forty-five days. For a while, Charles Ponzi succeeded by paying early investors with a portion of the proceeds flooding in from eager new investors, until he was finally exposed in the *Boston Post* by Clarence Barron; by coincidence, the same man who later founded *Barron's* magazine.

Ponzi, an Italian immigrant, depended on what students of the scam call "affinity fraud," appealing by word of mouth to members of one's own group. In Ponzi's case, those were fellow Italian Americans itching for riches.

Wood did not hook prospects with a hard sell; rather, he relied on his own aura of wealth, on word of mouth, and on impressive presentations in print and in person. He had hired a marketing guru to produce a glossy presentation depicting Wood in his "Tommy Bahamas" sand-colored suit, barefoot on our beautiful Naples beach. The quote above the picture reads, "If a man looks sharply and attentively, he shall see fortune." Jack Jr., Wood's eldest son and vice-president of market analysis and trading, is pictured in the brochure on a Harley, wearing a leather jacket. His chosen quote: "The greatest mistake you can make is to continually fear you will make one."

In retrospect, I wonder if Junior is a little more fearful today.

Malik Kasal, the inventor of the secret trading system Wood used, the Raptor, is pictured with an abacus (a Chinese invention). Douglas Endsley, VP for operations, came from the Kentucky horse country. Of course, the brochure depicted this handsome Southerner on the back of a beautiful horse. Douglas was touted as the company's top investor relations associate.

The final page of the brochure warned, "Past performance is no guarantee of future results. The Wood investment funds are speculative and involve a high degree of risk. Investors who participate must be prepared to lose all or substantially all of their investment."

Were there more clues to the fraud even in their brochure than anyone ever imagined? Did Wood taunt the intelligence of his investors by putting clues of the fraud throughout his materials, waiting for someone to catch him?

Only Wood knows.

Two months later, Wood's Heaven cigar bar and the contents of his plush offices were on the auction block to raise money for the swindled investors.

The year 2000 had started off with a bang of bad vibes and worse news. I was looking forward to vacation once our "selling season" was over—just a few more weeks. May would provide some peace and quiet at the clubs, and maybe all this publicity surrounding Wood and Eugene Gannon would quiet down.

On May 8, the Ethics Commission advocate reached a settlement agreement with an administrative law judge, in which Gannon, to avoid the hearing scheduled for mid-May, admitted four violations of the Florida ethics law and agreed to pay a $5,000 fine. Just when Gannon thought that this deal would allow him to move on with his life, on May 23, four of the commissioners voted on a resolution that asked Gannon to resign or face suspension by Governor Jeb Bush in light of his admission to the ethics violation. Gannon refused and said he would withdraw the settlement to have his day in court. He told the *Collier Enquirer* that he expected exoneration on all counts at the hearing.

On June 1, Florida's Commission on Ethics rejected Gannon's request to back out of his settlement. At 1:00 p.m. on June 2, Gannon was arrested as he left a downtown shopping center. He was charged with accepting unlawful compensation and reward for official behavior, a third-degree felony. Gannon was taken in handcuffs to the Collier County Jail. The news channels made an absolute spectacle of the arrest. This town showed no mercy to Gannon—especially in light of his former partner, Jack Wood, admitting to a Ponzi scheme. Was this just the tip of the iceberg? That's what I feared as I wondered, *What else can go wrong?*

Eighteen

As June unfolded, the media offered continuous coverage on both Gannon and Wood. Every day the front page had a tragic story of an investor who'd been duped by Wood, and equal coverage was provided to citizens who hated Commissioner Eugene Gannon. The *Collier Enquirer* made sure that everyone within a hundred-mile radius was aware of the fraud and government corruption occurring in our own little paradise. When readers began to get bored by the story, the reporters would dig a little deeper through what they called "investigative reporting."

On July 23, the *Collier Enquirer* revealed that Evan Hanover, another seated Collier County Commissioner, had received a hefty loan from Wood for his personal company, SmartKids. Hanover denied vehemently that he gave Wood or any of his companies favorable treatment as a reward for his commission votes and offered to cooperate with the state prosecutors to clear up any misconceptions they had developed against him. However, the paper made sure that this story, further proof of a corrupt county government, made the front page.

Had the county commission turned into a giant cesspool of finger-pointing and ethics violations? Anita Satterwhite, a seated commissioner, demanded that Hanover resign. Hanover refused and further complicated his stance by refusing to release his business records to the public. What was happening to our innocent Naples?

On August 6, 2000, the *Collier Enquirer* reported that Hanover voted on matters involving a Wood-backed development more than two dozen times and accused the commissioner of quid pro quo behavior.

On September 28, the state attorney's office arrested Evan Hanover and charged him with racketeering and three counts of unlawful compensation. He resigned the next day. The state attorney also said that Phillip Durkee, Peter's father, helped arrange the business loan from Wood to Hanover.

Was our sleepy little town really just a backwater good old boys network? Was this behavior "business as usual" for the commissioners? Get a little cash on the side for our "real" businesses and look out for the responsible corporate citizens of Collier County? After all, the commissioners had full-time businesses that they were running. The commission seat was a Tuesday meeting and, well, a part-time job.

While the paper kept Collier County whipped into frenzy over the ethics issues with the commissioners, it laid quiet on the Jack Wood front. What had happened to him since his tearful confession in mid-February?

He was arrested on October 19, 2000, and charged in the federal case: twenty counts of fraud and money laundering.

To close out the year, on December 12, Phillip Durkee was arrested and charged with conspiracy to engage in a pattern of racketeering. Gannon and Hanover were also charged because the state uncovered evidence of a check written from Durkee to Gannon for $2,165 for a commission on a real estate home sale and for his part in the business loan to Hanover. As the investigative reporting continued, it appeared that Phillip Durkee also gave Hanover a large price cut on his swank wedding reception in 1996 at Turtle Cove Country Club. Hanover, of course, denied that he knew anything about the discount.

I just knew that 2001 had to be a better year—there was no way anything could be worse. Little did I know that this was just the beginning of the bad news, not just for Wood and his crew, but for me as well.

Judge Faye Barrett, a retired judge from Miami, was selected to preside over this case of corruption in Naples. Governor Bush didn't want to risk that any of our local judges were also in on this "enterprise of corruption" and decided that a retired Miami judge would be a better choice.

Judge Barrett's first act was to throw the state attorney, Mike Pennino, off the case for a conflict of interest technicality.

Governor Jeb Bush appointed special prosecutor, Miami's own infamous Martin Strickland, to investigate the reports of widespread corruption.

Why, all of a sudden, did little Naples need all of these legal professionals from Miami? Our small town produced nowhere near the level of corruption that came out of Miami—but Martin Strickland was about to change that forever.

Peter and I watched with amazement. How could all of this be happening? I, for one, had never met any of the commissioners, except during the few meetings that brought Gannon into our office. I had never been to a commission meeting and really didn't have enough knowledge of civics to know how or why any of this was happening. It appeared that it all started with the filing of an ethics complaint about Gannon's involvement in a never-built golf coliseum, which led to an investigation by the state, which concluded that no direct quid pro quo occurred. Yet we had two commissioners under arrest for racketeering and conspiracy, tied up with Wood, a Ponzi artist who may have bribed commissioners, and Phillip Durkee, accused of brokering loans between Wood and commissioners!

Meanwhile, our third community was under construction; I just wanted to get back to work.

Judge Barrett and the special prosecutor did not have a good relationship. Barrett initially refused to allow Strickland contact with the former investigators who concluded there was insufficient evidence and had dismissed the case. That meant that he needed to gather new evidence.

On July 5, 2001, Strickland said he feared that the statute of limitations was about to expire. Judge Barrett relented, allowing limited contact with the former investigators to discuss the case.

As expected, on July 20, 2001, Wood pled guilty to federal charges of money laundering and fraud for swindling investors out of more than $150 million. He could face life in prison.

What a difference a little time makes. Just a few years earlier, Wood was the talk of the town, present at every high-end event, giving millions to charities. Now his publicity photo showed him in an orange jumpsuit, white socks, and blue sandals, shackled at the ankles and wrists. Who knew?

It was time for Wood to be charged by the special prosecutor in Collier County for committing racketeering and conspiracy with commissioners Hanover and Gannon and real estate mogul Phillip Durkee. The arrest documents said that Wood conspired to pay off Hanover and covered up a bribe to Hanover from Durkee. Wood was also charged with money laundering; remember the suitcase full of cash he brought back to Naples from Tennessee?

Just to be sure that every commissioner had been implicated in some form of corruption, Kenneth English, the final male commissioner (there were three men and two women on the CCBC), was arrested—for playing free golf. And he pled guilty! Now this young, up-and-coming career politician had a felony conviction for, yes, you've got it, playing a few rounds of golf for free. Does this type of activity sound anything like what some people in Washington D.C. do for a living? In Washington it's called lobbying, but in Naples we call it corruption. It is amazing what damage can be done to local businesses, personal lives, and an entire county when a visiting prosecutor offers his own unique interpretation of the law.

Of the five commissioners, all three of the men had been arrested and only the two women remained. They were both thoroughly investigated by the special prosecutor, and much to his chagrin he could produce little dirt on either of them.

This has to be the end of it, I thought.

Nineteen

The news struck—ten additional arrests in the Coliseum Golf corruption case were anticipated. The *Collier Enquirer* suggested the arrests could involve other high-ranking government officials—but whom?

Then the letter came.

Well, it was more of an invitation by the special prosecutor to meet with him voluntarily, without representation, of course, to see if either Peter or I could shed some light on some of the investigation.

Peter was quick to say that we had nothing to hide, which was, in fact, the case. What we didn't know at the time was the special prosecutor did not intend to leave us alone. He wanted to get as much information from us as he could before he slapped the cuffs on us too.

"Rosie, we've got to do this," Peter said as we pored over our invitations to meet with Strickland. "We've got to go down there and help this prosecutor understand that he's headed down a cul-de-sac—this case leads nowhere. There's no conspiracy. My old man is no more a mafia don than the man in the moon. They've pulled a few pieces of evidence together and made some very wrong assumptions. What we have to do is set him straight. And with our knowledge, we're the only ones who can save my father. At this point, I'm sure that the only tail Wood is trying to save is his own."

Peter waited with anticipation for my response.

"I don't know, Peter," I said doubtfully. "The idea of a letter of invitation to meet with the man who's arrested everyone in town? I just don't feel good about it. Maybe we should call Andrew and ask him what he thinks. If he says we should do it, then we will."

We made the call.

"Andrew, it's Peter and Rose, we've just received—"

"I know; I got an invitation to the party, too." Andrew laughed.

"Why in the heck would he want to talk to you?" Peter asked.

"Well, I am the attorney of record for your father, The Preserve, and Coliseum Golf. I guess I'm the man with most of the legal answers."

"Andrew," I began, "do you think that it's wise for Peter and me to meet with Strickland without an attorney?" I was hoping for a negative on that one.

"You two have nothing to worry about," Andrew said breezily. "You were both granted immunity when you testified truthfully with the former prosecutor. With any luck, you can help this misguided prosecutor and send him back to Miami."

"I'm ready to go," Peter offered. "Bring him on!" Peter would live to regret his burst of bravado.

I needed time to think about this. It was time to pray for guidance. I returned briefly to my office and clutched the Bible that had found its home on the corner of my desk. I closed my eyes and began to pray.

"Lord, why me? What possible lesson is there in this for me? Why must I come face to face with the enemy, the man that has cleverly pieced things together to build a case? I see no upside in speaking to the enemy. He will only twist and turn my words and use them against me. You know how he works, Father. Speak to me, guide me, and protect me."

I opened my Bible, searching for God's direction. I found myself reading Ephesians 6, and I began to search the text for my answer, my direction from God. *Let's see,* I thought. *Children and parents—that's not it. Slaves and masters? Hmm. I'm starting to feel like a slave.* Then it popped out as if God's almighty finger were pointing to the words, "the armor of God." I read the passage, verses 10 through 17, aloud:

> Finally, be strong in the Lord and in his mighty power. Put on the full armor of God so that you can take your stand against the devil's schemes. For our struggle is not against flesh and blood, but against

> the rulers, against the authorities, against the power of this dark world and against the spiritual forces of evil the heavenly realm.
>
> Therefore put on the full armor of God, so that when the day of evil comes, you may be able to stand your ground, and after you have done everything, to stand. Stand firm then, with the belt of truth buckled round your waist, with the breastplate of righteousness in place, and with our feet fitted with the readiness that comes from the gospel of peace.
>
> In addition to all this, take up the shield of faith, with which you can extinguish all the flaming arrows of the evil one. Take the helmet of salvation and the sword of the Spirit, which is the word of God.
>
> Ephesians 6:10–17

I wanted to cry. God was answering my prayers. His word was clear to point out that what I was about to enter was in fact spiritual warfare, and I needed to put on the belt of *truth*. I believed Peter and I were headed straight into one of the devil's schemes, but now I felt protected. I could only pray for my partner, Peter.

We both responded affirmatively to the invitation, and the prosecutor scheduled us on the same day early in September 2001. Strickland met first with Peter for two hours before he met with me. I assumed that since Peter's father had already been arrested, he wanted to ask Peter some personal family questions. Peter went down just after lunch, and I followed at 3:00 p.m.

I had been to the county administration building only twice before that day. The first time was to apply for my marriage license in 1990, and the other was when we hired Craig Delaney, then county manager, to be president of our company. He had held a press conference at the county manager's office to announce his departure to work for Wood Durkee Development Group and Coliseum Golf.

Now, as I approached the building, I missed the feeling of joy and pride that had surrounded me on my prior two trips. This time, I had a gnawing ache in my stomach. I was about to meet with a voracious prosecutor who believed that he had the power to pick the criminals, decide what crimes they committed, and then arrest them. He would save the proof of guilt and other such formalities for a later date.

As the elevator doors opened on the eighth floor, there was no sign of life. A handwritten sign taped on the double glass doors read "Office of the Special Prosecutor." *Should I knock?* I was about to go around the corner to see if there was another way in when Special Agent Fred Bare opened the door. "Hello, Ms. Visconti. Come on in, we've been waiting for you," he said.

Fred looked just like the character Norm on the TV show Cheers. He was the good cop in this game. I said hello and extended my hand. Fred grasped it and gently led me into a makeshift conference room.

As I entered the room, there were charts and graphs all over the walls. The only furniture was some cafeteria-style tables and folding metal chairs. A laptop computer and a phone sat on top of a stack of boxes that had been made into a makeshift desk.

"We're a little underfunded," Fred admitted, embarrassed. "The county gave us this floor, but there are no luxuries afforded to us Miami folk."

As I passed through the cavernous room, I saw The Preserve newsletters hanging on the wall, plus timelines, boxes, and papers everywhere. There were several plainclothes officers wielding coffee mugs in their hands and guns on their hips and all the attitude in the world. Then I heard Peter's familiar voice. *Thank God, he is still here.*

"Rosie," Peter hollered, "come on in here and sit down, you're gonna love this!" Peter was squealing with laughter.

Things must have gone very well, I decided, if Peter was laughing and joking with the officers. Suddenly I was struck with fear, remembering that Peter believes everyone is honest and forthright. He was the worst judge of character I'd ever seen. *What has he done?*

"Sit down, Rose," Peter said, inviting me into Mrs. Spider's Tea Party, a place where I was not interested in going. *Remember, Rose, only answer questions that are asked, offer no personal opinions.* I had to really work on my self-talk, as I was never shy about sharing my feeling or my opinions. Something told me this was not the place to be smug or sarcastic.

"Fred, close the door." Peter was already on a first-name basis with his new chum.

"We don't need to do that, Peter, it's only us here now," Fred responded.

"No, I want Rose to see your photo collection on the back of the door," Peter said. Fred obliged and stood quietly to see my response.

"Oh, my God!" I could not believe what I saw. There, on the back of the conference room door, was every person in Collier County being investigated in the Coliseum Golf case. A five-by-seven print of what appeared to be a driver's license photo was displayed for each. My eyes quickly raced row by row.

Jack Wood, Eugene Gannon, Evan Hanover, Kenneth English, Phillip Durkee, Peter Durkee, Craig Delaney, Nicholas Shubert, Andrew Shanahan, Rose Visconti—

Rose Visconti? That's me!

"Oh, my God, I'm a suspect?" The room filled with laughter at my expense.

Peter giggled as I sat in a state of shock.

"At least I'm smiling in that picture," I said. "Where was it taken?"

"That, Ms. Visconti, is your Florida driver's license photo," the special prosecutor said matter-of-factly as he entered the room. "Welcome to our humble offices," he added sarcastically.

I was quickly reminded of the mandate in Ephesians 6:16 to "take up the shield of faith, with which you can extinguish all the flaming arrows of the evil one." Martin Strickland looked to me to be one of those flaming arrows.

He was a disheveled man approaching fifty. His curly hair, hanging in limp ringlets around his head, was in need of a good clipping. He was an unattractive man without distinctive features other than glasses and a pug nose. Fifteen or twenty pounds overweight, he looked as if he survived on coffee and doughnuts in the morning and anything heated in the microwave for lunch and dinner.

I get a quick gut read on most people, and the minute I laid eyes on him I became uncomfortable, certain we were going nowhere fast. It was clear that he had already decided we were all guilty. Why else would he have our photos in five-by-sevens on the back of his office door? Peter and I were suspects. Strickland didn't even seem to pay much attention to our answers when he asked questions. He wanted us to understand the theory behind his questioning, but he really wasn't interested in our responses. He had already decided that we were going to be arrested and tried for a RICO conspiracy. He was also very fidgety—almost a case of attention deficit disorder, walking around, stretching his neck, rubbing his short, stubby little hands together, as if to say, "You're mine, all mine."

There were several FDLE agents taking copious notes—Fred as the good cop, Roger May and Joe Dihn playing the bad cops at the table. Fred would occasionally roll his eyes at them, but I'd seen enough cop shows to know that trick. "Trust no one" was my mantra.

"Peter," the prosecutor was saying, "I've got a few more questions to go over with you. Do you mind if Ms. Visconti is in the room during questioning?" Strickland was setting the stage for pitting one against the other, I felt.

"There is nothing that Rose doesn't already know, carry on," Peter said. He offered a pat on my back to console me following the photo display.

"Your mother had an account with Jack that had about $100,000 in it," Strickland said. "Do you know where she would have gotten that kind of money? I mean, she doesn't work, right?" Strickland watched Peter's face for any sign of distress.

"I don't know," Peter replied, nonplussed. "You should probably ask her."

"We will. We just thought you might know why your former wife would give your mother a $50,000 deposit." He had set the hook.

Peter rarely spoke of his former wife, Gabriella. They had divorced years earlier so that she could pursue her personal interests. The allegation that she maintained contact with Peter's mother, and that he was aware of it, surprised me.

Peter thought for a moment. "You know, Wood had closed the fund to anyone under $100K. I know Gabriella wanted to grow her alimony, so Mother must have offered to deposit Gabriella's money in her account in the fund, and that way she'd get in under the minimum deposits." Peter again suggested that Strickland talk to his ex-wife and his mother directly. Strickland's questioning style was to try to get different answers to the same question, proving that you were a liar and a conspirator.

"Don't you find it odd, Peter, that your former wife and your mother seemed to be playing around with $50 to $100K during the time that your father was virtually guaranteeing the loan to Hanover through Wood?" Strickland looked deep into Peter's eyes, awaiting a response.

"I knew nothing about this SmartKids deal until I read it in the *Collier Enquirer*. Father and Wood did not keep me informed of all of their separate business dealings, and I'm just as happy that they didn't." By now, Peter must have been wondering if this meeting was a good idea after all.

As I watched the skilled prosecutor bait Peter, I realized that there was really no good reason to be there without an attorney. I guess it was too late for me to excuse myself. *Just be wary of the enemy*, I thought.

Strickland would ask a question, then get up and pace around the room, sometimes leaving the room altogether. After one abrupt exit, he reentered the makeshift conference room. "We've got him," he announced excitedly, trying to scare us. "I knew it! Listen, Roger, Fred, I need you to take his statement. Joe, you stay here with these two." He motioned to Peter and me. "I'll be right back. This is great! Just as I suspected, Collier County has the worst public corruption I've ever seen, and now with a little Miami-style justice, they're caving in like crazy!"

Strickland turned on his heel and whispered to the two agents as he left the room.

Acting as if nothing had happened, the other FDLE agent, Joe Dihn, continued the interrogation.

"Tell me, Ms. Visconti, about your relationship with Craig Delaney."

Joe's red hair and freckles made him look younger than his years. He wore a crucifix that hung outside his shirt. He did not come across like a Christian to me as he peered at us. Yet I wasn't nervous. I was still holding on to the feeling that we were there to straighten out the misconceptions that these FDLE agents and their fearless leader, Strickland, had concocted. I knew that I had not committed any crimes and that the legal system would certainly protect innocent citizens from a Miami prosecutor trying to make a name for himself. "Well, Craig and I met at church in 1995 or 1996. We became fast friends; our children were the same ages. Our families enjoyed ski vacations and regular dinners out. We had a good relationship." That should be enough, I thought.

"Great," Dihn said, without looking up. "Now tell me about how Craig came to be the president of your company."

"Actually, we were trying to hire Rick Bernadino, one of Craig's employees at the county. Rick was just about to accept our offer to come to work for us, not as the president, more like the head of development and construction. We didn't have anyone with a background in permitting and agency processes. He was very familiar with those things and also with how to work with the county and with the Army Corps of Engineers."

"Right. Can you get to the part where you hired Craig instead?" Dihn tapped his watch; it was getting close to quitting time.

I decided to tell him the whole story. Why not? I had nothing to hide, and I went through all the details of hiring Craig, up to the part where we made our deal with him.

"Can you tell us what that deal was?" Dihn's face was beginning to show signs of fatigue, just as Strickland entered once again. He was like a revolving door. Maybe this was how he kept people on their toes?

"Oh I can't wait to hear this one," Strickland said. "Do you remember what his, as you put it, 'iron-clad' contract looked like?" Strickland leaned into his chair and smirked at me. Did he already know the answer? Of course he did; he was testing me.

"I believe his base was in the $150,000 range."

Fred interrupted. "Holy crap," he exclaimed, "that's ridiculous! Hey, if you add up all of our salaries, do we make that much?"

The room erupted in laughter.

"No," Strickland responded, "we're only defending the justice system, so we get just over minimum wage. I'm sorry, Ms. Visconti, please continue."

"We paid the insurance for his family, a key man life policy, the other regular perks—auto, gas, cell phone." They had a copy of his contract; why was I going through these motions?

"Tell us about Nicholas Shubert." Strickland seemed very interested in this question.

"I think he's a male chauvinist pig. The only thing he thought I was good for was fetching coffee and taking minutes in the meetings. You'll notice at the press conference, all of the 'boys' were seated at the head table. I was invited to hand out press packages at the door. He had very little use for women." I think I made myself clear on that one.

"Come on, Rose, are you suggesting that these men—Jack, Peter, Craig, Eugene, and Nicholas—did not treat you with proper respect as a partner?" Strickland's words oozed with sarcasm.

"No, sir, they did not," I said. "You see, I was missing a few body parts that kept me from playing in the sandbox with the boys. They are all a bunch of male chauvinist pigs, and Mr. Durkee here is the president."

"And I'm proud of it, too," Peter responded, with a "sooey," as any good pig would offer at such a moment.

A woman stuck her head in the conference room. "Excuse me, Martin," she said, beckoning him with her finger. He immediately left the room to see what new evidence had been uncovered by his trusty assistant. They were only there for a moment when Strickland returned.

"Listen, thanks for coming down today. Can you come back in a few days? We've got a hot lead and I've gotta go. Fred, will you tell Rose what you're looking for? Maybe she can pull some copies and files together." Strickland grabbed his tattered briefcase and headed out the door.

"Rose, Peter," Fred continued, "how does next Tuesday look?"

"I don't know, I don't have my calendar with me." I did not want to meet with these folks again without Andrew here.

"You give me a call when you get back to your office, and if you don't want to come back down here, I'd like to send an agent up to see you, go through some old files, if that's okay with you." Fred was acting like a real gentleman.

"Great," Peter said, "Rose will call you when we get back. She's the custodian of records, so it looks like you'll be dealing with her from now on." Peter appeared excited at the thought of passing the buck to me.

"I don't think so, Mr. Durkee," Dihn responded, with a "gotcha" in his voice that made Peter uncomfortable. "We've got more questions for you, too."

"Thanks again for coming down. Don't forget to call me, Rose," Fred said.

"I'll call you on Monday. It's already after five on a Friday, and I don't work on weekends—I've got children, you know." I had to set up some boundaries.

"Okay, I'll look forward to hearing from you. Have a nice weekend." Fred was out the door.

Peter and I walked to the elevator in a stupor. Our pictures were mug shots on the back of a door in a room filled with determination to charge people with racketeering and conspiracy. It was crazy. We agreed to meet at Peter's house after dinner to decompress. We needed to form our own strategy.

Twenty

As I drove home from this unsettling meeting, I believed myself to be a suspect. Anyone who was called in for an interview would see my photo on the back of the door—one of eleven people being investigated for the crime of bribing commissioners. My gut told me to go to the office and begin assembling my counterargument for Strickland. But it was Friday, and my family was home, patiently waiting for dinner.

After what just happened, my mind couldn't banish the thoughts and fears racing through it. That's what the enemy does: he never touches you physically; he just sets up circumstances around you that make you feel hopeless. What the enemy did not realize was that I had the Great Defender on my side.

Once I got home, I headed straight for a quiet moment in the only place where I knew I could be alone for a few moments: the bathroom. As I sat quietly thinking about the warfare that had taken place today, the words of Psalm 91 rushed into my mind. I had Bibles stashed everywhere for quick reference, and my "home office" was no exception. With a growing desire for God's protection, I read Psalm 91:

> Those who live in the shelter of the Most High will find reset in the shadow of the Almighty. This I declare about the Lord: He alone is my refuge, my place of safety; he is my God, and I trust him. For he will rescue you from every trap and protect you from deadly disease. He will cover you with his feathers. He will shelter you with his wings. His faithful promises are your armor and protection. Do not be afraid of the terrors of the night, nor the arrow that flies in the day. Do not dread the disease

> that stalks in darkness, nor the disaster that strikes at midday. Though a thousand fall at your side, though ten thousand are dying around you, these evils will not touch you. Just open your eyes, and see how the wicked are punished. If you make the Lord your refuge, if you make the Most High your shelter, No evil will conquer you; no plague will come near your home. For he will order his angels to protect you wherever you go. They will hold you up with their hands so you won't even hurt your foot on a stone. You will trample upon lions and cobras; you will crush fierce lions and serpents under your feet! The Lord says, "I will rescue those who love me. I will protect those who trust in my name. When they call on me, I will answer; I will be with them in trouble. I will rescue and honor them. I will reward them with a long life and give them my salvation."
>
> Psalm 91

I closed the good book and committed myself to dwell in the very secret place of the Most High God. Feeling spiritually protected, I prayed, "Lord, help me through this mess; help me to know that you are my protector and my guide. There is nothing that this one man can do that will harm me."

I left my home office with a renewed spirit as I headed to the kitchen to prepare dinner and spend some quality time with my daughters. Zack had been spending more evenings in front of the television and this night would be no exception. It troubled me that we both seemed unable—or was it unwilling—to repair our failed relationship. I felt as if my legal problem had invaded every part of my existence. I had to learn to separate the horribleness of the case from my family life; if I didn't everyone would suffer. The joy of the Lord would be my strength.

On Monday, I was at the office bright and early, pulling copies of the requested documents to show how ridiculous Martin Strickland's claims of a grand conspiracy were. Any one piece of evidence—if taken out of context—could be artfully construed to have a questionably criminal context, which is just what Strickland was doing to us. This unbridled prosecutor was taking highlights of business and commission meetings from the past five years and piecing them together to support his claims of an enterprise of conspiracy, of business people bribing commissioners for favorable votes.

Creating a RICO conspiracy was the only way that Strickland could accomplish two things: the first, to make a name for himself at the expense of innocent people; and the second, to elevate the charges to a RICO conspiracy so that he could get felony convictions, not just misdemeanors. The media weren't going to cover multiple court hearings for misdemeanors. Strickland needed to spice up the charges in order to have the kind of media coverage necessary to gain personal notoriety. It made me furious that a public official would use and abuse the lives of innocent people for his own personal career gain. There was no consideration on Strickland's part for the destruction of families, businesses, and personal lives that resulted from his outrageous behavior.

As I reviewed the list of the documents they wanted, I realized that I was going to be spending the better part of the day pulling four years' worth of files from our corporate office attic, which lacked air-conditioning. I wasn't wearing the right clothes for this task, but there was no time to lose.

I pulled the retractable stairs down from the small ceiling space and began my ascent to the history of our company—the truth. A wave of heat hit me in the face as I pulled myself up the rickety stairs, and the musty air took my breath away.

As I stood in the long, narrow attic space filled with boxes of old bank statements, contracts, blueprints, and all of our county submissions for both The Preserve and Oak Haven, I was momentarily overwhelmed. The boxes were not in any particular order, and it seemed that whoever was responsible for putting the boxes up here did not want to spend any more time than absolutely necessary. In the cramped space, the moldy, stagnant air made it difficult to breathe.

I had no time to begin organizing the files. I just needed to pull the years in question and begin assembling our case to prove to Strickland that he was way off base in his accusations. He needed to pack up his car and head back to Miami posthaste!

After I had been in the attic a few hours, Peter's voice echoed down the hallway. "Rosie, are you up there?"

"Yes," I responded. "You want to come up and help me pull these files?"

"No way. It's hot up there, and the weight of the two of us together could be dangerous," Peter offered with a laugh. "Come down here for a minute." Either Peter had news or he just wanted to give me a break from the polluted air.

I struggled to turn myself around in the narrow space. The stairs were almost a complete vertical drop, offering no easy descent.

"I just got off the phone with Special Agent Fred Bare. They want us to come back down tomorrow with the documents. Does that give you enough time?" Peter glanced doubtfully at his watch.

I sighed from frustration and exhaustion. "I don't know," I admitted. "You should see the mess up there. I'll make it work. I don't want them to go down this crazy path of conspiracy another day. The sooner I can show them how wrong they are, the better. If you get us lunch, I'll continue pulling documents. My stomach is making so much noise I'm having a hard time concentrating."

Peter chuckled. "I'll go to Subway. After we eat, we can assemble what you've gathered and take the boxes home with us tonight." Peter left, leaving me to the less desirable of the two jobs.

Over our subs, I said to Peter, "I'd like to make an inventory of the documents. I don't want to deliver originals without them acknowledging they've received them. I don't trust these guys any farther than I can throw them."

"I don't think you'll have time for that, based on the list you have there," Peter said, motioning to the faxed request from the state attorney's office. "We'll just take the box of documents and have them do the inventory list. Or, better yet, copy what they want while we're there."

"Peter, I don't want to spend any more time in that office than I have to.

Those FDLE agents and Strickland actually believe that we're mixed up in their grand conspiracy theory. Don't you get it? They think we're crooks!"

I tried to put some fear into Peter's heart. He was blindly trusting that these people had his best interests at heart. The only interest they had was putting as many faces as possible on the front page of the paper and gaining notoriety.

"What's on the list?" Peter slid the paper closer so he could review it.

"It looks like they've focused on your dad's road building company, Craig Delaney's contract and employment records, and anything to do with Coliseum Golf, of course."

I ignored my sandwich and continued searching through the musty boxes that we'd retrieved from the attic.

"Do you have all of this stuff?" Peter was always amazed at our level of organizational efficiency.

"Yes, and I'm putting it in order now. I should be done by 5:00 p.m."

I was feeling better about the documents. They clearly showed there were no shenanigans going on here.

"We can just leave from home tomorrow," Peter said. "They want us down there at 9:00 a.m., so take the box home with you." I could tell he wanted to help, but being the chauffeur was the best he could offer.

"Okay. If I find anything interesting, I'll call you. Otherwise, honk at my front door at 8:30." I added sarcastically, "We don't want to be late."

The next morning, precisely at 8:30, I walked out my front door with the box of documents in my arms, just as Peter was rolling down the passenger window.

"Come on, Rosie," Peter shouted, in remarkably good cheer. This guy is either drinking heavily or hopelessly naïve, I thought. "Let's go show this Strickland character the truth!"

I hoped Peter wouldn't offer too much information to Strickland. He had a way of saying far too much and offering his opinion very strongly. He sometimes came across as a little offensive, to say the least.

"Listen, Peter," I said, getting in the car with my big box of documents. "Behave yourself today. Remember what Andrew said? Only answer the questions that they ask you." I used my motherly voice to bring home my point.

"Oh, for God's sake, Rose," Peter said. "This guy is headed down a path to annihilate Father's business and, if he has a chance, ours. This is no time to be diplomatic. Strickland needs a relocation package back to Miami where he came from."

We sat in silence the rest of the way. Peter really was naïve enough to believe that he could bully Strickland out of his decision to go after us. I had a premonition that Peter's antagonistic attitude would only make things worse.

His tone changed as we pulled up to the meeting place. "We're here. It's show time!" Peter seemed excited about playing this very dangerous game.

As we entered the Collier County government building and waited for the elevator, thoughts began to race through my mind. *What are the most important things we can offer Strickland that will derail his one-track mind from thinking of us as criminals? He has predetermined our guilt. This is our last chance to expose the truth, if we can just keep him seated long enough to hear it.* I hoped Strickland was less fidgety in the morning and that he hadn't had too many cups of coffee. Suddenly, as the elevator reached the eighth floor, my mind flashed to my photo in the lineup on the door. *I'm a suspect! The government is after me! They think I'm a bad person!*

What was happening to me? My stomach suddenly felt queasy. There was the enemy again, trying hard to give me a spirit of doubt and fear. I knew that I had the power of God's Word to put my foot on the enemy's head and reclaim my victory. So I did; I visualized my next step to be on the neck of the enemy.

"Let's go, Rosie. Our FDLE agents await," Peter said as he held the elevator door.

"I felt sick for a moment there, Peter. How about you?"

"It's just your nerves. You'll be fine once we walk through that door." Peter tried to treat the situation lightly, for his benefit and mine.

"Good morning," Fred Bare offered as he opened the plain white door to their special offices. "Can I offer you some coffee? It's really bad, but it's all we have. You know, the Collier County folks aren't too happy to have the Miami squad over here." Fred continued talking as he poured the coffee into Styrofoam cups. "Sugar or powder creamer?"

"I drink mine black, thank you," I said.

"I don't touch that stuff, and by the looks of that pot, maybe you two should reconsider," Peter joked.

"I need it to start the old engine." Fred inhaled the aroma of the dark brew. "Come on in and sit down. I see you've brought a box of documents with you."

"Rose is very efficient, Fred. She'll show you guys that you're headed down a cul-de-sac. You're wasting your time with us." Peter was very matter-of-fact.

"I've heard a lot about Rose from several of the people we've already interviewed," Fred said sharply.

The tone of Fred's voice caused my stomach to drop. *Who has he interviewed? What did they have to say about me?* I needed to keep my composure. Fred was just fishing and he almost hooked me.

"Really, I'm sure it was all good!" I wanted to see what Fred would offer.

"Well, mostly." He smirked, knowing that he'd played this game far more times than I ever could or would. "There was one person who thought you were a pain. Do you remember Roxanne Bushey?" Fred wanted to play just a little longer.

I knew that name, and I wasn't surprised if she was criticizing me.

I nodded. "And I'm not really sure that she's all woman. The language that comes out of her mouth is worse than anything I've heard from any man on a construction site. She could make sailors blush."

Fred hooked me, damn it. I needed to cool my jets and not offer any derogatory comments—about anyone. He would use them against me when he interviewed them. This was his technique: to get you defensive and cause you to bring down another person.

"So, Rose, tell us how you really feel about Roxanne," Fred chuckled.

"Do you mean her company, Fred?" I asked. Two could play at this game.

"The company," he replied evenly. "You paid her company quite a bit for some services in 1997. Can you describe that relationship to me?"

Fred touched the tip of his pencil to his tongue and readied himself to take notes.

I launched into it. "Ed Mees, our project manager for construction development, was having a tough time working through all the permit requirements for The Preserve. This was the first time that he had been in charge of a project of this size, and he suddenly felt overwhelmed. We were falling behind schedule. The harder he worked, the farther behind he got. Someone introduced him to Roxanne. She was presented as an expert with the county and had the knowledge necessary to keep the project on track. Ed Mees and Peter met with Roxanne and hired her."

"So they hired her without your approval?" Fred was casting his hook again.

"As the owner of the company, Peter did not need my approval," I began, trying to remain patient and poised.

I knew I had to be very careful in how I worded everything I said, and I needed to keep my sarcasm to a minimum. Roxanne was only involved in The Preserve, and I wasn't sure what she had to do with the coliseum deal and Gannon. I began to realize that the prosecutor was reaching beyond the coliseum project to firm up the rest of his case.

I continued. "However, her fees were not budgeted. It was an expense that appeared to be inevitable, just much more than I thought it should cost." I was being very careful in my responses.

"What do you mean by 'more than it should cost'? Did you think she was ripping off your company?" Fred peered through his glasses, which I now noticed were heavily smudged with fingerprints.

"No, I did not suggest that," I replied emphatically. "What I will say is that with the fees that we paid her, we could have hired a high-powered person from the county, someone like Rick Bernadino, who would have had The Preserve's best interest at heart." This was a nice entree into why we tried to hire Rick.

"Good, you're ready to talk about Delaney being hired as your president." Fred was closing in on me. *How did we get into all of this so quickly?* My head was starting to swim.

"We were trying to hire Rick Bernadino," I explained, reminding myself to appear patient and calm. I glanced over at Peter, who was doing the same Silent Sam routine he'd been following in pretty much every interview. He figured that the less he said, the less trouble he could get into. Why was I feeling like I needed to help Strickland sort out the details of five-year-old history? His only goal was to create a crime and arrest us for it. I needed to keep my answer short and sweet. *That's a joke* I thought to myself.

"Rick was the head of Parks and Recreation at the county," I replied. "We knew that he was well respected and knew the ins and outs of Collier County planning and development. This was where our company was the weakest.

"We had people working for us that had never done a project the size of The Preserve. Because it was a development of regional impact at twelve hundred units, we were in foreign territory. We had to deal with agencies like the Army Corps of Engineers, South Florida Water Management, and the like. Rick had relationships with these groups or agencies, and we thought that it would be in our company's best interest to hire a professional who knew how to work the system.

"You can't beat the system, but if you've got someone on your side who knows it inside and out, your chances of success are far greater. We were fighting a bank's funding clock that was all tied to permits and progress. We did not have time or money to waste."

That ought to clear up any confusion about why we wanted to hire an ex-county employee, or so I thought.

"So, what you're saying, Rose," Fred offered, "is that you wanted to steal someone from the county who could use their influence with their old office pals to get you what you wanted. Is that correct?"

I suddenly realized that Fred was accusing me of participating in this crazy conspiracy theory they'd cooked up.

My eyes flashed. "No, Fred, that is not correct," I said, trying to control my anger and my fear. "Rick and I were friends, and he'd been working at the county for a long time. He was ready for a change from government to the private sector. He'd reached his earning potential at the county and, unless he was promoted to county manager, this was the best career move he could have made. I'm sure that throughout your stellar career you've been recruited by the private sector, haven't you?" As those words left my mouth, I realized that Fred was a lifer in law enforcement and would never have presented himself as "private" material.

"No, Rose," Fred answered bluntly. "I'm dedicated to fighting crime. Nobody has ever been successful at offering me money to change careers, to work for the 'other side,' as it were."

Fred was effective at setting his hooks, that was for sure. I had to continue to explain the truth, even if it was his job to twist it for his boss, Strickland. It probably surprised the prosecutor and his team that we were appearing without counsel to guide us or tell us when to stop talking. Oddly enough, Andrew Shanahan had suggested that we go without lawyers present. He felt that it would show that we had nothing to hide and were able and willing to show the prosecutor the holes in his case. Either Andrew was incompetent with his advice or he felt that we were so squeaky clean that we just needed to straighten this guy out. It was the last meeting we attended without our own legal counsel in the room with us.

As soon as thoughts of Strickland entered my mind, he passed through the door.

"Good morning, gentlemen, lady." Strickland bellowed as he entered the investigation room. "Has the Delaney story started yet? I didn't want to miss a thing." Strickland slurped his coffee steaming in a Frosty the Snowman mug. "Don't let me interrupt, Fred. Please continue."

Strickland pulled out his yellow legal pad and fumbled in his tattered briefcase for a pen. He scribbled with two or three before he found one that worked, returning each of the nonworking pens to his briefcase.

Fred nodded knowingly. "Oh, Rose here," he began, "she was just about to tell us how she was trying to steal Rick Bernadino from his county job to work for her, keeping her project on track."

Strickland smirked, as if this was exactly what he had suspected.

Emboldened by his boss's presence, Fred leaned in. "So, what happened with Bernadino?" he asked pointedly. "Why did he suddenly decide to stay at the county and not come to work for The Preserve?" Fred had his pencil poised for my response.

I cleared my throat before I answered. I knew from experience that Peter wouldn't be doing any of the talking.

"At the Coliseum Golf press conference in October," I began, "on the eleventh, I believe, Jack Wood and Peter decided to tell Rick's boss, Craig Delaney, that we were going to make Rick an offer that week. Craig suggested that they not offer Rick the job. Later, following the press conference he offered to become our president. After all, he knew far more people than Rick did, and his reputation with all of the agencies was outstanding."

Strickland interrupted my explanation. "Tell me about your relationship with Craig Delaney."

Peter piped up in my stead. "Well, today it's not the greatest," he said. "Rose had to, well, fire him about six months ago."

Thanks, Peter. The one time you open your mouth, you've got to make me look bad, so you can look like the hero. Thanks a lot.

"Really? Tell me about that, Rose." Strickland seemed to salivate. Had he just been offered an open vein from Peter?

"I did not fire him." I protested, cursing Peter silently. "His contract was complete," I explained, my heart pounding, "and, following the loss of the coliseum project, Wood Durkee Development Group did not have a need for a high-profile president like Craig. We were also in a financial crunch most of the time, and we needed to all be working managers. Craig, having been the county manager for ten years, was great at delegating and found it difficult to transition to the 'working manager' position. As a result, we did not renew his annual contract and paid out the six months of severance. He then did some work for Peter's father, and we participated in paying some portion of his salary for the permitting work that he did for our next project, which was Oak Haven."

That is enough, I thought to myself.

"So, would it be safe to say that you don't like Craig?" Strickland gave a wry smile.

"No, that would not be safe to say," I replied. "I like Craig. He is a good and faithful man. Our company just did not fit the profile any longer for a man of his caliber."

"So, you do like him?" Strickland was relentless. Either way, he won, it seemed.

"I… admire him," I said, choosing my words carefully. I didn't want to hand Strickland anything he could use against me, but it seemed that anything I said just made him salivate. "We had a very close relationship for a long time. We don't see each other much socially anymore."

I was saddened by this thought. *We had enjoyed a good friendship. This company has a way of quietly stealing parts of your life,* I thought to myself.

"We've interviewed about a hundred people at the county," Strickland told me, "and we've found only one person, Sonya White, who likes Craig. The general consensus is that he's an arrogant, self-centered person who only took care of people in the county who stroked him." Strickland actually giggled as he offered his findings.

"I don't know anybody at the county," I said defensively, "except Rick Bernadino, and he and Craig are like brothers. Did you ask him how he felt about Craig?" *Why am I engaging in this madness?*

"Yeah, we talked to him." Strickland offered a smirk and a nod, as if not even Rick liked Craig, not after he stole his private-sector job. "Let's move on," Strickland said. "We've got enough on Delaney already. Did you cover Roxanne Bushey yet, Fred?"

"Yep," Fred said happily. "Rose agrees—she's got the mouth of a sailor and overcharged their company."

"I never said that, Fred," I protested.

Fred winked at me and pretended to use his eraser on his notes.

"What else do we need with these two?" Strickland flipped through his legal pad of chicken scratch. I attempted to read his notes, but his handwriting was illegible.

"Oh yeah, Peter," Strickland said, turning to my partner. "Tell us about your father's road building company. Don't you own fifty percent of that company?" Strickland was setting up a serve to Peter. I hoped he was paying attention.

Peter nodded. "On paper," he began, "I own fifty percent, but I don't act as owner. Father has my name on many of his companies, some of which I don't even know about. He's getting older and wants me to be able to clean up the companies when he's gone, like an executor of his will."

"Don't you collect a salary and some health benefits?" Strickland pointed to some paperwork that he had in his folder.

"I don't think so. I get checks from here and there and just put them in the pot. My bills are always more than I make, so I'm always happy to take money from anybody."

Peter hesitated as those words left his mouth; he did not mean to sound like he'd do anything illegal. Strickland looked as if he'd just heard something juicy he could use later on.

"Did Wood know," Strickland asked, "that you owned fifty percent of the company when he signed the contracts for all the development work at The Preserve? Looking at it from his perspective, you stood to gain quite a profit from the work that your father's company was doing for The Preserve." Was Strickland setting up Peter as a scammer with his partner, Jack Wood, who scammed the wealthy of Naples?

"Wood was fully aware of my ownership and relationship with father's company. Besides, there was no real profit in the deal. As most road jobs go, time is your enemy, and in the summer, rain adds another element to slow down progress. The only real money that was made was paid to the on-site workers to keep the company alive." I could see that Peter's strategy was to defend his father's company. *So far, so good*, I thought. *Peter, just don't screw it up.*

"So, how does 'Father' stay in business?" Strickland asked, mocking the respectful way Peter spoke of his father. "The Preserve paid him a management fee. Can you tell me what that was for?"

"I don't think we've paid him anything, have we, Rose?" Peter looked to me for assistance.

"I think at the most we've paid him $6,000," I said. Strickland's direction did not feel good at all. I began to realize that Strickland's scope was far greater than Coliseum Golf, and we were going into very old Preserve business. *Why? Where is this headed?* I could tell that anything we said was being twisted to fit his theory. We needed to get out of here, and fast.

"The balance of the management fee," I said to Peter, "has been accrued on the books. The bank feels that management fees should come after they've been repaid." I hoped that helped Peter's memory.

"Why are we paying Father a management fee?" Peter asked me. The question certainly was not helping his credibility with Strickland.

"Hey, Peter," Strickland cracked, "how do you operate when Rose's not in the room?"

Ignoring the barb, I responded for Peter. "I'll answer your last question, Mr. Strickland," I said. "Phillip Durkee signed on the Heartland Bank and Trust note for $22 million as a personal guarantor. In exchange for his exposure—and there was exposure—he earned a management fee. As I recall, the total fee in the partnership agreement was $3.5 million, of which Phillip Durkee would earn twenty percent, or $700,000. Unfortunately, when Golf America took Wood's place as the guarantor, they also 'took' eighty-one percent of the management fees, or roughly $2 million. So, all told, Phillip could have earned about $200,000, but I believe that he only received checks totaling $6,000.

"The balance has not been, and probably never will be, paid. The Preserve did not perform as well as we'd projected, after the Wood fiasco and all of the refinance fees." I was very matter-of-fact in offering these statistics.

"What a great deal," Strickland mused. "So, if you're Peter Durkee's father, you can keep your company operating by forcing them to sign contracts, even if they are significantly higher than the competition's. Then you offer your signature on a loan document for half a million bucks. Father has done well with you for a son, Peter." Strickland really had his scope set on the Durkees.

"That's a joke," Peter retorted. "I'm sure if you check our files, you'll see that the bank required us to get competitive bids. You'll see that Father's company did not, as you suggest, stiff us for its benefit. You've really got this whole thing twisted, Mr. Strickland." Peter was entering shark-infested waters with this comment.

"We'll see about that, Mr. Durkee. I think that's all I have for today. Fred, you can finish with these two on your own. I've got to follow up on some of this new information." Without so much as a good-bye, Strickland left as abruptly as he had entered.

"Let's see what you've got in here." Fred began to pull folders out of the box.

"We did not copy these files," I said. I wasn't leaving the files unless they signed for every page. I felt they were perfectly capable of doctoring originals or destroying exculpatory evidence to further their cause.

"If you want to keep them," I told them, running out of patience, "you'll need to either copy them now or write up a receipt for every single document." I was not leaving evidence that proved our innocence in these guys' hands.

"Tell you what. We don't have a copy machine here. You know the Collier County guys aren't too happy about us stepping on their toes, so they don't offer too much help. Why don't you take this back to your office and copy it for us. And, if you're not too busy, our financial crimes specialist can come to your office and spend some quality time with Rose and the files. That way, you don't have to come down here again. You'll like Judith Binns. She's in the Fort Myers office. I'll have her call you, if that's okay. Rose, you can set a time that is convenient for you both. Does that work?" Fred was reverting to his kind, manipulative self.

"Sure," I said, "as long as she doesn't come to the office with a badge and a gun. You've upset our staff enough with all of your visits. Nobody likes to see people with guns and badges."

Fred laughed off my request. "The only weapon she'll have is a calculator. I told you, she's with the financial crimes unit."

"Great, I'll just take my box and be on my way. Have a good afternoon, Fred."

"Thanks, Rose. You've been a big help," Fred offered with another wink.

What did that mean? I would need to replay the meeting with Peter to make sense of it.

"Okay, Rosie. Let's get to the office. We've got a company to run." Peter was as anxious to get out of there as I was.

When we were safely in the car on the way back to the office, I turned to Peter. "I really don't think we should meet with them again without an attorney," I said. "Did you see any recording devices?" I was beginning to get that gut feeling that we'd made the wrong decision to meet with Strickland without counsel.

"We'll give Andrew a call when we get back to the office and see what he thinks. He's meeting with Strickland today, too. That should give us a clearer perspective on where this guy is going." Peter looked worried. "Why do you think Strickland is chasing Father so hard?"

"I don't know. Maybe Strickland's office has investigated some business deals that your father did with the commissioners that substantiates its case against them. The only way to get the commissioners is to get your father in a position to testify against them. Did you see any recorders?" I was still wondering if and how they would use the information we'd given them.

"No, and they never swore us in. I think it was just an interview. They wouldn't be able to use it like a deposition, just fact-finding, I guess." Our minds churned as we tried to understand the prosecutors' M.O.

"I'll wait to hear from Judith Binns, the financial crimes analyst and see if she offers any insight." I was ready to get to work and put this bizarre meeting behind me.

No sooner had I entered the office than the phone rang.

"Hello, my name is Judith Binns with the FDLE. Fred Bare said you would be expecting my call."

"Yes," I said. "What does your schedule look like and how much time do you need?" I wanted to set some clear boundaries with Ms. Binns.

"I'd like to come this afternoon, if it's possible, around two. I'll stay until about six, if you don't mind. If I don't get through everything, then we'll plan on Tuesday, too. Is that okay with you?" Judith was playing the same good-cop, bad-cop game as Fred and Strickland.

"Sure. I'd like to be prepared when you come. What exactly are you expecting to review?" I asked.

"All the bank statements for Coliseum Golf, The Preserve, and Wood Durkee Development Group. I'd also like any contracts between any of those companies and Phillip Durkee's companies, as well as the contract that you had with Roxanne Bushey and any canceled checks that you have to Andrew Shanahan or Evans and Dorne. That should be enough to get me started."

"I'll have the conference room set up. See you in about an hour." I hung up, wondering if they'd already scoped out our offices.

I buzzed Peter to see if he was in his office so I could fill him in on the Binns call. He was glad he didn't have any knowledge about the financial records of the company and that I would suffer this meeting alone.

As promised, Judith Binns arrived at 2:00 p.m. She was a nondescript woman, dressed in a dark suit and shoes—the typical accountant look. She spent the day reviewing and marking documents that she wanted copied. I spent about an hour answering her questions about checks, contracts, and the like, then agreed that she would return on Tuesday morning to cover a few remaining areas.

The next day, following another hour of questions and answers, Judith called me into the conference room to discuss some final issues. One of my accounting assistants was producing the photocopies that Judith had requested and was in the conference room re-filing some checks. "Rose," Judith said as she was putting her notes into her briefcase, "I've reviewed all the documents that the prosecutor has requested, and I can honestly say that I do not see where any crime has been committed here."

"Thank God!" I cried. "I mean, I knew that all along, but after one or two meetings with Fred and Strickland, those two could make you wonder about the Virgin Mary! Thank you, Judith."

I gave my assistant a smile, as she was there to witness this conversation with Judith. She smiled back at me, vindicated; she knew we were honest business people, not the crooks the prosecutor was making us out to be. Judith's statement left me feeling much better, especially after our meetings with Fred Bare and Martin Strickland. Maybe they would listen to one of their own. After all, Peter and I were suspects, so of course we would be defending ourselves. But now we had one of them to defend us.

Peter was also happy to hear that we'd been cleared by the financial crimes division and wanted to celebrate by calling Andrew. Certainly, by now he'd have a better sense of the prosecutor.

"Andrew, its Peter and Rose. How's it going?" Peter had relief in his voice, but only for a moment.

"Peter, Rose, you should not meet with Strickland again without an attorney. In my meeting with him yesterday, well, things did not go well. He thinks that I'm covering for your father and that I lied to him."

Andrew didn't sound optimistic. "I've contacted an attorney, and I suggest that you do the same—and fast."

"When Rose and I were there Monday, we offered to take a polygraph test. What do we do now?" Peter wanted to be prepared if they called to schedule.

"Don't do anything without an attorney, Peter. Do you hear me?" Andrew was adamant.

"I hear you. Who do you suggest we call?" Peter was beginning to feel worried about the quality of the attorneys in town. Naples, until now, did not produce enough white-collar criminal activity to attract top legal professionals. The other defendants had already hired the only one or two who did call Naples home.

"Your father's attorneys are in Tampa, and the one I've hired is in Miami. I'll do some checking and get back with you." Andrew sounded distraught.

"Peter, I'm calling Conrad," I said. "He'll know whom we should call." I knew I could trust Conrad Edmond, a valiant legal warrior who had always been there for us. Surely, he would know where to look or whom to recommend.

"Okay, call him," Peter said. "I'll go see Father to see if his attorney has any suggestions for us."

I got Conrad on the phone right away. "Have you talked to Andrew lately?" I asked.

"Yeah, he said that you and Peter needed a good criminal attorney. I searched the law directory, and I think you should use Wesley Driscoll. Do you know who he is?"

Conrad wanted to be sure that we knew Wesley Driscoll would not be cheap. However, he was world-renowned, and using him would send a very strong message to the prosecutor and the press.

"I've heard of him. Didn't he handle the Kennedy case?"

"Yep, that's him, and that's just one of his cases. He handles very high profile cases. Anyway, he's the best, if you want to win. It's just going to cost you." Conrad again wanted to prepare me for the shock of a criminal lawyer's pricing. "I've set up a meeting for you and Peter tomorrow."

"Tomorrow? Wow, that's fast." I was beginning to feel like the situation was spinning out of control. A wave of terror moved across my body as the thought of hiring a criminal attorney filled my mind. But I agreed to the meeting.

There's that enemy again, filling my mind with fear. I began to realize through this trial that the mind is the true battlefield. It is where the enemy can get in and cause fear, doubt, and unbelief. *I must have faith; I must close my eyes to the circumstances that I can see and trust that God, who promised my refuge under his wings, will protect me. I must keep my spiritual eyes on the Word.*

I remembered God's promise to me in Psalm 91 and made the words personal to myself. *Though a thousand fall at my side, though ten thousand are dying around me, these evils will not touch me. But I will see it with my eyes; I will see how the wicked are punished. If I make the Lord my refuge, if I make the Most High my shelter, no evil will conquer me; no plague will come near my home. For He orders His angels to protect me wherever I go.*

I needed those angels more than ever!

Twenty-one

Conrad Edmond suggested that I check out Wesley Driscoll's Web site. The firm's mission statement read:

> We specialize in representing individuals and companies confronting the vast power of the state or federal government and their law enforcement apparatus. We are dedicated to assisting those in the darkest hour of their lives, facing the possibility of losing family, fortune, freedom, or even life itself. When all seem against you and the might of the government bears down on you, you will find in us a friend, a counselor, and an aggressive advocate.

Was I really facing the possibility of losing my family, my business, and my freedom? I had not realized the severity of the situation until that very moment.

I found myself unable to pull away from Driscoll's Web site, which went on to demonstrate, in riveting detail, how a defense attorney must investigate criminal cases by sifting through evidence and preparing for trial—not unlike preparing for war. It showed how the principles of law, cross-examination, and evidence, as well as careful jury selection and skillful use of expert witnesses, can level the playing field to counter the enormous resources that state and federal prosecutors have at their disposal. The site made resoundingly clear the crucial role that criminal defense lawyers play in safeguarding the basic right to a fair trial for all.

That's all we could hope for now: a fair trial for all. What were we up against? A real estate deal that never got off the drawing board had suddenly turned into a RICO conspiracy case. We really did need Wesley Driscoll, or someone like him. Had we said too much to Strickland? Had we unwittingly laid the foundation for our own prosecution? I didn't get much sleep that night.

The next morning, Wednesday, October 10, 2001, Peter needed to sign some papers with Andrew at Evans and Dorne. We met at our offices, and I checked my voicemail before heading out the door. Much to my surprise, there was a message from Judith Binns at 7:00 a.m. She wanted to meet privately with a special agent and me first thing that morning. She made it clear that Peter was not invited to this meeting. What happened to that clean bill of health we'd gotten just the day before?

I went to find Peter to share the news with him.

"Peter, you're not going to believe this," I said. "Binns wants me to meet with her and another agent this morning—alone. I don't know why they'd want to meet me without you. I'm not going to return her call."

At that point, I felt that nothing good would come out of meeting for anyone without an attorney. I never returned Judith's call that day, and the events that followed that afternoon removed whatever option Judith might have offered me that morning.

"Fine, let's go. Let's call Andrew right now and let him know what's going on." But when Peter got Andrew on the phone, he received some astounding news.

"Hi, guys," Andrew said. "Listen, I just received a call from my attorney. They're going to arrest me tomorrow." Andrew's voice was hoarse, as if he'd been awake all night.

"For what?" Peter said, shocked.

"Not sure. We'll find out tomorrow. And, Peter, they're going to arrest you, too." Andrew tried to deliver the message gently.

"What? How do you know?" Peter was beginning to panic.

"Listen, just get down here. Sign these papers before we're all in jail." Andrew's request to wrap up the paperwork for an unrelated project was an attempt to add some levity to the situation.

"We'll be right there." Peter was ready to hang up but stopped himself. "What about Rose? Will they be arresting her, too?" Peter wanted to offer me some peace, if any were available.

"I doubt it. She really did not have any dealings with the Coliseum Golf project. My attorney didn't mention her name being on the list."

The list? Who else was being trapped in this crazy man's net?

"Topping the list is Craig Delaney, former county manager and president of Wood Durkee, followed by real estate developer extraordinaire Peter Durkee and his trusted attorney, Andrew Shanahan. Last, but certainly not least, is Nicholas Shubert, the father of Coliseum Golf. Don't forget, they've already arrested Wood, Gannon, Hanover, and your father. That's all I know." Andrew was out of breath.

"We'll be there in about twenty minutes." Peter was already standing up.

"Don't speed. They probably already have a warrant out for your arrest. You don't want to be booked before you've paid your criminal attorney his retainer!" Andrew laughed at his own morbid joke as he hung up the phone.

Once we arrived at Evans and Dorne, I huddled in Conrad's office while Peter signed his papers. I was genuinely afraid at this point. I had a financial crimes agent trying to track me down for a private meeting and a loose cannon of a prosecutor who believed I was guilty of a crime that I had not committed. I needed to remain in the company of a fierce attorney, and I knew that Conrad Edmond had more than his share of the aggressive advocate gene.

As I sat in Conrad's office, he handed me some background reading on Strickland, who had been involved in the Lil Tots case in Miami. A case summary document included an article on the case:

> **The Lil Tots Case**
> Our attorney general, Janet Reno, has been accused of managing Satanic Ritual Abuse (SRA) prosecutions (see "Trial by Therapy," Natl. Review, Sept. 6, 1993; "Justice Gone Crazy," *Readers Digest*, Jan. 1994.) One, the Lil Tots case, resulted in a conviction. Luis Quinonez is serving two life terms and a 165-year term. Lil

> Tots is often cited as a well-documented case because of the confession of Regina Mayo and the fact that one child tested positive for gonorrhea.
>
> In revisiting Lil Tots, it was revealed that much of the evidence in this case is extremely dubious. The gonorrhea test was later found to yield false positives one-third of the time. Regina confessed during intensive therapy sessions in which she was kept in isolation for almost a year, except for visits by her defense attorney, prosecutors, and therapists. Her attorney insisted on getting a confession and plea bargain as the only way out of a life prison sentence. His strategy was successful: Regina received a ten-year sentence and was released and deported after three years.
>
> More recently, Regina has recanted her "confession." She had initially refused to get involved, but more recently wrote a deposition describing how prosecution psychiatrists essentially "brainwashed" her. In addition, Quinonez's son has recanted all his accusations (he actually recanted immediately after making them, but nobody believed him). In recent depositions, he described how he made the accusations because interviewers would not let him leave the room until he told them what his father "had done."

Regina's attorney was none other than Martin Strickland!

"Holy smokes, Conrad! This guy obviously does not play by the rules." I thought I was going to puke.

"Listen, you need to know your enemy—that is the first law of war. You need to know that the guy you're dealing with will do anything to nail you. Don't trust anyone except your attorney. Do you understand? Now, I want you to read the entire file so that when you feel that Strickland's being nice, you'll remember what he did to Regina to get her confession." Conrad wanted to instill the fear of God in me ... and it was working.

As I reflected on what Conrad had just said about knowing the enemy, I realized that God had once again used my pastor's message to prepare me for the events of this week. Just days earlier Pastor Grant had read these words to us:

> Humble yourselves, therefore, under God's mighty hand, that he may lift you up in due time. Cast all your anxiety on him because he cares for you. Be self-controlled and alert. Your enemy the devil prowls around like a roaring lion looking for someone to devour. Resist him, standing firm in the faith, because you know that your brothers and sisters throughout the world are undergoing the same kind of sufferings
>
> 1 Peter 5:6–9 (NIV)

Just then Peter popped his head into Conrad's office.

"Let's go, Rosie. We've got to hire ourselves a criminal attorney," he offered with a laugh. Then he noticed that my face was drained of blood. "What's wrong with you?" he asked. "You look sickly pale. Are you okay, or is the stress getting to you?"

"Conrad just gave me a file on your favorite prosecutor. When you read it, you'll look like I do. Let's go, you can read while I drive."

I turned to Conrad. "Thank you for always being there for me, for always being many steps ahead to assure that my path is lit and safe. You are truly an angel. I love you, man." I had tears in my eyes, and suddenly I was unable to get another word out.

"I love you, too," Conrad said. "You're the Great Rose Visconti—don't forget that. And remember: Never let them see you sweat." Conrad offered a gentle hug as we left his office.

As we began to face the idea that we had to live and do business in a community where our faces were on the front page of the newspaper almost daily, the shock and shame of it all began to numb my defense mechanisms. The media had already convicted us, with headlines declaring that ours was one of the "largest institutionalized corruption cases ever seen." The letters to the editor and the paper itself, through its editorials, began to crucify us. We had unwillingly traded the title "Developer of the Year" for "pond scum."

The shock to our employees was enormous. We were a small company, a family-owned business that had strong ties with our staff members and their families. They were genuinely concerned for Peter and me but could not hide their own personal fears.

What if this prosecutor was successful in prosecuting us? How would our company survive? Should our employees remain loyal until the owners were carried away in shackles and handcuffs, or should they begin looking for new, more credible employment immediately?

Peter and I attempted to quiet our staff's fears and even went so far as to tell the most concerned employees that if they felt that leaving now would allow them to provide a safe and secure future for their families, we understood. I don't think anyone left under those circumstances. In fact, our entire staff, which consisted of more than three hundred employees, began to defend us, our company, and our commitment to excellence in Collier County.

The way the prosecutor and the media were reporting the "crime," you would have thought we'd overbuilt in each of our communities, that we'd destroyed protected animals and wetlands. On the contrary, we were building fewer units then were allowed under the permit in each of our allotted developments. We were providing more green space to Collier County than many other developments that lacked golf courses and consisted entirely of homes. We were increasing the employment base in the county and were involved in our community's education programs and charities. On top of all that, we did not receive any special favors or treatment from the county or from any commissioner. We followed the law to the letter.

The only crime I was aware of was Jack Wood's bilking two honest business people, along with some very savvy investors, of their savings and reputation.

Every time something hit the media about Wood, The Preserve residents felt a wave of fear that their investment was somehow at risk, their community tainted by Wood's fraud. I spent many hours, even days, talking through this issue with potential buyers. Convincing them was not easy, as they were all well aware that the person they were trying to believe had recently been arrested in a RICO conspiracy with Wood.

October 2001 continued to be filled with turmoil. Only eighteen days following our arrest, on October 29, Jack Wood was sentenced to seventeen years in a federal prison for his Wood Investment scheme. Many of his investors who had lost millions were at his hearing to give the judge reason to keep Wood for life. Their lives had been ruined, and they wanted this man to pay the price.

As the state continued its case against us, it needed a key witness. Who better to volunteer than Jack Wood? He knew his only hope to reduce his federal sentence was to cooperate, to bear false witness against us with the state.

In his handwritten letters to Strickland from the Collier County Jail, Wood wrote, "I will do whatever you need to assist you in the Coliseum Golf case. I will say whatever you need for me to say, in exchange for my R-35 sentence reduction."

In his no-holds-barred attempt to reduce his jail time, Wood became a jailhouse snitch for the prosecutor, even offering to use his "faith" to obtain inmate confessions for the prosecutors. They could save their souls through Wood's "ministry" and feel good about it as they sealed their own fate at the hands of the prosecutor. Wood was using a salvation message on the inside to save himself on the outside—if he lived. If any of the prisoners that he was ministering to found out that he was using their personal confessions against them, they would kill him—or have him killed.

Shocking news came on October 11, 2001, as Craig Delaney pleaded guilty to racketeering conspiracy. The prosecutor knew that he needed a more credible key witness than a convicted felon like Wood. As a recent convict of a federal crime, Wood did not look very convincing in his orange jumpsuit. I wonder how the jury would have responded to him when he stated his current address as federal prison.

Delaney was an upstanding citizen who had served his community as county manager, and now, under duress, he had to cooperate fully with prosecutors or face ten years in prison. How's that for a hammer?

During a series of depositions leading up to our trial, Craig was asked why he had pleaded guilty when, in fact, he was not. He explained that his attorney had told him that since he was a public figure at the time of the incident, there was greater than a fifty percent chance of conviction and that the fees for the case could be nearly $1 million. Craig had to weigh his decision, not wanting to subject his family to the financial strain or the chance that he would be serving time. Our attorneys suggested that Delaney sue his attorney for malpractice. Peter's attorney, Adam Woerner, only wished that Craig had been given better legal advice. If Wesley Driscoll's firm had been fighting for Craig, he never would have pleaded to a crime he did not commit.

Craig met several times with the prosecutor who was helping to form the case against us. We had been arrested with no solid evidence of a crime being committed. Now the prosecutor and his team of FDLE muscle needed to dig, looking for anything that might help them in their case.

In a series of interviews with the prosecutor, Craig had remembered the $200,000 loan from Mary Smith that Wood claimed to have brought in a suitcase from Tennessee. Craig thought that by mentioning this transaction to Strickland, he was able to demonstrate our honesty, proving that we would not accept cash without proper reporting and would never have participated in any money laundering. He wanted to prove that neither he nor I would accept such a large sum of cash from anyone without proper documentation. It was this piece of new "evidence" that Strickland was going to use to pressure Phillip Durkee into a plea deal. After all, now there was proof that Phillip had taken $200,000 in cash from Wood. He could really make this look bad and force Phillip into a plea. Strickland needed more credible witnesses than Wood; now he had Delaney and hopefully Durkee.

Strickland was interested in having as many of us as possible plea to anything. A large number of pleas would allow him to get everyone involved to testify against his big fish, Eugene Gannon.

To force Phillip Durkee to become a witness, Strickland wanted evidence from Wood to support charging Durkee with money laundering.

My evenings were spent pouring through the boxes of discovery material that had been provided to us by the prosecutor—his evidence in the case. I was searching for clues to anything that the prosecutor was fishing for in his interviews with his key witness, Jack Wood. I pulled the October 24, 2001, interview of Wood from his jail cell. This interview caught my eye as Fred Bare started out by explaining to Wood that Delaney had mentioned a point in time when Wood left town for a weekend and returned with a large sum of cash. Wood was asked only if he recalled going to retrieve the money.

"Oh I can't wait to read this one." I continued reading to myself as Jack's lies covered the pages of notes that followed:

> In late 1997, The Preserve was in need of money to cover expenses, and Wood discussed this with Peter and Rose. Mary Smith, an investor in Wood's fund, had previously expressed to Wood a desire to invest in real estate. Wood had Andrew Shanahan prepare a promissory note for $200,000. Wood took the note with him to Tennessee. Smith squirreled away $200,000 that she had not paid taxes on. Wood and his son drove to Tennessee to pick up the money, as he didn't want to fly with that amount of cash. The money was packaged in envelopes and organized into $10,000 packets.

"Hold on a minute" I protested aloud. "The last interview I read he didn't remember how the money was packaged. What a liar!" I continued reading silently:

> He brought the money back to Naples and met with Peter and Rose.

What! I never met with him. My head began to pound. *We told him to call Phillip Durkee; after that, Peter and I had no involvement! Oh, I have to start taking notes so that my attorney can discredit this liar as a witness, and fast! Let's see what other contradictions are in this little jail cell interview."*

> Andrew took the money and deposited it in the safety deposit box at Union Bank. Wood stated Phillip Durkee might have taken the cash to the Bahamas. Wood stated that Andrew, Peter, Rose, and Phillip all knew what was going on.

"What was 'going on'? I thought the scum bag was covering his mystery wire transfer that never came!" I blurted aloud.

Armed with fresh ammunition from Wood's jailhouse interviews, Strickland filed new charges of money laundering to squeeze Phillip Durkee just a little bit harder.

Phillip Durkee had been fighting with Strickland over these charges of racketeering and conspiracy since the previous year. He had been arrested December 12, 2000, and he, too, was feeling the financial squeeze caused by his criminal attorney's monthly fees. Strickland called Durkee to arrange a meeting at which they could discuss new charges of money laundering and conspiracy; charges that Strickland had gathered from his meeting with Delaney and which his key witness, Jack Wood, had now verified.

Phillip Durkee agreed to a special meeting with FDLE and Strickland on October 31, 2001. Phillip's attorneys would carefully navigate their client though this shark infested meeting. When asked about the $200,000 cash transaction, Phillip Durkee's answer was recorded in his interview as follows:

> He received $200,000 in cash from either Jack Wood or Andrew Shanahan as "collateral" for a $200,000 loan that he had made to The Preserve. He said that he asked Wood if the money was clean, and Wood told him that it was from a wealthy woman who had been hiding the money from her husband and was now investing the money into the Wood stock account. Durkee said that he assumed that Wood credited the woman's account for the $200,000. He, Durkee, put the money into his safe deposit box at

> Union Bank, which is in the same building as Andrew Shanahan's office. When he received the cash, he called a "banker friend" and asked him what he should do with the money. His banker friend told him to spend it. Over the next three years, he used the money for personal expenses, although $50,000 was taken out and brought to the Bahamas. Durkee had copies of the promissory note from The Preserve to him for the $200,000 loan.

The meeting concluded with Strickland suggesting that Durkee strongly consider a plea deal. The evidence that he laid out for him included a check for $2,165.00 written to Gannon marked "commission." There was also the deep discount on Commissioner Hanover's wedding and the personal guarantee on a loan to SmartKids, Hanover's company. That loan, arranged by Durkee through Wood, was never repaid. He also appeared to be the author of the partnership structured for the Coliseum Golf deal that gave Commissioner Gannon a no-money-down, ten percent interest in the project. Things were not looking good for the seventy-five-year-old developer, but he was not giving in to the pressure. Not yet.

Strickland decided to hit Phillip Durkee where it hurt. He had evidence that Durkee's wife, Ann, deposited $50,000 into an account with Wood's fund; it was this $50,000 that Wood suggested guaranteed the loan to Hanover. Maybe Durkee would be motivated by the arrest of his seventy-year-old wife as a co-conspirator. Would that get this stubborn old man to move into the state court and testify against his son? The threat of arresting Ann worked. Phillip Durkee entered a plea of no contest to racketeering conspiracy on November 5, 2001, and, just as in Delaney's deal, he promised to cooperate fully with the investigation—or go to jail. He was sentenced to four years' probation and eight months of house arrest, along with a $75,000 fine.

Following Phillip's plea deal, November was a fairly quiet month. The attorneys were busily filing motions to dismiss the case on the grounds that there was no evidence of a crime. On December 3, 2001, Judge Faye Barrett dismissed conspiracy charges against the remaining five of us (Peter Durkee, Andrew Shanahan, Nicholas Shubert, Gannon, and me), calling the charges "vague." She left in place racketeering and influence peddling counts against Gannon. Strickland was surprised at the ruling and vowed to re-file the charges against the defendants within thirty days.

"We will clean up the weaknesses the judge seems to see in the information," Strickland said to the *Collier Enquirer*, adding that he expected new charges to trigger another round of defense protests. He also said that if Judge Barrett subsequently threw out charges in another round, he would appeal her ruling.

This minor victory thrilled us. The justice system was working, and—finally—we were being treated fairly. We expected to be completely exonerated. All of the Collier County cutthroats and the *Collier Enquirer* owed us an apology.

Apology? No way is the Collier Enquirer *going to apologize to anyone*, I thought to myself as I entered the front door of New Hope Ministries the following Sunday morning and was given a welcoming hug by a smiling woman who handed me a copy of the weekly bulletin. I was so thankful that God had led my family to this church and to this pastor. Grant Thigpen truly loved and cared for his congregation; it was evident in the way that he walked up and down the aisles during praise and worship, greeting and touching as many people as he could. Not only was he a loving pastor, he was a gifted Bible teacher. In the time we had been attending New Hope, I had learned how to pray, how to put on the full armor of God, and how to stand on his covenant promises.

I remembered how I initially thought that New Hope Ministries was an odd name for a church, but now, as far as I was concerned, it had more than lived up to its name.

Twenty-two

On December 4, following the judge's dismissal of the charges, a front-page editorial ran in the *Collier Enquirer*:

Justice Is Far From Finished
Though Monday's dismissal of some charges in the Coliseum Golf case can be confusing, citizens who have stuck with the story of scandal and corruption for nearly five years remain focused on what's most important—justice and government free of sleazy deals.

Thank goodness Special Prosecutor Martin Strickland vows to at least re-file or, at most, pursue them to a higher court following Judge Faye Barrett's dismissal of all of the charges against three of the accused, Nicholas Shubert, Andrew Shanahan, and Rose Visconti, and some of the charges against Peter Durkee and ex-county commissioner Eugene Gannon.

It was Gannon's attempt to work with Shubert on a golf coliseum concept and use it to become limited partners with developers Durkee and Visconti that prompted criminal investigation since June 1997; Shanahan is the attorney of Durkee and his father, Phillip Durkee, who also is a developer and already has been found guilty in the case.

Yet Judge Barrett wants more information—more details, more facts—from Strickland. The timing of her decision is unusual. Citizens believe that fuller disclosure is what trials are for, so that evidence and rebuttals can rise or fall on their merits in full public view.

Still, there is encouraging precedent. At least once before,

> Judge Barrett has raised the bar of performance for Strickland, and he had risen to the challenge. When he came on the job in April from Miami, Barrett ordered him to stay at arm's length from investigations already done by SW Florida State Attorney Mike Pennino, who was thrown off the case for a conflict of interest, buying stock in a firm hyping a second attempt to build Coliseum Golf. He did manage to find, where Pennino found nothing criminal, widespread influence peddling and money laundering and racketeering. No wonder Strickland put his finger on the culture of corruption that became a way of life for those who asked for and got the public trust—only to treat citizens and their business with contempt. Some Coliseum Golf charges are dropped. For now.
>
> Surely this case is not over yet.

On December 5, the newspaper printed a correction and clarification on the inside back cover of the paper in 6-point font:

> An article on 1A of the Tuesday, December 4, edition incorrectly stated that a racketeering charge against Peter Durkee still exists in the Collier County public corruption case. Durkee only faced a racketeering conspiracy charge that was dismissed by Judge Faye Barrett on Monday.

On December 19, as some sort of sadistic early Christmas present, Strickland re-filed all charges and added new counts. Just when we were celebrating our victory, the prosecutor who had the funds and the ability to accuse us, decided to play Scrooge. How, I wondered, did just one man possess the power to destroy our reputations, our business—our very lives—with nothing more than an accusation?

Our attorneys urged us to put the case out of our minds and try to enjoy the holidays. They continued to encourage us that the charges were bogus and that they would fight this battle in the proper playing field, our United States system of justice. However, my faith in our justice system was faltering, to say the least.

On January 12, Peter and I found ourselves back in Courtroom 2A in front of Judge Barrett, once again entering our pleas of innocence in response to the re-filed charges. We considered ourselves lucky that we did not have to be reprocessed, even though this was just a formality of the court. After we entered our pleas, our attorneys told Barrett that they planned to file legal challenges to the new information. They would use similar arguments as last time, insisting the description of the charges was too vague for them to understand and defend.

Both Woerner brothers, the defense attorneys for Peter and me, announced plans to argue that Strickland's office didn't have the legal authority from Florida Governor Jeb Bush to file charges of conspiracy to money laundering against us. We were thrown into a whirlwind, unsure of where we were headed. We had no idea why our lawyers were arguing about legal authority. We had no involvement in money laundering—or racketeering and conspiracy, for that matter. However, once you've entered the criminal justice system, you fight every charge on legal authority. It was no longer whether you were innocent or guilty; it was now a game of legal maneuvering.

I knew without a doubt that Jason Woerner was the best at this game, and I was thrilled that I was his number-one cause. I was still in shock that I had entered the criminal justice system. Justice seemed very far away—and very expensive. Joking over lunch following the January 12 hearing, Adam Woerner said we were "innocent until proven indigent," with a laugh. Defending ourselves had already cost us nearly $350,000, and we had been in court only twice. I was almost afraid to ask just how much Adam thought the final tab would be. In the end, when pressed, the attorneys' estimates were based on dismissals, depositions, trials, and the like.

"Just save every dollar you make. Your freedom will depend on it!" Adam offered with gallows' humor.

It took until February 13, 2002, for Judge Faye Barrett to rule that the new Coliseum Golf charges barely passed muster, telling Strickland that his charging document was "not a legal work of art." However, Judge Barrett made clear that the charging document, the second filed in less than two months, was just barely adequate to allow the five-year public corruption case to lumber into its next phase, called discovery. This phase takes several months and involves depositions of witnesses and the state providing copies of its evidence to the defense.

Strickland accused Judge Barrett of intentionally criticizing him in her written ruling. He also said his office was researching whether to ask her to recuse herself for throwing out the previous charges. In his statements, Strickland sounded like a little boy whose feelings had been hurt by a girl spurning his affection:

> If you read the first one, she took a shot at me in it, and she took a shot at me in that one, too. I think the judge takes personal shots at me whenever she can.

Strickland and Barrett's personalities were obviously clashing, and the media, fueled by Strickland, began to report that the judge was showing favoritism to the defense. Strickland said Judge Barrett wouldn't give the state a fair shake and filed with the appellate court to boot Barrett off the case.

February was filled with motions from our attorneys in response to Strickland's latest charging document. It was late February when the defense pressed Strickland to release the discovery the prosecution had gathered to support the charges. The prosecutor sent sixteen thousand pages of documents; box after box arrived. I knew I had to go through every page; if there was anything in the boxes that appeared to be inappropriate, I was determined to find it.

The flood of paper was obviously part of the prosecution's strategy. The boxes had no rhyme or reason. There were multiple copies of the same documents and copies of every calendar that Eugene Gannon ever owned, including hundreds of blank pages. It looked as if they'd copied anything and everything they could get their hands on, threw all the papers in the air, then picked up sixteen thousand pages at random and neatly boxed and numbered them as evidence. None of it seemed to lead anywhere.

I began to assemble the "discovery" in a way that I could make some sense of it. I was ready to act as legal assistant to the Woerners, to do as much research as possible on this case. I knew more about The Preserve project than any associate ever could.

I needed to save money wherever possible and my husband, who was an employee of the company, needed to find a new job. Durkee Development Group had no future as long as Peter and I, the principals of the company, were under the RICO shadow. But Zack found it difficult to find new employment; it seemed the case had damaged his name too. I suppose no other developer in town wanted to chance hiring the husband of Rose Visconti. It was just too scary to be that close to a prosecutor who thought every developer in town was illegally schmoozing the commissioners.

Our marriage was continuing on the downhill spiral it had begun five years earlier. The stress of the trial and my personal stress trying to run a company under extreme conditions—no financing available to accused felons—caused Zack to talk to me less and less. It felt as if there were a gigantic magnetic force hard at work in our home. When I entered a room, Zack would leave it. Eventually, I slept in the spare bedroom or conveniently fell asleep while reading to Taylor in her room.

The silence between Zack and me seemed deafening at times. The startling reality that Taylor was growing up in the dysfunction of our marriage was becoming more and more obvious. She'd happily spend time with either Zack or me, but never the two of us together. It had been this way as long as she could remember. What a horrible disservice we were doing Taylor! We were setting the most important example she would use for what a relationship between man and woman, mother and father, looked like. Would she grow up and look for an empty relationship because that was all she'd known?

This madness had to end soon. All I could do was pray. My mental muscle had lost its fight with Zack. I had tried for so long to gently encourage him to re-spark the romance we had lost. I don't think either of us had the heart to completely surrender our pride and our identities, not even to save our marriage or to save our daughter from the pain and anguish that a divorce would bring to her. How selfish and stubborn we were.

Enough dwelling on things I could not change, but I had to focus on my freedom.

My first assignment from Jason Woerner was to set up a spreadsheet that showed every vote before the commission for a real estate development. First was just The Preserve. Then we expanded it to any and all developments that had had a petition before the board or the planning council for zoning or permitting.

It was clear that Eugene Gannon had begun to abstain from voting in early January 1997 on any projects that Peter Durkee was involved in. Although he had suggested that the county attorney said it was not necessary for him to abstain, he avoided any potential conflict if and when the Coliseum Golf deal came to fruition.

By day, Peter and I attempted to keep our company running. At night, we reviewed discovery documents, trying to keep ourselves out of jail. We had no time to lose. If there was evidence that would exonerate us, it needed to be presented as quickly as possible to the judge.

Sixteen thousand pages and no end in sight.

Twenty-three

My home life, of course, was deeply affected by the trial preparation and the fear of what the future would bring. Each night, my family would leave the dinner table, disappointment etched upon their faces, knowing that Mommy was about to disappear into the garage to look at boxes of papers. Taylor was too young to understand the depth of what her mother was facing. I tried to be a mother when I returned from work, making dinner and chatting with Taylor, but I was always silently calculating how many hours I would have in the boxes before I dropped from exhaustion. Zack was as supportive as he could be. He'd read to Taylor before bed and do his best to let me know that he was concerned about how I felt.

Our dog, Genevieve, a two-year-old white Labrador, was due to have puppies on Valentine's Day. That gave Taylor and Lauren much to get excited about. Taylor was thrilled at the thought that she would have so many puppies around the house to play with, even if it was only for a few months. Lauren, who was living in a nearby condo we had purchased as an investment, was attending Florida Gulf Coast University and was looking forward to keeping a puppy for herself. After all, she explained, a nineteen-year-old college student living alone could benefit greatly from a watchdog. I knew that Lauren was having enough of a struggle just taking care of herself without adding a puppy to the mix. Her schedule included going to school during the day and going out partying at night. Somehow, a baby mammal with a small bladder didn't seem to fit too well with her lifestyle.

As the blessed day approached, Zack left on a golf week with some pals, promising to be home before the puppies arrived. His timing was impeccable. Just after dinner, Genevieve began nervously pacing the house. Zack had built her a whelping box and had put it in the corner of our bedroom. We led Genevieve there and began the watch. We invited a few friends and family members who were anticipating the birth to witness the miracle. Peter's sister, Deborah, who is a registered nurse, was adopting one of the puppies and was on hand to assist as necessary.

Everyone knew I was no good with blood or a dog in distress. Deborah, with stethoscope in hand, climbed into the box with Genevieve and assisted with each birth. Nine beautiful puppies graced our bedroom on Valentine's Day.

Lauren was right by Deborah's side, counting the puppies. We'd promised eight puppies, so Genevieve would have to overproduce for Lauren to get her own—and she delivered. The runt, Tank, was Lauren's new baby. Although he was the smallest, his stocky legs and rough and tumble entry into this world gave him his name.

I would not trade one sleepless night with those puppies. For eight weeks, the love, licks, attention, and smell of puppies filled my life. I made the gruel for their feedings and I loved bath time, which we called "puppy car wash." The family enjoyed all of the excitement and love that these nine little bundles of affection provided.

We had visitation time each night when the soon-to-be adoptive parents could come and play with their babies. When they were old enough to move to the lanai, we installed a baby fence to keep them out of the pool. Labradors love water and the pool was just too enticing for the nine little creatures. They were so much fun to watch—jumping, rolling, chewing, chewing, and more chewing. We had to replace all the patio furniture once the puppies had been relocated to their adoptive homes. It was a welcome, wonderful distraction from the pressures of life.

Easter was the appointed time for our little ones to move out of their mother's nest and into their new homes. The day the last puppy left, I felt my heart tear apart. These little bundles of fur had provided an unconditional love, tails wagging each time they saw me. Now I had to return to the harsh reality of my life. It was a quiet, cold existence between Zack and me once again. Taylor no longer had the distraction of the puppies to play with and nurture. The birth of the puppies had been a miracle, a wonderful escape, but now the puppies were gone.

I came to rely on music, especially that of Jim Brickman, a romantic pianist, to soothe me during the stressful times in the garage with the sixteen thousand pages of discovery.

One spring evening following dinner, I camped out in the garage with my Jim Brickman CD and a glass of wine to resume the search for justice and truth. It was ninety degrees in the garage and the oscillating fan did nothing more than move the stale air around me. As I looked down at my hands, the paper cuts were many, and my cuticles were bleeding. The only evidence of a crime was that I needed a serious manicure.

I had developed a process of numbering the boxes then re-creating boxes by defendant. That way, I could assemble evidence or lack of evidence and answer questions quickly if Jason Woerner had any. I was startled when the door from the house swung open.

"Hi, Rose, how goes the battle out here?" Zack said. "I just put Taylor into bed; she'd like you to tuck her in and give her a kiss. Is there anything I can do to help you out here in command central?"

"Thanks for asking, Zack, but I'm not really sure what I'm doing, so I don't know how you could help at this point. I'll go kiss Taylor goodnight. I could use a breath of fresh air and a hug." I left Zack standing in the garage surveying the papers lying everywhere.

"Where is that sweet little girl of mine?" I asked as I pressed my hands all around her little body hidden under the covers. "She must have been swallowed up in the bed!" Taylor could hardly stand the tickling and began to laugh and squeal, "Do it again, Mommy!"

"I came in here to put you to bed, not wake you up, silly. Will you give Mommy a big hug and kiss before you lie back down? Your special hugs and kisses are what keep me going every day."

Taylor looked up at me. With her beautiful green eyes and her curly blond hair spread across her pillow, she looked like an angel. "Good night, Mommy, and don't you work too late in the garage. It's really hot out there, and I think there are bugs too!"

"Okay, Sergeant Taylor," I said, saluting. "I won't stay out there for more than one hour."

When I returned to the garage, Zack was still there. "What are you still doing out here?" I asked. I was hoping to get some work done, not fight with him.

"Well, I know how much you like this Jim Brickman CD, and I was listening to the radio, and guess who's coming to the Philharmonic?" Zack held up two tickets to the concert with a smile.

"That's great; I'd love to see him live." I felt a wave of panic rush over me. Zack and I going to a romantic night of Jim Brickman's music? *Hopefully, he'll just enjoy the music and not be "moved" by it.*

"I made reservations for dinner before the show, and the babysitter's all set," Zack said proudly.

"Who's sitting?" I wouldn't let just anybody take care of my angel.

"Nora Coppenhaven, you know, she lives at the end of our street. She's great, but we can't be out too late; it's a school night." Zack said.

"You know Zack, maybe we should just eat here with Taylor. That way she won't be alone with the sitter so long." I was looking for ways to get out of dinner. Why bother eating out at a nice restaurant with nothing to talk about except the case?

"I was just trying to reach out, Rose, but obviously you're not interested. Do you want to take your sister to the concert instead of me?" Zack's feelings were obviously hurt.

"Don't be silly," I said. "I appreciate the concert, and I think you will too. I just don't want to leave Taylor alone that long, that's all. Don't make it more than it is, Zack. It's not always about you."

The night of the concert arrived, and we decided to join Taylor in a McDonalds delight at home. She was excited that Nora was going to be playing with her and letting her stay up past her normal bedtime.

"Now, Taylor, you be good for Nora, and remember bedtime is 8:30 and not a minute later."

Taylor looked at me and gave me a wink. "Okay, Mommy, I'll go straight to bed." She ran over, gave me a big hug and kisses, then reached over, and took Zack's hand. "Daddy, you hold Mommy's hand. She needs lots of love." *How did Taylor notice this lack of physical touch in our relationship all of a sudden?*

"Okay, Taylor, Daddy will hold Mommy's hand," he said. Zack's hand felt cold and unwelcome in mine. But for Taylor's sake, for the thirty seconds that it would take us to get to the door, we could do that much for her.

As soon as we cleared the front door, I grabbed my purse to keep my hands occupied. Zack jumped into the car, and not another word was spoken until we arrived at the Philharmonic.

"Do you want me to get you a drink before the show?" Zack asked.

"Sure, I'll have whatever you're having, as long as it's not beer. I don't want to have to run to the bathroom; I don't want to miss a single song of the concert." I offered a smile as Zack stood in the long line for a glass of wine.

The bells chimed, letting us know that show time was five minutes away. I was so excited. I had all but forgotten about my nightly dates in the garage with sixteen thousand pieces of paper. This night would be just Jim Brickman and me—oh, yeah, and Zack.

We had gone for so long not loving each other, not touching each other, that when Jim Brickman encouraged the audience to hold hands and enjoy the romance of his music we looked at each other with confusion and dismay. How sad our life had become. We each felt cold and isolated, but neither of us felt responsible or capable of extending a hand of healing. We just gave each other a sad smile and focused on the music, arms folded tightly, sending a clear message.

Brickman played beautifully. As we enjoyed the music I wondered, *Lord, can this marriage be saved?*

Twenty-four

As we drove home from the concert, I had that haunting "mother feeling" about Lauren. I had not been able to reach her throughout the day, and at 10:00 p.m. as we left the Philharmonic I thought I'd try her one more time.

Part of me was angry with her for being irresponsible. After all, she had an eight-week-old puppy in her care. How could she not be home all day? I promised myself that if she did not answer this time, I was going to repossess the dog in the morning and find a suitable home for Tank. Her school days and partying nights were just not going to work with a dog.

"No answer," I said to Zack, my voice chasing away the uncomfortable silence in the car.

"Who are you calling at this hour?" Zack asked.

"Lauren. She hasn't returned my messages all day. I'm worried about her, but really worried about Tank. Can you imagine the mess in the condo if she's left the dog alone all day?" I shuddered at the thought. "Do you think we should stop by the condo to check on the dog?" I hoped Zack would agree.

"No. If you start that now, you'll never stop, and Lauren will have you taking care of the dog." Zack was adamant.

"Okay, I'll just worry all night and hope for the best in the morning."

"Your sarcastic tone does not affect me, Rose. Save it for somebody else." After the wonderful evening at the Philharmonic, Zack's tone of voice was a rude awakening to the real condition of our marriage.

I was glad the ride home was a short one; the silence in such a small place was difficult. We were lucky that our babysitter lived at the end of our street, and Zack quickly offered to take her home. While he was gone, I thought I'd try Lauren a few more times.

What if she's dead somewhere? Should I call the police and report her missing? The thoughts, the horrible thoughts that possess a mother's heart and mind when she cannot locate her child, were haunting me.

I knew that all I could do was get down on my knees and pray for Lauren's protection and God's intervention, wherever she was and whatever she was doing. I used Psalm 91 as the basis for my prayer: "Lord, you are my refuge and my fortress; it is in you alone that I put my trust. Please send your angels of protection to guard Lauren and keep her, watch over her, and protect her from evil and from harm. I offer her life to you, Lord. Keep her in your care."

I climbed into bed, closed my eyes, and continued to pray until I fell asleep. I had to push the negative thoughts from my mind. They continued to try to overtake my prayers of intervention. What kind of spiritual warfare was brewing? Why did I suddenly feel under attack—again?

When morning arrived, I was eager to dial Lauren's cell phone one more time. Even if she was completely hungover, she could at least grunt, and I'd know she was fine. Once again, however, I got her voicemail.

"Hi Lauren, it's Mom again. I'm worried sick about you. I've tried for twenty-four hours to reach you and you're not calling me back. If you don't call me in the next thirty minutes, I'm going to your condo to see if you're okay." Fear ripped through my mind.

"Any news from Lauren?" Zack asked as he walked into the kitchen.

"No. And I don't know what to do. I think I'm going to drive by her condo after I take Taylor to school. I'm hoping her car will be there. If it is, I'll be patient and wait for her to call me. If it's not, then I'll call all of the hospitals in the area." I was beginning to get a sick feeling in my gut.

"Oh, Rose, don't overreact. She probably partied last night and had the sense to spend the night wherever she was. Be glad she didn't drive drunk. That's all you'd need is to have your daughter's picture alongside yours on the front page, with her there for killing someone."

Zack's voice faded as I left the room.

“You’re always so positive when it comes to Lauren.” I retorted.

“Have a nice day. Call me if you hear anything from Lauren.” Zack was trying to recover from his blunder.

“I will, thanks. Come on, Taylor, we’re going to be late for school.” I needed to switch gears to keep Taylor on track.

After dropping Taylor off at school, I drove by Lauren’s condo to see if her car was there. I was running late for a meeting at the office, but if I could just see her car, maybe I’d feel some relief.

As I turned into her complex, my pulse quickened and my mind was fighting between wanting to kill her and hug her. After all, how hard is it to return a call to your mother? I had left over twenty voice messages, with none of them returned. As I turned the corner, I began to pray. “Lord, let her car be there, please.”

No car.

In a continued panic, I pulled into her spot to turn around. Maybe she would just be pulling in after a long night of drinking.

No. All hopes were beginning to fade.

I dialed her cell phone again, and as tears began to well up in my eyes, her voicemail answered once again. Should I leave another message, or should I call the police?

“Hi, Lauren. It’s Mom, for the thirtieth time. Will you please just call me and let me know you’re okay? If I don’t hear from you in the next hour, I’m calling the police.”

Even if she were in a drunken stupor, at least she’d call me to avoid being hunted by the police.

It was time to call the hospitals. I called both of the community hospitals in Naples, but no one fitting her description had been admitted. My chest began to feel as though someone weighing three hundred pounds had taken up residence on it. I didn’t feel strong enough to handle any more tragedy. The stress of the arrest and its effects on our business had landed me at my stress limit.

As Lauren failed to reappear, or even to call, I began to pray. “Lord, I don’t think I’m up for another trial just yet, so if you could, protect Lauren wherever she is. Send your angels of protection to her side. Bring her home now. She is your child and you have great plans for her life!"

I knew that the only way I could leave the battlefield of my mind, where Lauren was dead, was to pray. God would deliver her. I had to stand in faith that his will would be done. I opened my Bible to the book of Isaiah and read God's promise:

> Do not be afraid, for I am with you. I will bring your children from the east, and gather you from the west. I will say to the north, "Give them up!" and to the south, "Do not hold them back." Bring my sons from afar and my daughters from the end of the earth—everyone who is called by my name, whom I created for my glory, whom I formed and made.
>
> Isaiah 43: 5–7

My work that day was minimal, I tried to do heavy brainwork but found myself unable to concentrate. Late in the afternoon, my cell phone rang. The caller ID said "Lauren." *Thank God.*

"Hi, Mom, it's me," said a very faint voice that barely resembled Lauren's.

"Where have you been? Are you okay?" I was ready to move from "I'm glad you're alive" to "I'm ready to kill you."

"Where is Tank? Have you left that puppy home alone all this time?" I hadn't even given Lauren a chance to answer before I fired off a few more questions.

"Mom, listen for a minute." Her voice was weak. "I'm in very bad shape. I'm going to have a friend take me to the condo to get Tank and then bring me to your office." Lauren's voice again faded as if she were still drunk or high.

"Where are you? I'll come get you." I began to panic.

"I'll be there in about thirty minutes. Just wait for me there." Then she was gone.

What was going on? Where had she been? She had left Tank alone all day and night!

"I'm going to have to find a home for the dog. There is no way that puppy should have to suffer because Lauren is irresponsible." I realized I was talking out loud when my sister Aly popped in.

"Who are you talking to?" she asked.

"I was talking about Lauren to myself. She's been out all night and left the puppy home. I'm sure the dog has destroyed the house, between going to the bathroom and chewing. She is just unbelievable." I was releasing the stress of the last twenty-four hours.

"Remember, Rose, the most important thing is that Lauren is okay. The dog will survive. But you're right. She can't take care of herself, much less a dog." Aly was always good at helping me keep things in perspective.

I sighed and continued. "She's having someone bring her to my office. Evidently she is not fit to drive, or her car was left in the trail of partying last night and she doesn't know where." I was thankful that I had heard her voice and that she was at the very least alive.

"I'll be here for a little longer. Do you want me to wait until Lauren gets here before I leave?" Aly was always there to lend a shoulder

"Yeah, just in case." I did not know why I said that, but I was glad I did.

"I'll be in my office. Call me if you need me or when Lauren arrives." Aly patted my back before leaving me alone with my thoughts.

I sat in my office watching out the window for Lauren's arrival. I seemed to have enough sense to call Zack and ask him to pick up Taylor from school and to update him about Lauren, what little I knew.

Zack agreed that we needed to find a new home for Tank, and quick. He offered to go to the condo with Taylor to clean up after the poor dog. I thought better of that. I knew that if there was any real damage, or if the party had started there, that I would never hear the end of it.

"No, thanks, Zack. I don't know what to expect. Why don't you take Taylor to McDonald's for dinner? As soon as I see what Lauren's state is, I'll call you back." I tried not to sound like the director, as Zack had so frequently called me.

"Okay," Zack said, sounding concerned. "Taylor and I will go to

McDonalds for dinner and then wait to hear from you at home. Are you okay? You sound stressed."

"I'm torn between a sense of relief and being totally angry with her. I'll have to work out all these emotions before she arrives." I peered out the window and felt a flutter of hope. "It looks like a car pulling up now. I'll call you later."

I jumped out of my chair to see a young girl pulling Lauren out of the car. I waited to see if they needed my help. I soon noticed that Tank was in Lauren's arms and realized that might have been the reason she'd had trouble getting out. I ran to the door to let them in.

"What is wrong with you, Lauren?" I exclaimed as tears began to run down my cheeks.

She could barely hold her head up, and her friend was holding her up under her arm. Although it was apparent that Lauren was under the influence, I still had no idea what influence she was under.

"Take her in my office. Right this way." I put my arm under Lauren's other side and yelled for Aly to help.

"Oh my God, Lauren. What's wrong?" Aly said as she raced to her side.

"Take the dog, Aly, and put him in my office." I wanted to get Lauren to a chair and fast.

As soon as Lauren's friend had settled her in the chair, she bolted to the door before I'd even learned her name. She obviously did not want to be involved in any part of what was going to happen next.

"Lauren, look at me." I was on my knees holding her head, which hung heavy between her shoulders.

"I can't." Lauren groaned.

"What do you mean you can't? What did you take? Aly, we need to get her to the emergency room."

"No," Lauren protested. She paused before continuing. "I tried to kill myself last night. I should be dead."

"That would be impossible. I was praying prayers of intervention over you." The tears raced down my cheeks, but I knew that I had to be strong.

"Well, that explains it," Lauren said as she drifted in and out of consciousness. "You and God got in my way."

Aly grabbed her cell phone and stepped into action. "I'm going to call Dr. Burkhalter. He'll look at Lauren confidentially and tell us what to do next."

I was trying to wrap my mind around what was happening, wondering what might have occurred last night to cause Lauren to want to kill herself. She had been working with a psychiatrist, Dr. Tolar, on issues of feeling abandoned by her own father and the subsequent difficulty in her strained relationship with her stepfather. While these were serious matters, I didn't see how they could possibly be connected to the events at hand.

"Have you been seeing your psychiatrist, Lauren?" Maybe she could provide some insight as to why my child had decided to take her life.

"Yes. Maybe you should call her." Lauren was crying out for help.

Thirty minutes after I'd left a message at the doctor's office, I received a call back.

"Hi, Mrs. Visconti. This is Katerina Tolar. Is there an emergency with Lauren?" I heard a soothing voice say.

"Yes, she is sitting here in front of me and just told me that she attempted suicide last night." I felt a shock wave through my entire body as those words left my mouth. Thank God she was sitting in front of me alive!

"Let me talk to her." Katerina suddenly had command in her voice.

"Lauren, Katerina wants to speak with you." Lauren was barely able to lift her arm and had to use both hands to hold the phone to her ear.

All I heard was Lauren mumbling a series of yeses and nos. Then she handed the phone back to me and dropped her head between her knees in exhaustion.

"Mrs. Visconti, I've spoken with Lauren, and she said that she did not feel like she wanted to take her life right now, so you're safe to take her home. We'll set an appointment for tomorrow. If you'll bring her down, we'll see if we can get to the bottom of this." Katerina's voice was matter-of-fact.

"What do you mean? Should I sleep in the same room with her, just in case?" What could have been so bad that Lauren wanted to die?

"You should keep a watchful eye on her until you bring her here tomorrow. I've got another appointment waiting. Is there anything else?" Katerina was in control. I was not.

"No, thanks. We'll see you tomorrow." I was in shock and disbelief. Was I overreacting to the situation or was this doctor not taking Lauren's situation seriously?

Lauren had been sitting in my office for thirty minutes with no improvement when Dr. Burkhalter arrived. He had just been to my office earlier in the week when I was having chest pains from the stress of the trial and our "on its last legs" business. Dr. Burkhalter was both a wonderful friend and a trusted and professional doctor.

"Well, what have we here?" Dr. Burkhalter shouted as he pushed my office door open.

"I just got off the phone with Lauren's psychiatrist, who said that even though Lauren attempted to take her own life last night that I should take her home. But, Doc, by the looks of her, she can't even stand up."

Dr. Burkhalter shot me a reassuring smile and guided me to a chair on the other side of my office. "You sit down and let Doc have a look. So, Lauren, can you look at me?" Doc was kind and gentle as he brushed her hair from her face.

"No, I can't move," Lauren replied.

"Lauren, what did you take? What is in your system right now?" Dr. Burkhalter asked as he reached for a pen and paper.

"Well, I drank about a case of beer. Then my roommate—well, ex-roommate—and I got into a fight. She was throwing ashtrays at me, beer bottles, anything she could get her hands on. Then she left. I was really upset and depressed when she left. She was the world to me." Lauren stopped and tears began to flow.

I was more than a little confused. Roommate? She didn't have a roommate. After the description of the fight zone, I was glad that Zack hadn't gone for the clean-up duty.

"Go on, Lauren," Dr. Burkhalter prompted.

"I called another friend who told me to meet her at another party. When I got there, I was really upset about the fight. At that party, there was a guy who was a cancer patient. He had morphine. I talked to him about wanting to kill myself. He wanted to die, too, and handed me two morphine pills. I took them with a bottle of vodka. Then I passed out, for what I had hoped was forever."

"How could I have missed all of the warning signs?" I blurted.

"Rose, it's not about you right now. Let's see what we need to do to get Lauren to the hospital." Dr. Burkhalter led the way, redirecting me out of my self-absorbed state and reminding me what was truly important just then: Lauren. "I'm going to call Dr. Moschetti, the doctor you saw this week about your chest pains. He should be able to come right over and take a look at Lauren. He'll know better what we should do next."

As Dr. Burkhalter dialed Moschetti's number, I stroked Lauren's hair, wondering what had gone so terribly wrong. I was so thankful that God had answered my prayers and that my daughter was still alive.

"Dr. Moschetti will be here in fifteen minutes," Dr. Burkhalter said as he hung up the phone. "Lauren, you need to stand up for me, okay?"

"I can't. After I took the morphine, I started puking. I've been puking for five hours straight. I don't have the energy to open my eyes, much less stand up." Lauren rolled her eyes in an effort to retain consciousness.

Dr. Burkhalter watched out my office window for Dr. Moschetti. I think we all knew that taking Lauren home would be a tragic mistake, but none of us wanted to be the first to suggest the emergency room.

"He's here," Dr. Burkhalter said as he left my office to let Dr. Moschetti in. His departure also provided the opportunity to fill in Dr. Moschetti on Lauren's condition.

"Hi, Rose," Dr. Moschetti began. "How are *you* feeling?" Dr. Moschetti was a young and handsome doctor, just over thirty, and it became clear quickly that he was kind and concerned about my health first, before we even began to discuss my daughter.

"Hi, Doc," I said, trying to sound more courteous and cheerful than I felt. "I was doing much better before my baby showed up about an hour ago."

"Lauren, I'm Dr. Moschetti, a friend of your mother's." He extended his hand, but she did not budge. "I'm just going to take your vital signs, okay?" He reached for her wrist to take her pulse, but she remained stock-still. When he looked up at me, I could tell by his gaze that there was reason for concern.

"Rose," he said, his tone urgent, "listen. Lauren is in really bad shape. You need to take her to the emergency room immediately. I'll call ahead so they know you're coming and give you special treatment. You realize what this means, right?"

Dr. Moschetti looked at Dr. Burkhalter with concern. According to Florida law, someone who attempts suicide and voluntarily checks into a hospital cannot check out until a psychiatrist examines her and concludes that she is not a threat to herself or others. Dr. Burkhalter responded for me.

"Yes, she knows," he said, "but she also wants to save her daughter's life. She'll get her down there right now."

Dr. Burkhalter pressed his hand on my back as if to say, it's time to go now.

Aly and I stood up simultaneously. We weren't sure what the doctors had meant by their nebulous last comments. We only knew that getting her there was top priority.

"Lauren, we're going to take you to the emergency room now," Dr. Moschetti informed my expressionless daughter. "You just have to walk with your mom and Aly on either side. We'll get you into the back seat and you can lie down until we're there, okay?"

Lauren nodded in agreement.

"Rose, I've called ahead," Dr. Moschetti told me.

"Thank you for everything," I said, emotion welling in my throat. "I owe you one." I was so thankful that I had such wonderful doctors as my friends.

"You can set me up for a round of golf when this is all over, okay?" Dr. Moschetti was doing his best to keep spirits high.

"You got it. Anytime."

I managed a weak smile as I started my car, then pulled away. I turned my attention back to where I was needed most.

"Well, Lauren, you'll be feeling better in no time!" I said, trying to keep her engaged because the doctors had warned that she could slip into a coma. All I got in response was a moan.

As promised, when we pulled up to the doors of the emergency room, an orderly was ready to meet us. I was glad that Aly and I did not have to help Lauren out of the car by ourselves.

"Okay, miss, if you'll just sit up," the orderly said. "I'll help you into the chair."

The orderly had no idea how bad Lauren's condition was.

"I don't think she can hear you," I said, "and, if she could, I don't think her body is capable of movement without assistance right now." I watched helplessly as the orderly attempted to coax some reaction out of my daughter.

"Okay, then we'll just pour her right into this chair and, if you'll meet me inside, you can fill out all of the paperwork."

The orderly's accommodating and kind demeanor made me wonder how often he saw young people in such a condition. As we entered the emergency waiting room, he directed us to an open window to provide the insurance papers.

The admitting nurse's tone was quite severe compared to that of the orderly.

"Since she's an adult, your daughter is going to have to sign the admission papers. We'll bring them into her room once you're in there so that you both understand what she is signing." Her eyes met mine and I had the strange feeling that I was somehow being reprimanded.

"Why are they making such a big deal about her admission?" I asked Aly as we walked down the hall to what would be Lauren's room.

"I don't know," said Aly, "but now that you mention it, maybe that is what Moschetti was talking about when he asked if we knew what this meant. We're about to find out, sister."

As we stepped into the room where Lauren was being assessed, I felt a sudden sense of relief. I no longer had to hold it together and make decisions about her health. She was now in the hands of professionals.

A young physician pulled back the curtains and greeted us. "Nice to meet you, Mrs. Visconti. Can you tell me what happened with Lauren? She still looks pretty out of it."

I reiterated what Lauren had told Dr. Moschetti but did not have much more to offer.

He nodded. "We'll pump some fluids into Lauren," he said. "She's definitely dehydrated. We'll also run some blood tests to see what exactly remains in her system.

I called Zack and gave him as much information as I had and promised to update him with any new news as it happened. Then I spoke with Taylor to calm her fears about her big sister. I wanted so badly to hug her, to tell her how much I loved her and that nothing in life was ever so terrible that you should ever consider taking your own life. But she was so little that she would be more confused than comforted by such a conversation.

My job from then on was to make sure my girls knew how much I loved them and how much God loved them. On those things they could always depend.

Just then, a nurse stepped into the room and began to hook Lauren up to wires and IVs. Although the hospital staff was kind, they weren't very willing to offer information. You practically had to drag it out of them.

"Can you tell me how she is doing?" I asked the nurse, hoping for some nugget of insight. "I haven't seen her eyes open since she came to my office four hours ago."

"We're refilling all of the fluids that she lost through the vomiting," the nurse replied. "Do you know if your daughter uses drugs regularly?"

"I don't think so, but after today I can't be sure." I didn't want to fool myself.

"Do you know if she has an eating disorder? It appears that she has a lot of damage to her esophagus. Have you heard of bulimia? She's barely a hundred pounds." The nurse looked over her glasses at me for some insight.

I thought back to the last several months and could recall a few times where Lauren's eating habits had worried me.

"Since she graduated from high school, she's lost over forty pounds. She's had several incidents where we had to call the paramedics because she passed out. In both cases, I knew she had been taking diet pills. When I read her the symptoms of an eating disorder a few months ago, she got very defensive and refused to acknowledge that she had all of the symptoms. She's nineteen. She doesn't live at home anymore. There is little that I can do for her, other than pray, which lately I am doing more and more."

I had to stop. Tears were welling in my eyes, and I found it impossible to speak.

"Thank you," the nurse said her voice softer now. "I know it's hard. I have a young adult of my own. You're right, once they're on their own, the only hope you have is your faith. Hold tight to it now. You're going to need it."

The nurse clicked her pen, gave me a sympathetic nod, and left the room.

I heard Aly exhale a barely audible "wow" as reality set in. An eating disorder, drug abuse—could this be true?

"I'd often thought that Lauren was getting too thin," Aly mused. "But she looks so much better than when she was, well, fat. I hope this will be a wake-up call for her." Aly stroked Lauren's hair.

Hours in the emergency room passed without any visits from our doctor. Lauren had regained consciousness and was actually getting hungry. I went to the cafeteria to find something for her to eat. Upon my return, the doctor was talking to Lauren about her attempted suicide.

"Lauren, tell me, did you knowingly attempt to kill yourself?" The doctor looked at Lauren with compassion and concern.

"Yes, I did." Lauren's answer was matter of fact.

"Do you still feel like you want to end your life?" He looked deep into her eyes as he asked the question.

"No, I don't think so." Her eyes dropped to her lap.

"Here's the deal, Lauren. The state requires us to keep you under observation if you have attempted suicide. This is for your protection, you understand. I'm going to need you to sign these papers to admit yourself into the hospital tonight."

The doctor handed Lauren the form and she signed it without hesitation. She knew that she was in no condition to go home. Being in the hospital gave her a sense of security, possibly because she was so far from the people—her "roommate," the person who'd given her the morphine and whatever other crazies I'd yet to hear about—who had made her life so unbearable.

It wasn't long after she had signed the form that an orderly came to transfer her from the emergency room to the fifth floor. As we all piled into the elevator, I looked at my little girl and knew that God had saved her, that his mighty hands were on her and on me. He knew that I could not have taken on any more. The elevator doors opened and my heart dropped as my eyes focused on the sign that informed us where Lauren would be staying: "Psychiatric Ward."

My mind reeled with thoughts of what they were going to do to her once she passed through the solid steel doors.

The orderly pressed the call button to let Lauren in. "This is where you'll have to say goodbye to your mom, Lauren."

"No way. I made a deal with my mother that if I agreed to stay, she would stay overnight with me. If that's not the deal, I'm going home."

Lauren shot up on the bed on which she was being wheeled. She looked about ready to sprint down the hallway when the orderly informed her that my staying would be impossible.

Just then, an angel of a nurse passed through the steel doors. "What seems to be the problem, Lauren?"

"I'm not going to stay here five minutes without my mother. If she can't stay, I'm leaving. That's it."

Lauren acted as if she were in control.

"Let me see what I can do for you," the nurse said reassuringly. "Mom, will you come with me for a minute? I will see what I can do to make this easy for Lauren, but if she tries to leave, we'll have no choice but to Baker Act her."

The looks on our faces told the nurse that neither Lauren nor I had any clue what was about to happen. "Lauren, we'll let your mother spend the night. She'll have to sleep in a chair in your room. Mom, is that okay with you?"

"Fine with me," I replied. Aly and I made plans for her to take my car and return around 8:30 the next morning with a sausage McMuffin, a large coffee, and a change of clothes. Then I hugged her goodnight and whispered in her ear, "I thank God for you, my sister."

Aly bent down and hugged my daughter just inside the psych ward doors. "I love you, Lauren. You're going to be fine. I've got extra prayers covering you tonight." For the first time all day, I saw tears forming in my sister's eyes. She left the ward before the full storm broke loose.

As the nurse escorted us to the room, Lauren held my hand so tightly it started to go numb. I patted her hand and offered her that look of comfort that said Mommy would not let anything bad happen to her. She was scared, very scared. As we walked into the room, the tears began to stream down my face. The room was stark white. There were no sheets on the bed, no mirrors, not even a toilet seat. There were surveillance cameras over the bed and in the bathroom. Although the surroundings struck fear in me, I knew that I had to remain positive and not let Lauren see me cry. I quickly wiped my tears and helped her into her bed.

The nurse explained to Lauren that she was on suicide watch, which meant that every fifteen minutes they would come into her room and move her around to be sure that she was okay. If she needed to go to the bathroom, she would need to call the nurse to accompany her. Lauren was mortified.

"It's okay, Lauren," I said, still holding her hand. "I'm here and you're going to get the help you need. What happened to you tonight is very serious and this is the best way, the only way."

"I'm leaving with you tomorrow, period!" She lay down on the bed, angry and afraid.

"Goodnight, sweetheart." I kissed her head and patted her back like I used to do when she was little. *What has happened? What could have been so horrible that Lauren wanted to end her life?* It was a long night in the two hard chairs that the staff had put together to make a "bed" for me. But I wasn't going to complain. At least I was able to be with Lauren.

The next morning, I was thankful to see the sunrise. As I rubbed the sleep from my eyes to get a closer look at the glory of God's new day, the jail-like bars across the windows obstructed my view. I wondered if I was having that horrible nightmare of being in jail. *Oh Lord, save me from this hell! Protect my children and me.* It seemed I was surrounded by spiritual warfare at every turn, but I was determined not to fall victim to it. I was strong in my faith and ready for the day.

I had to try gingerly to raise myself out of the chairs because my legs were half asleep from the hardness against my bottom all night. I made my way to the bathroom and realized I, too, needed a nurse to let me in. I used the call button, and within seconds a nurse with a gentle smile was there to open the door. To help shake off the events of the night, she gave me a toothbrush and soap, for which I was grateful.

I had been standing at the window for about thirty minutes marveling at the sight of dawn when a man entered the room, clipboard in hand.

"Hello, I'm Frank. I'm a nurse practitioner specializing in psychiatric medicine." He didn't once glance up from the clipboard as he offered his credentials.

"Nice to meet you, Frank," I extended a hand. "I am Lauren's mother, Rose."

"You must be pretty special to have been granted permission to spend the night here with Lauren. That is strictly against hospital rules."

Frank was not a happy camper. He went over to my daughter's bed to wake her. "Lauren, you need to wake up now. We have some forms to go over and you have a schedule of programs today." Frank spoke with an authority that said he knew how to treat people in this wing.

"I'm not staying today," Lauren replied succinctly. "I said I would stay the night, and I'll be leaving with my mother as soon as my paperwork is complete." She stretched in the twin bed.

"I don't think so, sweetheart." Frank's gaze was that of a parent who'd caught his child with her hand in the cookie jar. "Here's the deal. You attempted suicide. The hospital cannot discharge you until *we* are sure that you are no longer a danger to yourself. That means you'll be here for the better part of three days for evaluation."

Lauren shrieked. "I signed myself in, and I will sign myself *out*. You and my mother can't keep me here against my will." Lauren leaped off the bed and headed toward the bathroom as if she'd said her last words on the subject.

"I'm afraid that's not correct, Lauren." Frank had probably had such a confrontation a hundred times before and so took none of her bad attitude personally. "You have two choices. Choice number one: You stay here under your own free will, except that you don't leave until we say you can leave. On the other hand, choice number two, I can *and will* Baker Act you, which means you will be in the custody of the state until *they* say you are okay to leave. Except, instead of this comfy hospital, you'll be a special guest at the state facility, which makes this place look like the Ritz Carlton. So, Lauren, which will it be?"

Lauren's eyes were imploring as she turned to me. "Mom, tell him we're leaving." She began to cry and hoped that I could change the course of what was about to happen.

My heart broke to speak the words and my voice cracked as they came out. "I can't, sweetheart. You heard Frank, and I think you're much better off here. I called Katerina Tolar last night, she said she will come over as soon as she can to see you."

Frank turned to deliver my orders. "Rose, you're going to have to leave soon and begin operating under the ward's visiting hours. You'll need to bring Lauren some clothes for the next few days, and we have some specs you'll need to follow. No drawstring pants, no belts. I've got a whole list for you."

He didn't have to tell me that the wardrobe specs had been implemented to limit any future suicide attempts.

"Why don't you come back around dinner time with all of her personal effects?" he added.

Just as I was walking out of Lauren's room, Katerina Tolar arrived. I stopped her before she went into Lauren's room. "Hi, Katerina, I'm Rose Visconti, Lauren's mother. You will be a welcome visitor for Lauren. She's not very happy with being 'committed.' Maybe you can help."

Katerina shook my hand, her eyes conveying her condolences. "Rose, if there is anything I can do—"

"Yes, there is. Somewhere, I'm not sure where, there's been a huge breakdown in Lauren's life—eating disorders, drinking, depression, now attempted suicide. Where do you recommend I go from here?"

"If you can afford it, The Meadows would be the perfect place for Lauren. Check out their Web site. It is difficult to get in. You'll need to have her admitted from here directly for them to take her. If you get started now, you may be able to work out a direct transfer. The facility is in Arizona. Let me know if I can help. I'm going to check on Lauren now. Good luck."

Katerina offered a shrug as she entered Lauren's room.

Aly, who had arrived as planned, was waiting by the nurse's station and offered a puzzled look at Katerina's comment.

I turned to Aly. "What do you think she means about affording it?"

"Rose; these last twenty-four hours have been so weird that I don't know what to think. How about I drop you off at your car, it's still at the office. Then you can go home, shower, and change and start researching The Meadows."

Once I finished my application for Lauren's acceptance to The Meadows, I realized what Katerina was talking about: they didn't take insurance. They needed a wire transfer of $35,000 before Lauren was officially accepted into the thirty-day program. Between my legal fees and now The Meadows fees, I needed to begin borrowing from my retirement account.

Days after Lauren's admission to the hospital, she was discharged for transfer to The Meadows. Lauren and I headed for the airport and began our journey. We pretended we were on our way to a vacation spot in the desert. We arrived in Arizona, rented our car, and headed to the hills of Wickenburg. The two-hour drive was filled with laughter and some tears. As we neared our destination just before midnight, Lauren feared that the separation anxiety would be too great for her. I assured her that she would look back over this time in her life and be so thankful to have left all of life's baggage in the desert.

We arrived at The Meadows, a beautiful ranch-style community with a few dorm-like buildings. We took Lauren's suitcase and headed for administration and admittance. I could sense Lauren's fear rising by how much tighter her grip of my arm became as we entered the building. A couple of nurses sat in the reception area to offer a warm hello. They were expecting us and quickly began the admittance process. "Welcome to The Meadows, Lauren," the staff exclaimed as she entered the room.

"Thanks." Lauren offered a weary smile.

"If the two of you will have a seat right here, we'll get all of Lauren's information. Mom, we'll have you out of here in no time." The nurses knew the sooner I left, the better it would be for Lauren.

"Take your time. I'm in no hurry," I responded.

Lauren read all of the papers carefully this time so as to leave herself a way out if she changed her mind. She signed all of the papers with tears in her eyes. She knew that her mental health depended on this stay, but the "victim" inside of her wanted to run and hide as she had in the past.

We said a tearful goodbye to each other, and I flew home to Naples.

The first week at The Meadows was very hard. Lauren would cry and plea for me to come save her from this place. I had a peace that she needed to be there to face the demons that were haunting her. This was a once-in-a-lifetime chance for healing. Most people carry baggage with them all of their lives; Lauren had been given the opportunity to leave her childhood demons in the desert. I called her every day and sent her care packages and flowers to keep her spirits high.

During the third week of her stay, we were invited to attend Family Week, a special time designed to provide a safe way for the resident/patient to confront her family with all of the issues that she had uncovered in her therapy.

Zack wondered why Lauren's natural father had escaped the confrontation. Lauren did not feel that she was emotionally capable of facing him. They had not seen each other for over a year and she felt abandoned. Being at The Meadows offered her an alternative, and even satisfying, method of dealing with her father.

We arrived at The Meadows on Mother's Day. I was so happy to be celebrating this special day with my eldest daughter alive. As she came out to the courtyard to meet us, she looked so beautiful. She was herself again. The Meadows had worked a miracle.

We had a wonderful lunch and toured the property. It was a healing place, with many quiet respites. The landscape reflected the reds and oranges of the sun, with cactus and other plants dotting the landscape. The atmosphere was quite different from Naples; it had a peace that was shining in Lauren's eyes.

Family Week opened with Lauren telling her story to the group. Hearing her little voice crack through the tears caused me great anguish. She revealed a sense of abandonment by her natural father, and the fear that I, too, would leave her one day; of being overweight and teased not only by kids at school, but by Zack; of feeling like she was standing in the way of happiness for our family, that she was responsible for our marriage being awful.

Could we be forgiven, not only by our children, but also by our heavenly Father? Certainly all of Lauren's experiences were not part of his plan for her life. His plan was to protect children, to love them and raise them up in faith so they would not depart from it.

I had faith that Lauren would survive this horrible time and that she would be a mighty warrior for God. I believed he would save her not for me, but for him, so that she could be an angel in someone's life—she could share her success story of total healing.

Twenty-five

A drop of being arrested, a pinch of your daughter attempting suicide, a dollop of seeing yourself plastered across the evening news as a money launderer—now it was time to add a dash of business pressure. Richard Zuker, our Minneapolis, Minnesota, partner in The Club at Oak Haven, called on May 6 to deliver an ultimatum.

"You and Peter need to find someone to take me out of Oak Haven. Can you find somebody new, and fast?"

"It's nice to hear from you, Mr. Zuker," I replied, the sarcasm clear in my tone. The last time we had any substantive conversation he was refusing to help us fund our legal defense with future profits.

"I understand your desire to disassociate yourself from Peter and me," I continued, "but I've got to be honest with you. No bank will lend us money. We've had some significant struggles since our arrest, as I'm sure you can imagine."

I would have bet money that he had hardly given it a thought. He said nothing, so I plowed ahead.

"The bank won't even advance further funds under our development loan at Kings Palm (our third and what would be our final gated golf course community) until they get more comfortable with our situation, if that's possible. The only chance we'll have is another private investor. However, there is no way another investor will pay what you are owed. The 24.9 percent interest has eaten up any potential profit. You'll have to decide what you're willing to take and what the timeline is. Once you've done that, give me a call and I'll set up some meetings."

Across the miles, I could almost hear the gears in his head turning, trying to decide how to play me.

"How am I going to do that?" he asked. *Ah, he's decided to play dumb.*

"You've got a team of accountants and lawyers," I reminded him. "I'm sure they'd be happy to run some numbers and give you the proper advice."

He was sorely mistaken if he thought I'd do his dirty work for him.

"Can't you or Frank Rupp run some numbers and then my folks can look at them?" he asked, sounding increasingly distressed.

"Richard, as I'm sure you're well aware, we're all very busy and under a tremendous amount of stress. I'd greatly appreciate it if you'd try to find someone in your own organization to do this. Besides, it wouldn't be right for us to discount your number. There's already enough tension between us." I wanted him to know that I did not appreciate the way he handled our request.

"Okay," Richard finally drawled in his Minnesota accent. "I'll see what I can do, but I want out of Oak Haven by October first, or I'm taking over."

Richard did not take long to send a demand letter with the details of his plan. In short, we had repaid the $40 million of principal and now he was owed about $24 million, all interest on the money we borrowed to develop the property (three years at 24.9 percent on $40 million). He was willing to take $18 million by October 1, 2002, but only if we had a check in hand, no contingencies.

It was May 6. How would we find a new investor, one who would believe we were innocent of all of the RICO charges, in five months? If we didn't meet his demands, we would be forced to surrender our stock in Oak Haven, and Richard would become one hundred percent owner.

"Wow, now I really feel the love," I fumed as Peter read his copy of Richard's letter. "Can you believe this? He's going to steal Oak Haven if we don't find somebody to take him out."

Unlike me, Peter refused to be blinded by anger and sprang to the defense. "Rosie, start going through your Rolodex for private investors." Peter knew that it was a futile exercise, but we had to try. The fact that he still held some hope enabled me to take up the investor search with renewed vigor.

I met with everyone I could drum up, from private bankers and restaurant owners to the Ritz Carlton, who needed a golf course for overflow guests. We operated Oak Haven with Ritz Carlton standards and had, in fact, hired most of our restaurant and service staff from there. I left no stone unturned, but nobody was willing to pay the price Richard was asking. This came as no surprise. The September 11 terrorist attacks had touched everyone financially. There were no businesses willing to risk $18 million on an industry that was totally dependent on second-home buyers and the luxury of golf.

Every aspect of my life seemed to be slipping from my grasp. Just when I'd think the situation couldn't get any worse, I'd be proven wrong again. I felt helpless and thought it might be worthwhile to see a psychotherapist. A friend suggested Gabriella Whittle, praising her as an angel straight from heaven. Within a week of my first call, I was sitting in her office, lulled by the soothing sound of her voice. As we discussed the many black holes that had become my life, I felt some of the pressure escape my body, if only for that one hour a week. Between refueling with the word of God at church and seeing Gabriella on Fridays, my weeks seemed almost joyful. I was being tested and, as far as I could see, I was passing with flying colors. Most people subjected to the kinds of pressures I had would be crouched under their desks with a bottle. I was counting it all joy and standing on God's promise: Consider it all joy... whenever you face trials of many kinds, because you know that the testing of your faith develops perseverance (James 1:2). If God be for me, who could stand against me?

I realized that I needed to run both our company and my life as "business as usual" or face an utter collapse. I ran the same daily meetings, met with the project managers and club managers on site, volunteered for the Make-a-Wish Perfect Season Miami Dolphins charity fundraiser, and even managed to squeeze in a concert by Chicago, a favorite band from my high school days.

June arrived in the blink of an eye, and our lender began to apply pressure to pay off our loan at The Preserve. It would mature on July 1, and we owed about $3 million. Our only hope of paying them off was to sell the last commercial piece of land that we owned, which had been available since 1997, or find another bank to refinance.

Our criminal case continued through the constipated bowels of the justice system, moving ever so slowly and with excruciating pain. The amended charges that the prosecutor filed against us following the dismissal of the original charges included a charge of money laundering. Thus began my education as to what a RICO charge did—and didn't—constitute.

The Racketeer Influenced and Corrupt Organizations Act, enacted as Title IX of the Organized Crime Control Act of 1970, was originally designed to combat organized crime. RICO requires that the government "prove the defendant, through the commission of two or more acts constituting a pattern of racketeering activity, directly or indirectly invested in, or maintained an interest in, or participated in, an enterprise, the activities of which affected interstate or foreign commerce."

From a legal defense perspective, the key here is the phrase "through the commission of two or more acts." Since the $200,000 cash transaction that Wood orchestrated did not go to anyone in the "enterprise," which was the Collier County Commission, it could not be considered a predicate act under RICO. That meant that what Peter and I were charged with was only one act, and therefore clearly didn't fall under RICO. No matter how many times I reread the description of the charges before us, I couldn't see how we could be held under a RICO violation. Why were we even talking about money laundering when there wasn't any?

Wait a minute . . . RICO was considered by both the public and the media as intended to combat traditional organized crime and its infiltration of legitimate enterprises. We're being charged like a mafia family. This is an outrage! Since the $200,000 transaction did not involve the enterprise, The Collier County Board of Commissioners, we began filing motions to have it excluded from the charges. I struggled with the mentality of legal merit over the truth. Back in January, my attorney filed what was called a quo warranto, which in layman's terms is an extraordinary procedure used to prevent an official or legal entity from exercising its authority in an unlawful manner.

The *Collier Enquirer* reported our lawful defense this way:

> **Coliseum Golf: Defense continues legal challenge to corruption charges**
> **Thursday, January 24, 2002**
> **By Hugh Glimes**
> The defense attorneys in the Coliseum Golf public corruption case have filed a new barrage of legal objections seeking to win dismissal of newly re-filed charges against their clients.
>
> Included in the requests, filed this week in Collier County Circuit Court, is a motion that notifies Judge Faye Barrett that Coliseum Golf co-developers Rose Visconti and Peter Durkee have asked the Florida Attorney General's Office to intercede. The attorneys want proceedings to determine whether the special prosecutor has the legal right to file a money-laundering conspiracy charge.
>
> Miami attorneys Jason and Adam Woerner argue Miami-Dade Assistant State Attorney Martin Strickland doesn't have the authority under his office's appointment to the case by Gov. Jeb Bush to charge a crime they argue has nothing to do with Coliseum Golf or any public officials.
>
> The charge, which is among 17 filed against 10 co-defendants in the sweeping, four-year probe, alleges Visconti, Durkee and Andrew Shanahan, a Naples attorney representing Coliseum Golf developer Phillip Durkee, worked together "to create phony loans to hide the laundering of $200,000 cash, which was obtained as part of an organized scheme to defraud" between August 1, 1997, and December 2000. The charging document refers to it as the $200,000 Durkee/The Preserve loan.
>
> Strickland has argued his office was appointed by Bush in April 2000 in two broad executive orders charging the prosecutors with ferreting out public corruption in Collier County. The Coliseum Golf case has already netted no-contest

or guilty pleas from two former Collier commissioners, a former county manager, real-estate magnate Phillip Durkee, and investor Jack Wood.

All have pleaded to a racketeering conspiracy charge and are not expected to be sentenced to jail or prison. In exchange, each agreed to cooperate with investigators, possibly including providing information about other public corruption.

So Strickland cites the wording of the governor's order, which gives his office the authority to investigate and prosecute "all matters pertaining to or arising from" the Coliseum Golf public corruption and racketeering cases "as well as matters arising from or relating to the Collier County Administration."

Visconti and Peter Durkee's attorneys argue the money-laundering charge "is outside the scope of the executive order." The governor assigned Strickland's office to the case after Barrett ruled Southwest Florida State Attorney Michael Pennino, whose office oversees Collier, had a conflict of interest. Pennino invested in a company that was the developer for the second set of failed plans for Coliseum Golf, which would have been a spectator golf arena near the Collier-Lee County border and a stop on the professional golf tour.

"The private loan transaction...was not the basis for the disqualification of State Attorney Michael Pennino, nor does it justify the assignment of an outside prosecutor," according to the Woerners motion.

Also, the Woerners and the attorneys for two of the other co-defendants have filed court papers seeking dismissal of the main charge, the racketeering conspiracy. The attorneys for ESPN founder and Coliseum Golf idea man Nicholas Shubert and former Collier County Commissioner Eugene Gannon have filed motions to dismiss that charge.

All the attorneys give similar arguments to what prevailed before when Barrett threw out the charge—that the charging document, refiled Dec. 20, is so broad and vague that the defendants can't understand the allegations or defend against them.

The motion was heard as a separate civil case by Judge Matthew Tamayo on August 14, over half a year after the motion had been filed. Judge Tamayo ruled against us, dismissing our motion, and Strickland immediately asked the governor to expand his authority to include any and all matters pertaining to and arising from Coliseum Golf.

Following this temporary defeat, Peter and I joined Adam and Jason Woerner for lunch and began preparations for the upcoming depositions. After placing our orders, Jason got right down to business. "All right, you guys," he said as he flipped through his papers. "Let's go over whose depositions we've taken. We've done FDLE Agents Roger May, Fred Bare, Joe Dihn, Judith Binns, and Craig Delaney."

"That Delaney deposition was incredible," said Adam. "You can tell the guy was a politician for ten years. I gave him every opportunity to say that he was not guilty, and he slipped all around it." Adam shook his head in disbelief as he took another bite of his sandwich.

"Craig has to make it through this deal with the prosecutor," Jason explained. "He's probably scared that if he said anything contrary to his deal, then it's off to jail for him. I bet Strickland would love to violate him."

"What exactly do you mean by 'violate'?" I could only imagine the worst possible definition.

Jason explained that "violate" is a term used when the prosecutor can re-impose the suspended sentence after determining that the defendant has violated the terms of his plea deal. He raised an eyebrow. "What did you think it meant?"

I looked at the three men seated around me at the table and felt my face grow warm. I decided the question was better left unanswered.

Jason continued. "Strickland would love to violate any of the flips—that's legal jargon for someone who was a defendant and has 'flipped' to the prosecutor's side through a plea deal and will testify for the state." I appreciated the way Jason navigated us through the legal quagmire without making us feel like chumps.

"I hear that Nicholas Shubert is working out a plea deal with Strickland, too," Adam mused.

"No way," Peter said. "He'll never give up the fight."

"Well, his attorney said that he's going to plead on August 27—that's next week." Adam's eyebrows lifted. "Are you ready for a plea deal, Peter?"

"Heck, no!" Peter pounded his fist on the table, the indignation burning in his eyes. A few of the other restaurant patrons turned in our direction. "I'll go to the bitter end with that jerk. He's taken my business and my money. But I'm getting my reputation back. He'll have to apologize publicly to me!"

"That will never happen," Adam said flatly. He put down his fork and stared at Peter as if he were an unruly pupil. "If you think for one minute that if the charges are completely dropped the *Collier Enquirer* will report that in large font on the front page, you're dreaming. And furthermore, Mr. Durkee, the residents of Collier County who think you're a sleazy developer will always think that, even if the charges are dropped. They'll just claim you had a great attorney, which is in fact the case, and that you bought your way out of the charges. So if the only reason you're not taking a deal is to prove to Collier County that you're innocent, save the money. Go on lavish vacations. Take that $25,000 that you pay me each month and give it to your kids or a charity. You will not buy back your good reputation in Collier County. Period." Having said his piece, Adam returned to his lunch.

"Wait a minute," Jason interrupted. "What kind of deal is Shubert taking?"

Adam gave him a hard stare as he finished chewing. "He's going to plead guilty to two reduced counts of making false statements in the Coliseum Golf stock fraud case against him. I think they refer to that as 'Coliseum II.' The prosecutor is going to drop all charges against him in the corruption case, our case. I think he'll get two years' probation as part of the plea deal."

"What?" Peter practically shouted. He sounded positively apoplectic. Once again, heads turned in the direction of our table.

"He's the father of Coliseum Golf. If they drop all of the charges against him in the corruption case, how does that look for us? After all, he was the one who had Gannon for a partner." Peter was seething as

Adam explained the situation. "When you're ready to take a plea deal, Peter, you let me know." He offered a smile.

"There are only three ways out once you've been arrested," Adam continued. "One, plea deal. Two, trial. Three, judge dismisses the case. There is no chance that Strickland will just say, 'Oh, you were right. These two didn't commit a crime. Sorry for the inconvenience.' So, Peter, Rose, you both need to think about what's important to you. When you want to see what Strickland will offer, call us. Otherwise, we fight like dogs and take Strickland every chance we can get."

I drifted into my own thoughts as the conversation between Peter and Adam continued on the legal battle. My heart suddenly began to race; my face turned hot, and my eyes began to tear as I realized how hopeless my marriage had become.

Jason noticed that I had mentally checked out of the conversation. "Rose, are you okay?"

I allowed myself a small sniffle. Better a drizzle than a full-out rainstorm. "Yeah, I was just thinking about my marriage and the mess my life is in." Jason reached over and patted my back.

I dabbed at my eyes with my napkin and offered what I hoped was a convincing smile.

"Where is that situation now?" Jason asked interrupting my thoughts.

"Actually," I said, feeling stable enough to resume the conversation, "I've hired Naples's best divorce attorney, Nolan Masure. I need to protect myself now. If I don't, how will I pay you, Jason?"

"Definitely meet with that guy. You don't want to miss a payment!" Jason winked at me and continued to eat his lunch.

These guys had seen so much in their careers that our little case was nothing more than a pastime to them.

Then I was lost again in my own thoughts. I understood that God was working on exposing all of the dark little corners of my life, one by one. He wanted me to see each of them for what they were and to depend solely on him for the answer. I began to realize that God was stripping me down to the bare bone so that he and he alone could see me built up, renewed for his glory. *I hope he hurries,* I thought. *I don't know how much more I can stand.*

Zack had moved from our home to Lauren's condo during the first few weeks of August, with Lauren moving back home following her stay at the Meadows. Even though the change in living situations marked a definitive division in our lives together, I could at least get the peace I so desperately needed. I had to explain to Taylor why her father and Lauren had switched homes, and in time she grew accustomed to visiting him.

Zack decided that we had been emotionally and physically divorced for so many years, and if I was now going to cause us to be "financially divorced," he could find no good reason to remain married. It was obvious that neither of us had what it took to salvage our relationship. There was no trust, no compassion, and no love. The greatest asset that we had was Taylor, and we knew that she would survive as long as we remained civil to each other.

Once Zack had come to that conclusion, we both switched into lawyer mode. I wanted to make the proceedings quick and painless, not another publicity stunt for the *Collier Enquirer* to salivate over. I was ready to be fair.

Zack could not afford to buy the house and it made sense for Lauren, Taylor, and me—not to mention our three dogs—to remain there. My attorney advised us to have the house and the condo appraised for the calculations of assets, and I had to have my business valued. As far as I was concerned, each of the clubs was a liability, not an asset, since I signed personally on every one. The debt topped at nearly $100 million. My attorney filed for the divorce on October 4, just two days before what would have been our twelfth wedding anniversary.

Zack had started working again and was able to pay his attorney fees and condo-related expenses. I maintained our home and all of the expenses that entailed. I just wanted an end to the whole ordeal. I didn't care what he took as long as I had one less attorney billing me at the end of the year. Our divorce was final December 17.

Twenty-six

In my business life, the Oak Haven debacle still distracted me from my other legal misadventures. It was now mid-summer, and I couldn't find a private investor to take out Zuker's position for $18 million. I was fighting for my freedom against a crazed prosecutor who had one of the devil's favorite henchmen (Wood, that is) as a key state witness ready to lie about anything to have his federal sentence reduced. I had our lender coming down on us to pay off the note at The Preserve, and our lender on our third and final property, Kings Palm, notified us that it could not lend us any additional funds until the criminal case was settled. I came across a Bible verse that said, "For the revelation awaits an appointed time; it speaks of the end and will not prove false. Though it linger, wait for it; it will certainly come and will not delay" (Habakkuk 2:3).

God is never late, not one minute. But he sure is never early, I thought to myself. Still, if he didn't hurry up, we were going to lose Oak Haven. Maybe that was his plan. Maybe he was saving me from that project, from further debt and a strained relationship with Zuker. Who knew?

Whatever God's plan might have been, I kept calling and meeting with any investor who would listen to me. Finally, on September 29, God delivered in the form of Aaron Monroe, a Southern gentleman, probably in his late sixties, who had developed one of the most exclusive golf clubs in Naples. He saw Oak Haven as an opportunity for his investors to add another eighteen holes for their members and have an award-winning clubhouse to boot.

I tried to hide my desperation during our first meeting, but I also knew better than to hide the facts from a potential investor. "Mr.

Monroe, I really appreciate you meeting with me under the circumstances. I must tell you that I am not a pressure salesperson, but we only have twenty-four hours left, and then Mr. Zuker takes the keys. So if you're at all interested, please, please tell me."

Mr. Monroe was like an angel, calm and gentle. "Miss Rose, I am interested, but I can't sign a contract today. I can give you a letter of intent. Will that do?"

"I'll ask. The terms clearly state that it must be a bona fide contract, but with your reputation, Zuker may be willing to take a letter of intent. If you send me one, I'll fax it over to Zuker and his attorney to see if they'll accept."

"I'll do it as soon as I get back to the office, Rose." Monroe stood and, as befitting a Southern gentleman, pulled my chair out for me. "You get back to your office and tell Peter the good news. I'm sure you both could use some of that."

It had been so long since I'd smiled that my grin hurt my cheeks. "That's truer than you can imagine." I shook his hand and sped back to report to Peter.

"You're not going to believe this," I said as I entered the office. I relayed the results of my lunch with Monroe. Peter knew him as one of the old timers who had developed Naples along with Peter's father in the early eighties.

"As soon as the fax arrives, we'll send it to Zuker. Let's call him now just to give him the good news!" Part of me wanted to rub his nose in our success, to let him know that someone who did not know us personally believed in us, in our work, in our innocence.

We called Richard and were shocked to find out that he was not interested in a letter of intent. We had to deliver a bona fide contract or surrender our stock by 5:00 p.m. the next day. Peter and I suddenly realized that Richard didn't want to sell his interest in Oak Haven; he wanted to take ours and was betting that we would never successfully take him out. We later learned of his master plan. He and his son Billy were about to launch Zuker Development Group, and they needed finished communities to hang their hats on. Oak Haven, our crown jewel, would be their first prize.

Giving up Oak Haven feels like having to sell a child into slavery to pay a debt. I cried. I got depressed. What was next? All I knew was that our business, the thing to which Peter and I had dedicated our professional lives, was being taken from us.

After Zuker's taking of Oak Haven, the hardest meeting I had to hold was with my staff. It was all I could do to contain myself. I told them that had there been any other way, we would have chosen it. First, Peter and I had lost our freedom and our reputation, now we were losing one of our clubs, our finest work. The looks on their faces told me they were as heartbroken as I was. Then they began to think about what was going to happen to them. Would Zuker run the club to the same level of standards we did? Would he keep them all or fire them because of their loyalty to Peter and me? They had a million questions we couldn't answer.

Zuker insisted that we manage the facility until year's end and then he would decide the fate of each employee. He still had the upper hand in our situation. He was our personal lender for our equity at Kings Palm. Yes, of course the interest rate was 24.9 percent! I could just see it: Kings Palm was next on his list. I wasn't going to give up so easily this time. I would fight back, but with what?

As we were struggling with the emotion of losing Oak Haven, we also faced the one-year anniversary of the day of our arrest. It was hard to believe that an entire year had already passed and that so little headway had been made. Although the depositions had proven informative, not one FDLE agent would declare under oath that Peter or I had committed any crime. When we asked why, if that was the case, we'd been arrested, we were told it was because of one man—the special prosecutor, a man with such unlimited power that he was able to instruct law enforcement agents to arrest us with no evidence of a crime.

Our attorneys remained positive and continued to assure us that the case would be dismissed soon due to lack of evidence. What the prosecutor was hoping for was that as each of us ran out of money, the idea of a plea deal would get sweeter and sweeter.

Just two months later, Kings Palm was teed up to enter the Zuker portfolio.

I decided to talk to Peter about making some other changes. "After Zuker has taken two of our projects, the only thing we'll have left is The Preserve, and there's nothing there for him. We won't need this big office, either. Maybe he'd like to take it off our hands, too." I was beginning to feel an odd sense of relief. Since our arrest, we'd been struggling for over a year with banks, investors, and residents. Maybe if Zuker would completely buy me out, I could work out my time at The Preserve, be normal, and fight the lawsuit without total exhaustion.

This time, though, because we had never taken a salary from Kings Palm, we would walk away with some cash. At this point, that was all we needed. With the money to pay my legal bills, I could redirect my prayers to more important issues.

Great minds sure do think alike, because Peter already had a plan in the works. "I'm glad you mentioned that, Rose. You know how Zuker is; he's a bottom feeder. If we don't have another offer on the building, he'll try and take this for the balance on the mortgage. I've got a prospective buyer that's offered us just over a million, including all the furniture, computers—everything. What do we owe anyway?"

"I think it's just over $750,000 so it'd be great if we could make a $300,000 profit." I shrugged. "Sad for you, though."

"Why sad for me?"

"One hundred fifty grand goes a long way with Jason Woerner. You, on the other hand, with Wesley Driscoll's firm, you'll spend that in two months," I said with a chuckle.

"Ahh," Peter said, allowing a smile to break. "Did you have to ruin my dreams of buying something? We might as well just sign the checks over to them. Better yet, have it distributed directly to them on the closing statement." I was glad Peter was able to find humor in our situation.

"I've asked Frank Rupp to negotiate with Zuker for my final interest in Messina, the last piece of undeveloped dirt I have any part of," I said. "What do you think?" I was ready to move on, and the sooner I could get a deal the better.

"Like I said, Rose, he's a bottom feeder. Be careful. Your interest in Messina is worth millions. You'd be better off holding on a little longer. Once we get all of the required development permits, we'll be rich! The two projects Zuker's already taken are nothing compared to the flip we'll do on this property." Peter leaned back in his chair and clasped his hands behind his head. "Go figure, we work our tails off for three years building Kings Palm and Oak Haven, and we get next to nothing on one and absolutely nothing on the other."

"That's not entirely true. We got to keep our founding golf memberships at Oak Haven," I reminded him.

Peter smirked. I wondered if he was imagining what it would be like to actually tee off on our old property. "As I was saying, on Messina we contracted the land, sold it before we technically owned it, and we'll make a handsome return without ever turning a shovel. That's the kind of projects we need to be doing. You can shove this blood, sweat, and tears crap." Peter was pleased with his last deal. He had done the inconceivable.

"I'd happily take a few million today over waiting for twice that when and if the permits come through. A bird in the hand is worth two in the bush." Was I being crazy?

"You'll be lucky if he offers you a million. Without the permit in hand, he won't see the value the way we do. Don't do anything stupid, Rose," Peter cautioned. "With the cash you'll get from the building sale and your interest in Kings Palm, you should be able to wait. We should have our permit by April or May of next year. Hold tight. Don't let that SOB steal any more from you." Peter wagged his finger at me.

"Okay, we'll see what Frank works out. Maybe we'll be pleasantly surprised." But I knew better.

Peter was right. Zuker wanted me to agree to sell my interest for $2 million with no guarantee that he'd buy it. On top of that insult, he wanted the first right of refusal. Did he really think I was stupid or was that merely his negotiating style?

I was, nonetheless, offended.

Twenty-seven

As we moved into November, our case seemed to have stalled. Then, on November 10, 2002, Martin Strickland requested that former Collier County Commissioner Evan Hanover be sentenced immediately as punishment for violating his plea bargain deal. He asked Judge Barrett to sentence Hanover to fifteen years in prison for lying under oath and rendering himself useless as a witness for the state. Months ago, Hanover had entered a plea bargain of no contest and agreed to serve 364 days in jail on a work-release program. When I heard about Strickland's demands, I was reminded of Adam and Jason's declaration that he was always ready to violate a flip.

Strickland, in his long quest to find support for his RICO case, had counted Hanover as an important witness. That is until September 25 when Hanover was deposed by the defense attorneys and told a very different story than Strickland expected to hear. In an attempt to save himself, Hanover formally corrected his testimony on October 11, but the damage to his value as a witness for the State had already been done.

We had all been present at Evan Hanover's hearing, which gave us our first glimpse of the special prosecutor with the gloves off and bearing his teeth for all to see. Up until now, we had heard nothing but banter in front of the judge. But today, Strickland's goal was to see Evan Hanover behind bars for lying to him. He wanted to demonstrate his legal prowess and give the rest of the defendants something to think about.

During the hearing, the courtroom was filled with more than fifty people, some arriving an hour early. A dozen members of the media buzzed about interviewing people, hoping as usual to be able to print some new dirt.

As Peter and I sat quietly in the back row on the butt-numbing benches, we watched the parade of private attorneys, prosecutors, public defenders, clerk personnel, judges' assistants, residents, and paralegals settle in. Eugene Gannon entered through the large wooden doors and took a seat toward the back of the courtroom. Each time the broad doors swung open, our heads turned.

Finally, Gregory Hatley, the attorney representing Hanover, entered, followed by Hanover and his wife, Susan. Hanover, a tall man, wore a dark suit and a nervous look. He kissed his wife, whispered something in her ear, and then joined Hatley toward the front of the courtroom.

The crowd attending the hearing suddenly frightened me. As I looked around the room, I realized that the audience did not consist of concerned citizens rooting for fair treatment to the accused. The spectators were angry, told by a year's worth of *Collier Enquirer* articles that they had been robbed—robbed of the just services of these elected officials. They were there to see a hanging. My mind began to swirl out of control; I closed my eyes and began to pray for peace. Suddenly the calm, the peace that only God can bring, poured over me like a sweet spring rain. Psalm 35 had become my mantra, and I began to say it to myself:

> Contend, O Lord, with those who contend with me; fight against those who fight against me. Take up shield and buckler; arise and come to my aid. Brandish spear and javelin against those who pursue me. Say to my soul, "I am your salvation." May those who seek my life be disgraced and put to shame; may those who plot my ruin be turned back in dismay. May they be like chaff before the wind, with the angel of the Lord driving them away; may their path be dark and slippery, with the angel of the Lord pursuing them
>
> Psalm 35:1–6

Peter gently tapped my arm to redirect my attention to the courtroom.

I had my peace now. I was not filled with fear looking at the people who'd come to witness a hanging; they could not harm me. I dwelt in the secret place of the Most High God.

In this hearing, the court rules allowed former commissioner Evan Hanover to testify one way in a sworn pretrial statement and completely change what he said two weeks later. However, the attorneys argued that Florida law didn't allow the former Collier County commissioner to knowingly give false testimony in the Coliseum Golf public corruption criminal case in which he was charged.

Strickland said that lying is just what Hanover did, taking steps to change his pretrial testimony only after the prosecution pointed out those lies to him. As a result, Strickland declared, Hanover should be sentenced to fifteen years.

Strickland stood and turned toward the media so they could get an updated headshot. Only then did he address the judge. "This defendant," Strickland boomed as he pointed at Hanover, "in the face of warnings, with incredible impunity, egotism, and disregard for truth and honesty, chose to stay with his discredited story. Hanover's late arrival at partial truth does not change the consequences of his action."

The judge listened carefully to all of the testimony at the hearing and refused to sentence Hanover immediately. This was a blow to the prosecution's power. Judge Barrett traditionally took time to review all of the evidence, apply the law, and later render her decision. I was thankful that she was sitting our case. Her decision, she notified all present, would be rendered on January 10, 2003.

I was glad that we had attended the hearing. It showed me that Strickland could perform like a rabid bloodhound hot on the trail of his wounded prey. What would he do to us?

Just before Christmas, we finalized all of the negotiations with Richard Zuker for the purchase of our Preserve office building and the Kings Palm development. A brand-spanking new year lie before me and with it new hopes. My divorce was final, I was selling all the projects I owned, and I was going to start 2003 with only one headache, the criminal case. In comparison to what I'd survived in 2002, that situation was a relief.

No sooner had we begun celebrating the start of a new year when a reminder popped up on my computer screen: "11:00 a.m. Hanover sentencing."

Peter and I exchanged glances. "Do you want to go, or should we believe what we read in the *Collier Enquirer* on Saturday?"

He practically threw his hands in the air. "Rose, are you nuts? Of course we're going. This will be the first time we see Judge Barrett in action. Up until now, the motions and hearings have been boring. I don't want to be like the rest of those bloodthirsty Naples residents just out for the entertainment. I want to see how Martin Strickland acts under pressure."

I agreed to go, even though I saw it as just another opportunity for the media to snap pictures of us.

Judge Barrett read part of her nine-page ruling. Hanover would not be going to state prison. He was sentenced to a year in the Collier County jail and might be eligible for work release. Hanover supporters in the courtroom expressed relief. Anti-Hanover forces looked at one another in dismay. They had come for blood and had not seen so much as a scratch. I hadn't realized that I had been holding my breath until I was finally able to exhale. In essence, Judge Barrett had declared that Hanover's plea agreement fell apart because he wasn't technically compelled to tell the truth about himself, only about other defendants.

The crowd remained to watch as Hanover was fingerprinted and led through the dreaded side door. From a holding cell, he would walk to the jail. I hoped to never have the horrible experience of walking that hallway again.

As Peter and I left the courtroom, many angry Naples residents were in the hall providing statements to the press. "They all get off scot-free. No one gets anything in Collier County!" one man raged. "And I thought New York was corrupt!"

When the reporters spotted us, they rushed forward with their microphones and cameras clicking. "Any comments from you two?"

Before I could say no, as we'd been instructed by our attorneys, Peter started in. "Oh, I can hardly wait for our trial. I bet they'll have TVs set up in the hallways to accommodate the angry residents." Peter laughed and slapped me on the back.

I waited until we were out of earshot to give it to him. "That's great, Peter. Maybe they'll print that in tomorrow's paper."

"I hope so!" Peter shouted joyfully. "The people of Collier County have failed to understand that the *Collier Enquirer* is not a real publication. It's no better than the *National Enquirer*."

I rolled my eyes. Peter failed to realize that the paper had the power of the pen and did not need or want to tell both sides of the story. The prosecutor's side was selling papers—that was all they cared about. The fact that the paper, without a trial or even any evidence, had already tried, convicted, and sentenced us proved that it was nothing more than a rag. Will the residents of Collier County one day demand more from their news reporters? I doubt it.

As we had expected, Judge Barrett took a beating from the *Collier Enquirer*, and just five days after her ruling in the Hanover sentencing, she quit the Coliseum Golf case. The previous Friday, Strickland had had harsh words for Barrett, saying she favored the defense. Strickland noted "hostile relations" between him and Barrett and stated that he'd unsuccessfully sought to have her thrown off the case, claiming she was biased.

On Wednesday, however, he was uncharacteristically measured in his reaction to the news. "We are definitely not displeased," he said. "I think the reasons are obvious. I'm not going to say anything else that might prejudice this case or this judge. We hope it will start up again with a clean slate and go forward to its culmination."

In a phone interview with the *Collier Enquirer*, Jason Woerner praised Barrett and bashed the paper. "Judge Barrett was a dedicated, fair, and courageous judge in this case, in the face of unfair criticism and overt pressure by the *Collier Enquirer*. In final analysis, we are confident that no matter which judge hears this case, Rose Visconti and Peter Durkee will be vindicated."

Peter and I were shocked to hear of Barrett's resignation. We had spent the last fifteen months watching Barrett in court and could only imagine what a new judge would cost us in terms of time and money. The Woerners soon told us that we would have to ask the new judge to move the trials to Miami. The publicity in the case had poisoned the Naples jury pool.

I knew immediately that they were right. Peter sighed as he calculated how much time a move would set us back, but he agreed. He then called Andrew Shanahan to get his take on Barrett's resignation. What he said wasn't what Peter and I wanted to hear.

"I don't think it's good," Andrew said, obviously reluctant to further dampen our spirits but unwilling to falsely bolster our hopes. "We really thought she was fair and understood the case. It must have been the stress of Strickland trying to have her removed. Her statements hurt his ego, but they were still the truth. He claims she consistently demonstrated her disdain for him through her tone of voice. I especially loved the part where he whines about her attitude and rolling her eyes when he spoke. If he only had eyes in the back of his head, he would know that everybody in the courtroom did just that. I think that he's just trying to judge-shop."

"Do you think we should ask for a change of venue to Miami?" Peter asked.

"I was born and raised here, and it's here that I will be tried," Andrew said defiantly. "I'm not running from this crowd of pumped-up *Collier Enquirer* bullies. I'll have my day in court right here. My doing so will really help you guys, too."

"How's that?" Peter asked.

"If the four of us are all tried together, I can't testify on your behalf. If we file a severance motion to have me tried alone, then I can be called in your defense, and vice versa. I know the defense team is working on that right now. I also know that Strickland has argued to keep the case in Collier County. He must really like it here. Either that or his boss wants to keep him out of Miami as long as she can."

"On what basis could he object?" I asked.

"He doesn't feel that Miami would offer a jury pool of similar demographics to Naples. He's probably right. The new judge, Heyward, is from Sarasota. Sarasota has a similar demographic to Naples, so that may be an option for you guys." Andrew was always thinking as our lawyer.

"Our trial was scheduled for March," Peter said. "I guess this change of judge and venue crap will move that date out, don't you think?"

"I'm sure it will delay it. I'd like to just get it over with." Even over the phone, I could picture Andrew's look of frustration—furrowed brow, pinched lips, and red cheeks. "I've already spent over $500,000, and we've just completed some depositions. I can only imagine what it will cost once we get into trial mode."

"We're right behind you on the fees, even if we don't have three attorneys show up for every hearing," Peter joked.

"I've asked them not to, but I'm only the client," Andrew shot back. "They don't listen to me."

"Well, we just wanted to get your insight before we called the Woerners. You have a nice weekend and don't spend any money eating out. You'll need it for your defense fund!" Peter ended the call with a laugh. "Well, Rosie, a new judge that we need to research and a new town, Sarasota. Have you ever been there?"

"Nope," I said. "I hear the parents of retired Naples residents live there. They call it God's waiting room."

"Great, maybe they'll all take their Geritol, turn up their hearing aids, and wheel into our trial. You have to be careful what you ask for sometimes, or you just might get it. Remember, it was Father who requested Pennino be removed from his case. And what he got in his place was our friend Strickland. We may want to give this some thought over the weekend and call the Woerners on Monday."

We called it a day—at the office, anyway. I still had some Internet research to do on our new pal, Judge Heyward.

Twenty-eight

I arrived home from the office intent on sneaking in a few minutes to learn about Judge Heyward. A hungry daughter eager for some quality time distracted my sleuthing, however, with "Mommy, let's eat at Taco Bell." *Ugh*, I thought, *how can I sway the taste buds of an eight-year-old?*

"Come on, Mommy!" Taylor called from the kitchen. "I'm starving." Taylor loved the soft tacos and the cheap toy that came "free" with her meal.

"I'll be right there," I sang back. "I need to print something, and then we can go." A little reading material would make the fast-food dining event a little more palatable.

"You said that an hour ago! Come on, Mommy. I'm hungry." I marveled at how adept my youngest had become at using guilt to get me to move at her command.

"I'm coming, I'm coming. But when we get home, I've got to do some research on the computer. We have a new judge on our case and Mommy needs to see what she can learn about him, okay?" This was a preemptive attempt to avoid her disappointment in case she wanted me to watch cartoons with her.

"Okay, but let's go now." She grabbed my arm and pulled me out the door.

Zack and I had settled on an unusual visitation schedule that he discovered while reading up on children of divorces. We agreed to co-parent, which meant that we would share Taylor fifty-fifty throughout the year. The thought of not seeing my youngest child for seven days at a time was too much to bear, so we used Zack's plan: three days, two days, two days, and three days. It was so confusing that I had to have a calendar to figure it out. I couldn't begin to imagine how Taylor felt.

But no matter how hard I tried to consider my daughter's needs, I could think only about how much I needed her around me. With the trial preparation weighing heavily upon me, her presence was a much-welcomed reprieve. I needed her unconditional love, her sweet little arms to hug me. I needed the love that only my children were able to give to me. I realized that all the love that a mother pours into her child is returned a thousand-fold throughout her life. Now, just when I needed it most, I was receiving my reward.

As we pulled into the Taco Bell parking lot, Taylor surprised me. "Mommy, I know that you don't like the way it smells in there, and I know that you've got to learn about your new judge, so let's go through the drive-thru and get you home!" I felt my heart give a little pang as Taylor smiled up at me and patted my hand.

"Thank you, sweetie," I said, hugging her by the neon glow of the outdoor menu. "That's so nice of you to think of Mommy. But I don't need to get to work so fast. I want to spend time with you. How about after you eat, we'll take the dogs for a walk together. Then when we get back, you can pick out a movie."

I was rewarded with a grin that could have lit a city block. "Really, Mommy? Let's watch *Homeward Bound* again!"

"You're the movie director. You can pick anything you want—after you take a bath. Then you'll be ready to snuggle up on the sofa with me to watch the movie."

"Can I take a bath in your big tub? And will you put the special bubbles in and light the candles?" Taylor used the smile she knew was my weakness.

"Sure, sweetie." I would have filled her bath with champagne had she asked for it. Candles and bubbles! I knew I was probably creating an eight-year-old with a budding high-maintenance problem, but my baby deserved it.

Once we'd returned home and Taylor had gorged herself on Taco Bell food, I ran her bath like a dutiful mother. As soon as she was settled into her bubble paradise, I heard Lauren calling that the phone was for me.

When I picked up the phone and said, "Hello," I heard the click of Lauren hanging up the extension. Then Zack's voice droned on the other end of the line.

"I see Lauren hasn't changed much," was his warm greeting. "Her phone skills still stink."

I forced myself to be civil. "What can I do for you, Zack? You certainly didn't call to discuss Lauren's phone etiquette."

I felt heat rise in my cheeks and my heart began to pound. No matter how hard I tried to ignore it, Zack's negativity always got to me.

"I heard about the judge quitting, so I figured you'd be working all weekend on your case, as usual." His familiar tone of reproach hung in each word and alerted my defense systems.

"What does that have to do with you?" I shot back.

"I don't want Lauren watching Taylor, and I thought if you needed to work, I would trade weekends with you. I have some plans for next weekend and it would help me out to switch."

"So you throw some blame and shame on me for working on my case, and the real reason you want to switch is to accommodate your social schedule?" I could hear the anger in my voice grow despite all my efforts. "I'll have to see about that, Zack. I don't know what my schedule looks like."

"Why are you being such a witch about this? I just need a schedule change and you're playing 'control freak' again. We're not married anymore, Rose. You can't control me!"

I nearly burst into laughter at his calling me a control freak. I supposed everything I did as far as he was concerned fit that label. "What are you talking about?" I said. "You call me, slam my daughter, slam me, and then ask for a favor? You are a piece of work, man. I'll check my schedule and get back to you." I needed to end the madness before it escalated into something far worse.

But as usual, Zack needed the last word in the conversation. "You know, Rose, you'll spend the rest of your life single. You're so stubborn that I don't think anybody could get along with you. It's you, Rose, who is the piece of work!"

Before I could respond, he hung up. Knowing Taylor would be occupied in a sea of bubbles for at least twenty minutes, I went to my desk.

As I sat staring into the computer's blue screen wondering why my entire life had exploded, I thought that maybe Zack was right. Maybe I was the problem. Maybe my personality had caused my marriage to fail and my business to crumble.

What lessons am I missing, Lord? What do you want to reveal to me about my personality? Do I have a prideful attitude or am I trying to maintain some control in my life when you want me to let go completely and allow you to be the center of my life?

Instead of searching for information on the new judge, I decided to seek out some insight on me. I logged onto Google and typed in "Christian personality profiles." It wasn't the world's view on my personality that I was after, but rather God's view. I wanted to know what areas of my personality were in desperate need of improvement. Perhaps another Christian could offer advice on the subject of me.

The first listing on the search was "eHarmony." I clicked, unsure of what sort of site it was. The first words on the site read:

> When you're ready to find the love of your life. See why eHarmony.com is the fastest growing relationship site on the Web. Take the eHarmony Personality Profile and get instant, objective feedback on yourself and how you relate to others. The eHarmony Personality Profile begins the exciting journey toward finding your true love.

The search for my true love would have to wait until the other complications in my life had been resolved. What I needed right now was objective feedback on me, and how to relate to others. I pressed on and read about eHarmony's unique method of matching singles. This wasn't exactly what I'd been searching for, but it was close enough, and the promotional copy sold me.

"That's it!" I yelled out loud.

"What's it?" Lauren startled me as she walked into the den.

I quickly minimized the screen. "Oh, nothing."

"What did Zack want?" Lauren asked, her voice dripping with condescension.

"He just wanted to swap weekends with me." I got up from my chair to attend to Taylor.

Lauren followed me down the hall. "Don't do him any favors, Mom."

I stopped and turned to face my oldest, offering a reassuring smile. "Don't worry, sweetie. Your mom's a little tougher than that." I put a hand on her shoulder and looked right in her eyes. Her scowl began to soften. "Want to help me get Taylor out of the bathtub before she looks like a raisin?"

She took my hand from her shoulder but gave it a quick squeeze as she did so. "Love to."

"Hi, Sissy!" Taylor's angelic face popped up through the massive bubbles that the jets had tripled since I'd left.

"Are you ready to get out and snuggle on the couch with Mommy and me?" Lauren needed Mommy time, too, and was happy to watch anything on the boob tube.

"Yeah, look at my fingers. They're all wrinkly!" She wiggled her digits happily. Taylor loved her bath once she was reconciled to taking one.

We dried her off and then went through the final preparations for family movie night. I just needed to write down this Web site for my late night entertainment.

"You girls get the popcorn started. I just have to shut down the computer."

I didn't want to leave any evidence on the screen, since Lauren also used my computer. She was curious enough to look through my files.

I quickly jotted down the information and headed for the sofa with my girls. By 9:30 I was dozing off and Taylor was fast asleep. I carried her to bed, brushed her curly blonde hair from her eyes, and kissed her soft cheek.

"Good night, my love." I stroked her hair, prayed for her sweet dreams, and left the room on tiptoe. Somehow, no matter how deeply she appeared to be sleeping, she'd call my name just as I reached her door—but not tonight. The hot tub, candles, and movie had put her into a deep sleep.

I returned to the family room thinking I needed to move Lauren into her bedroom so that I would have absolute security when I turned the computer on. All I needed was her staring over my shoulder while I completed an in-depth personality profile. I convinced her to watch her own television, and she responded by asking to sleep in the next day.

"I'm just going to smoke a cigarette before I go to my room, so don't lock me out."

I despised the habit not only because it made her stink, but also because it was a poor example for Taylor. Lauren was forbidden to smoke in the house and could smoke on the porch only as long as she cleaned up her butts.

"I'll do a final check of the doors after I take my shower. I'll say good night and tuck you in, too, baby." I knew that Lauren craved special treatment. The traumas in her life had retarded her maturation to the point where I often forgot which was the younger daughter. The counselors thought that until Lauren healed, these maturity issues would remain stagnant. It broke my heart to see Lauren missing out on being independent. I could only pray that in time she would overcome the problems in her life and take control.

As I had promised, I walked through the house, checking every door to be sure it was locked. I think that Lauren was always worried that one of her drug dealers would find her and break in. I secured the alarm and knocked on Lauren's door. She was already tucked into her bed with the TV on and looked about ready to fall asleep. I kissed her forehead, pulled the covers up to her chin, and wished her sweet dreams. Then it was off to my secret profiling.

I turned the speakers on the computer all the way down so Lauren wouldn't hear that I was still awake. The excitement was building as I waited for the page to load. I couldn't have cared less about finding a soul mate. I just wanted to move onto the profile.

The questionnaire displayed on the screen came with a message: "This test will take approximately one hour to complete." It was almost 11:00 p.m., but my adrenaline was pumping. Who is Rose? I was about to have a twenty-nine dimensional look into my behaviors and personality to see what I could do to be a better person. *Has the stress of the trial and family problems changed me, made me so hard-hearted that I am unlovable,* I wondered. It was time to find out.

I carefully considered every question and answered each one honestly. I figured that most people completing the questionnaire were doing it to meet Mr. or Ms. Right, a fact that could definitely sway your answers. I, however, wanted to know me for *me*. If there were areas of my life that needed improvement, I would address them for me—not for Zack or any other man. This matter was between God and me. If he chose this Web site for any reason other than to correct some of my personality traits, that was up to him and him alone. The only soul I was searching for was my own.

Time flew by, and I completed my test. I pressed the send button and waited for the results. In no time, my ten-page personality profile was ready for printing. The results were amazingly accurate. It showed my strengths and weaknesses, how people could communicate better with me, and how I could improve my communication skills.

eHarmony's next message stated: "You are now being entered into our matching database so that you can find your soul mate for life."

I turned the computer off for the night, climbed into bed, and began studying the results of my test. I started to think how online dating might introduce me to someone I could talk to about something other than the trial, someone who hadn't been corrupted by the *Collier Enquirer*. I must have fallen asleep right after that thought, because I woke with the papers still in my hand. The test must have given me some sense of peace, because I don't think I moved all night. I quickly hid the papers in my nightstand and made up the bed. Just then the phone rang, and

I realized I hadn't returned Zack's call about the weekend switch. Now it was Saturday morning.

I began the conversation with a short apology so as not to rile him, then told him we could swap weekends if he liked. If I was going to test my abilities to change, who better to test them on?

But Zack had rearranged his schedule and told me he no longer needed to switch. Without so much as a thank you, he told me just to leave things the way they were, then clicked off the line. I shrugged off his rudeness, not wanting anyone, let alone Zack, to get the best of my emotions.

After getting off the phone, I thought about logging onto eHarmony before the girls woke up. Although just hours earlier I'd been interested only in my personality profile, I'd begun to warm to the idea of a faraway machine grinding out a list of possible soul mates. Then I felt my nerves tingle, not so much out of anxiety but because I wondered what would happen if somebody I knew found out about my Internet dalliances. I could just hear Aly, who I was sure would concoct scenes of dates with mass murderers and rapists. I decided to keep the whole thing to myself.

I came back to reality long enough to revert to my pragmatic self. *I should really use this quiet time to research the new judge. I don't need to waste time playing around on some dating site while I am fighting for my freedom.*

I went to the Google search engine and typed in "John Heyward." It returned several legal sites with information about where he went to school and his last few cases. Then I recognized a name: Janie Fulton. I clicked on the link and read about a girl who wanted to divorce her parents. The judge who granted her wish was none other than our own Judge Heyward.

Florida Court Sides with Janie Fulton

Source: All Things Considered (NPR) A judge in Sarasota, Florida, ruled today that 14-year-old Janie Fulton, who was switched at birth with another baby, will not be forced to visit her biological parents. A judge ruled that her birth parents have no legal rights to Janie, who has lived with another family all of her life.

> Sarasota County Circuit Court Judge John Heyward ruled that if Janie Fulton were forced to visit with her biological parents it would cause the 14-year-old girl mental, psychological, and emotional harm. "It means that children aren't considered property by the courts in this county on this circuit and they have individual rights that need to be protected and that are recognized by the circuit courts of the 12th Judicial Circuit."

I didn't know how I felt about the decision. On the one hand, Judge Heyward hadn't bowed to pressure by the press, which made him an ideal choice after the *Collier Enquirer* had hounded Judge Barrett so badly. Judge Heyward appeared to know the law and did not feel pressured by traditional family values, biological parents, or teams of lawyers. Although he may have been a little quirky, he seemed fair. I printed the story for my files and e-mailed it to Peter, Andrew, and the Woerners.

The hardest part of my whole ordeal was the waiting, although the cost was a close second. Our combined legal bills had topped $500,000 and now we had a new judge who needed to be brought up to speed, which would cost us in both time and money.

I tried to shake the negative thoughts and remind myself it was the weekend. I shouldn't waste another brain cell on anything that didn't bring my girls or me some degree of pleasure. As I made the daily walk down our three-hundred-foot driveway to get the newspaper, I prayed, as I did each day, *Lord, please don't let my face be on the front page.* Each time that I found myself staring back in grainy black and white, I knew it would mean an uncomfortable breakfast in town.

Some of the retired people in Naples suffered from a terminal case of impoliteness. They stared and loudly voiced their disbelief that I would eat in public. "What gall!" they'd gasp and then hold up the paper to see if it really was me. I had become inured to their insolence, but it was painful for my children. I picked up the Saturday paper and felt my stomach sink. The choice of a new judge on our case had landed us on the front page again.

I managed to convince Taylor that the drive-thru was a superior option to eating in the restaurant. She was happy to accommodate my request, so I threw on my shades and was off to McDonald's with the newspaper. Despite my low opinion of the local rag, I couldn't help reading the articles about us in case a reporter actually dug up a new piece of information. As badly as the paper wanted to convict us, they would print anything that would show the judge as favorable to the prosecution. But all I found was the same old news printed under a different headline.

I tossed the paper into the backseat of my car as I approached the pick-up window. The McDonald's staff was always just as polite to me as to the next customer. I was tempted to honk and wave to the patrons in the restaurant as I drove off, but I fought the urge. There was no winning with some of the old folks. Although they had more than enough time to attend a hearing to see how biased the paper was, they preferred to believe the trash they were being fed while they played golf six days a week and rested on the seventh.

After Taylor had downed her customary two bites of pancakes, I hurried her off to wash up, and then went to Lauren's room to see if there was any chance of rousing her before noon. All I got were grunts and the covers being swirled over her head in protest to my intrusion.

"We're going to go out for a while. Call my cell phone when you wake up, okay?" Taylor and I were gone until almost dinnertime, so we picked up baked chicken, macaroni and cheese, and salad at a local deli and headed home. When we walked into the house I found Lauren headed for the home office. "I'm going to check my e-mail on your computer, okay?" she asked when she saw me.

My heart began to race. Did I leave out any evidence? Or worse, did I leave up the eHarmony screen? "Wait a minute, Lauren. No food in my office. You eat out here, and you can use my computer when you're done." I raced into my office to make sure the coast was clear.

"You're acting weird. Is anything wrong?" Lauren inquired upon my return.

"No, of course not. What do you mean weird?"

"You freak out when I'm going to use your computer like you're hiding something."

I could feel her eyes follow me as I picked up around the kitchen in an attempt to be nonchalant.

"Nope, I just don't want food in my keyboard, that's all." I wagged a playful finger at her and hoped I wasn't overdoing it. "When I'm finished putting Taylor to bed later tonight," I asked, "do you want to watch a movie with me?"

We watched Lauren's favorite—a selection from the Lifetime channel, which had become something of an addiction for her. Then I sent her off to bed early to avoid any Sunday morning arguments.

Church was more inspirational than ever. I needed the refueling of the Word in my daily life. I needed Pastor Grant to remind me that I was more than a conqueror and that with God anything was possible.

I usually found myself moved by the Spirit during the praise and worship portion of the service. God had a very special way of comforting me with song. He knew that I needed to hear his words in a way that spoke to my heart, mind, and spirit.

My name and face had made headline news on almost a daily basis for more than a year now. There were times when I thought I could not take another day or stand another moment. Then I would go to church to hear the anointed word of God preached through Pastor Grant. Without fail, I would leave each service reassured that God was at work in my situation and armed with the strength to continue believing him for the victory.

That evening, the girls and I took the dogs for their nightly walk. Then Taylor began her tub time, and I began to feel the sadness of the impending separation from her. The next morning I would drop her off at school and would not see her again until Wednesday. I knew that I could call her, but that seemed unfair to Zack. He gave me the quality time with few interruptions; I needed to reciprocate. I took extra time to read to Taylor and even gave her a manicure and pedicure. She loved having her feet rubbed, and it gave me time to record the feelings that would have to last me for the next three days. God had given me the motherly ability to record smells and senses so that when missing Taylor was too much to bear, I could close my eyes and recall the foot rub or holding her hand as we walked the dogs.

I tucked Taylor into bed, kissed her good night, and together we said our prayer of thanksgiving and special protection for when she was not with me. I was careful never to let her see me get sad.

I needed to be strong. The pain of the divorce for me was not the loss of my marriage—it was the loss of my baby. If my heart was breaking each time she moved between homes, what was happening to her little heart? I knew that a lot of prayer, prayer for healing her little heart, was the only thing I could offer her.

I went into the kitchen, poured myself a glass of wine, and headed for my office. It was time to prepare for the week.

Once seated at the computer, I felt a stronger compulsion to check for any soul mate matches than to do my work. To my excitement, fear, and surprise, I did in fact have an e-mail from eHarmony: "You have a match."

I was paralyzed. *What now?* I pressed the link to the eHarmony site and waited patiently. There was limited information—just a name, occupation, and state. My potential soul mate was a teacher in Alberta, Canada. I supposed that another country was far enough away for safety. The next step in the eHarmony process was a series of multiple-choice questions that allowed you and your match to test the water. You did not communicate directly with your match. eHarmony acted as a go between so that at anytime if you thought your match was not for you, you simply turned off communications. It was nice to have the go-between say, "Sorry, Charlie!"—but in a nice way. Not only that, but the system could help answer questions without your ever having to go on a date. The mere thought of dating sent chills up my spine. What I had seen going out with my friends while I was married was enough to scare anybody.

I began by answering the first three multiple-choice questions. They included questions such as, "If you were going on a weekend getaway, it would be (a) white water rafting, (b) a weekend at the cabin with no TV, (c) bungee jumping, (d) staying at home and sleeping in all weekend."

After I answered the questions and had the chance to ask my own, I turned my attention back to my battlefield. I needed to focus on getting my reputation back, winning the case, and getting on with my life.

Twenty-nine

The next day, Peter and I drove to Jack Wood's first round of depositions, reflecting on the craziness of the entire situation. We were about to confront the man we had once believed held the power to help Peter develop The Preserve, thus re-igniting Peter's career as a prominent real estate developer in Naples. Wood, however, had gone from being the talk of the town—donating millions to charity, working with Big Brothers/Big Sisters, and an after-school educational mentoring program—to being led in and out of court hearings as a shackled criminal decked out in a bright orange jumpsuit. We weren't sure what to expect as we neared the court reporters' offices located across the street from the courthouse and jail complex.

We had only seen our nemesis once since the indictment, at our arraignment more than fifteen months earlier. On that day, as he took center stage in the courtroom, Wood had a sinister look in his eyes. We knew he had promised the prosecutor, who stood resolutely alongside him, that he would help convict the other defendants in order to reduce his own federal sentence—even if it meant, as he'd done before, lying under oath.

Strickland would do anything he could to get as many of us as possible to plead to something—anything. He'd been sent to Naples to clean up corruption and, even if it meant fabricating evidence, he was going to arrest and try us. We knew Strickland could manipulate Wood, his key witness, who needed what only Strickland could give him—an R-35 reduction recommendation on his twenty-year federal sentence in exchange for his cooperation in the Coliseum Golf corruption case.

We arrived about ten minutes early to the four-story building that housed Executive Court Reporting and waited outside for our attorneys to arrive from Miami. We didn't want to chance seeing Strickland without our attorneys present. The Woerners provided a sense of protection and security from the aggressor; Strickland was not afraid to operate outside the box of proper rules of order. He was like a junkyard dog, baring his teeth, always ready for attack against anyone who stood between him and a conviction.

The Woerners arrived right on time and had a good laugh at Peter and me for waiting outside. In their eyes, the prosecutor was little more than a buffoon, and they enjoyed toying with Strickland at any opportunity, of which there were many. I shuddered each time they made him look foolish, fearful that he would exact his rage on me, since the Woerners were out of his reach.

The Woerners' legal prowess was far superior to Strickland's, whose lack of performance and zeal relegated him to life as a state employee.

His current position as a state prosecutor was a huge career improvement over his prior service as a public defender. You get what you pay for with a court-appointed defense attorney like Strickland, as Regina Mayo had found out in her Lil Tots case. Strickland did not do her any favors as her attorney. The only thing Strickland was interested in was helping his boss, Janet Reno, secure a conviction against Mayo's husband, and he cooperated in locking up his own client in solitary confinement for nearly a year until she "remembered" her testimony.

"If Strickland were any good as an attorney, he would have gone private," Adam Woerner laughed as he patted Peter on the back. "He's always taking shots at the defense attorneys about their fees and how ridiculous they are. That's because he's pulling in what I made as a law clerk!"

Adam shook his head as he opened the door to the deposition room. "He made his choice, now he has to live with it. Too bad he's so damn angry all the time; it makes it hard to demonstrate good lawyering when your opponent always has his underwear in a wad." I agreed with Adam; Strickland did always focus on the success of others and how unfair that seemed to him. His courtroom performance was weak and so were his interrogation skills. He was so paranoid that it probably rendered him undesirable for a private firm. How would we work around Strickland's feelings of inadequacy? We'd have to rely on the real professionals, Adam and Jason Woerner. I had prayed for them the night before as I was praying God's Word over today's deposition.

> Contend, O Lord, with those who contend with me; fight against those who fight against me. Take up my shield and buckler; arise and come to my aid. Brandish spear and javelin against those who pursue me. Say to my soul, "I am your salvation." May they be like chaff before the wind, with the angel of the Lord driving them away; may their path be dark and slippery, with the angel of the Lord pursuing them. Since they hid their net for me without cause and without cause dug a pit for me, may ruin overtake them by surprise—may the net they hid entangle them, may they fall into the pit, to their ruin
>
> Psalms 35:1–8

The deposition room held a long table with room for sixteen participants, as well as a row of chairs against the wall for overflow. The court reporter was already set up to transcribe the deposition at the far end of the room, a position that gave her the ability to see each of the participants as they entered so she could record their particulars. She requested that the witness and his attorney sit closest to her so that she would not have to strain to hear their answers. The Woerners placed themselves strategically so they could hear all the whispering from either Strickland and his assistant or the witness and his attorney. Peter and I sat in the peanut gallery, allowing room for the other defense attorneys to sit behind both Jason and Adam to answer any questions or give them insight for questions.

As the appointed time drew near, I developed a sense of uneasiness. I had not seen Jack Wood in more than a year and, after reading his personal interviews with the FDLE agents, I wondered what jail time had done to him, not to mention what it had done to his testimony, especially since there were so many contradictions in his statements. Had the agents been thorough enough to see the glaring lies they were being fed?

I had been present during all of the FDLE agents' depositions, and it was clear how they felt about Strickland. He acted like a jerk to everyone, not just his suspects, and he had used his position of power to humiliate his underlings.

My thoughts were jolted as two FDLE agents opened the door; the sound of chains dragging on the tiled hallway reached the deposition room before the prisoner was even in view. Pressed between the two FDLE agents was Jack Wood in a bright orange jumpsuit, hands cuffed in front of him and attached by a chain to his ankles. It was a sight to behold. This man had once worn only Armani suits and expensive Italian leather shoes. I would have called it a fall from grace, but considering Wood's background, grace was a state with which I was certain he had never been acquainted.

Wood had aged since his confinement to county jail, which had begun more than a year earlier. The lifestyle he had once lived had been taken from him, just as he had stolen it from his innocent victims. He was now nothing more than a common criminal; someone who had to be shackled whenever he left the jail. The man who had once spoiled himself and his entourage with $100-a-glass wines, caviar, and imported cheeses served on the finest Wedgwood china was now getting his food served in tin bowls. I was surprised that the once-trim Wood was now sporting a potbelly, considering the quality of prison food.

Wood did not make eye contact with us as he entered the room, and for a moment, I imagined that his shame had caused him to spawn a conscience. I was glad, though, that he did not look at us. I pulled out my notebook full of his prior interviews with the FDLE agents, ready to point out any contradiction to our attorneys.

Just as Wood settled into his chair, he asked Agent Fred Bare to release the cuffs on his wrists. "As long as you don't try to make a break," Bare laughed as he turned the key to release the prisoner's hands.

"How can I with these shackles on my feet?" Wood asked, clinking his ankles together for effect.

The door swung open with a bang as Strickland pushed his way into the room, his obsequious assistant, Ericka Haack, in tow. As far as I could tell, Haack's only purpose was to take notes and whisper into Strickland's ear to try to make the defense attorneys think they knew something we didn't. She was an easy one to figure out. After taking notes, she would leaf back through her steno pad, then lean over to Strickland and whisper some trifling bits of information. Strickland, in return, would nod his head while his toady would giggle, as if to suggest she had just caught someone in a lie. This charade looked even sillier played out in a room filled with the finest criminal attorneys in the country.

Haack was a plain-looking woman in her early thirties. Her dirty blond hair was not professionally coiffed, and her eyebrows were in need of some serious shaping. The overgrown eyebrows were emphasized by her poorly applied bright blue eye shadow and bright red lipstick. Her shoes were scuffed, and even though she wore a business suit, she always appeared sloppy, as if her clothes were never ironed or just too big. In most conversations she took a defensive posture, always making excuses for "her office" when scheduling mishaps occurred. She was happily Strickland's whipping girl, the person he blamed for anything that went wrong. At least fifteen or twenty years Strickland's junior, Haack seemed either to be enamored of his legal advice or completely smitten by him personally. Neither choice was terribly smart.

"Hello, everyone," Strickland bellowed. "Is everyone comfortable? The temperature, I mean?" Strickland patted Wood as he laughed.

"Hey, Martin, can I get a hot cup of coffee?" Wood asked, reaching an un-cuffed hand forward. "The stuff they serve in jail isn't drinkable."

"Fred," Strickland ordered, "grab Jack a real cup of coffee so we can get started. Let's see who's not here yet." Strickland scanned the room as he jotted down notes.

The door opened slowly, as if the arriving guests knew they were late. It was Andrew Shanahan and his pack of lawyers. No wonder Andrew's legal bills were so high: at each hearing and deposition he had at least two attorneys in tow.

"Sorry we're a little late, Martin," said Della Hollinger, one of Shanahan's lawyers, as she opened her briefcase and plopped binders and highlighters on the table. "We're trying to save our client some fees by driving over each morning from Miami."

Hollinger was a pretty woman in her mid-to-late thirties, a cross somewhere between Jennifer Lopez and Gloria Estefan. Prior to becoming a top Miami criminal defense attorney, Hollinger had been a prosecutor for the state and had worked closely with Strickland. She knew all of his weaknesses and was not afraid to attack them, as long as it benefited her client. She had long, brown hair that reached to the middle of her back and a beautiful face.

Having three children had taken a toll on her figure, but her inner beauty seemed to overshadow that. Hollinger used her looks to lure the prosecution into thinking that she was just another pretty face, and then—wham!—she'd whip out a fierce attack that caught them completely off-guard. She was also very effective with the witnesses, whom she made feel very welcome. She thanked them for their time and truthful testimony and made gentle eye contact as she led them down her carefully planned line of questions. The other attorneys were far more aggressive and did not take the time to calm the witnesses. They were happy to let Hollinger warm them up before they each went in for the attack.

"And last, but not least," Strickland said sarcastically, "the mayor of Fort Myers, Mr. Patrick Wurster. Where is your client, Mr. Mayor?"

"Mr. Gannon is just parking," Patrick replied. "He'll be right in. Sorry we're late."

Patrick Wurster, who had been mayor of Fort Myers years ago, had become Fort Myers's most prominent criminal defense attorney. The country music jams that oozed from his black Cadillac Escalade were so loud that even my teenager would object. He wore the finest suits, accessorized with alligator boots and obnoxious country belt buckles. His deep voice and Southern drawl demanded attention.

"Yeah, Ericka and I saw your TV commercial at 6:30 this morning. What a hoot!" Strickland cracked.

Wurster eyed him cautiously. "Are you two an item, or is the state short on cash and you have to share a room?"

Haack blushed, but Strickland offered only a smile. Neither of them admitted or denied the accusation, but Strickland was quick to turn everyone's attention elsewhere.

"Ladies and gentlemen," Strickland said quickly, "let's get it together. We're already thirty minutes late getting started and with four or five attorneys asking questions—"

"What's the rush?" Patrick said. "Does your key witness have a curfew?"

"I control this witness," Strickland replied. Lowering his voice for effect.

"I bet you do, Mr. Strickland, I bet you do." Patrick turned his attention to the court reporter. "Did you get that comment from Mr. Strickland on the record?"

"Enough pleasantries, folks. Let's get started." Strickland seemed to suffer from attention deficit disorder as he paced the room. "Who will start this deposition?"

"If you all don't mind, I'd like to start." Della Hollinger was ready to warm up her victim.

"Do any of you object?" Strickland asked the other attorneys.

Adam didn't even look up as he answered. "That's fine. Go ahead, Della."

"Good morning, Mr. Wood. My name is Della Hollinger and I represent Andrew Shanahan. How are you this morning?" She smiled as if genuinely interested in his response.

"I'm much happier sitting in this room than in a jail cell," Wood responded, "so I guess I'm doing just fine. Thanks for asking."

"For the record, Mr. Wood, can you please state your full name and address?"

"Sure. Jack Wood. I guess my present address is the Collier County Jail." Wood smirked.

"Thank you. Now, Mr. Wood, the first line of questioning that I would like to ask you is in reference to the $200,000 cash transaction. Are you familiar with that?" Hollinger once again served up a gentle question to the witness.

In a quiet voice, Jack responded, "Oh, yes, I am very familiar with that transaction."

"Mr. Wood," Hollinger continued, "raise your right hand so the court reporter can swear you in, unless that has already been done before I arrived."

"No, we have not yet sworn in the witness," Strickland said officiously. It seemed as if Strickland hoped that no one had noticed the oversight of this formality, which would have given his witness freedom to lie without fear of punishment. "Court reporter, if you'll do the honors."

Wood was sworn in. "Mr. Wood," Hollinger asked, with a swift appraising glance at Strickland, "now that you've sworn to tell the truth, let's move on to the questions. How did you meet Mary Smith?"

Wood's demeanor changed right before our eyes. It was as if we were watching a patient with multiple personality disorder. His physical form began to change: his eyes narrowed, and his face reddened and glistened with perspiration. His lips pursed tightly as he sat up erect, almost lunging forward toward Della. Then Wood sat back in his chair and began to unfold the story, or at least his latest spin on that story. "I met Mary Smith through a fellow who worked in our office, Douglas Endsley. He was good friends with Mary's daughter, Hannah, and I think it was Hannah who initially opened an account with us."

"And how much did Hannah or Mary open the account with?" Hollinger continued.

"I don't remember offhand," Wood stated. "I think it started small, maybe $50,000. Over the course of time with us, they deposited over a million dollars."

"Was that including the $200,000 cash that is the subject of my questions today?"

"No."

"Mr. Wood, do you know what the source of the funds that the Smith's invested was?"

"Hannah represented that her mother had some settlement from a prior marriage. Mary later confirmed this when she visited me in Naples. She was also running a business. She was into natural things and herbs, and she performed high colonics."

"Mr. Wood, do you know if high colonics require a license?"

"I don't know. I would think that if you were going to cleanse someone's colon, you'd need some sort of permit or license." Wood glanced around the room to gauge the response to his joke.

I had never heard of high colonics and leaned forward to the Woerners for an explanation. As the entire room broke into laughter, Jason had the opportunity to graphically describe the procedure to Peter and me. I was shocked. Suddenly this investor, who Wood had described years ago as a retired woman past sixty, was now a woman with a hose in her basement of her home flushing out people's colons for cash? Then he had the gall to continue his lie that we were all fully aware of her "activities." I felt slightly embarrassed for a moment that I was the only one in the room that had never heard the term. I guess my reaction should have clued in the prosecutor that I did not have any prior knowledge of Mrs. Smith's basement bowel business.

Hollinger quickly resumed control and continued the questions. "Mr. Wood, did you think anything of it, other than that it was a funny way to earn money?"

"Yeah, she told me she always did that business in cash to avoid paying taxes on it." Wood's eyes narrowed as he realized that Hollinger was the enemy, quite possibly a smarter one than he'd given her credit for. He needed to pay closer attention.

"She also told me—" Wood continued, "it was sort of humorous to me, because she's an older lady—that she had done this refunding scam where she would buy stuff on sale from one department store and then return it to another one and turn it in for a higher amount of money. She said she actually made a lot of money off that."

"Are you suggesting, Mr. Wood," Hollinger asked, "that Mrs. Smith made over $200,000 performing high colonics and refunding schemes?"

"Oh, yeah. She made over $100,000, maybe $200,000, doing this. She was very active at it, and she told me at some point she got busted by store security in Indianapolis and that they didn't end up prosecuting her, but they said if they ever caught her doing it again, they would," Wood said, smiling.

"So the high colonics were something she was performing in her home?"

"Yeah, she performs it in her basement. That always brings a chuckle from people. I'm not sure I'd want to go in her basement to get high colonics." Wood was clearly enjoying the build-up on this $200,000 money-laundering transaction.

"I wouldn't think you'd want to go anywhere to get high colonics," Hollinger said as she jotted some notes. "So that I am sure about your testimony, let me repeat what I understand back to you, okay?"

"Sure." Wood's eyes narrowed as he realized he needed to listen carefully to her summation.

"You met sometime with Mrs. Smith in Naples around 1995 or 1996 and while driving from your home to the clubhouse, she just volunteered all of this proprietary information about her refunding scheme and, to your suggestion, illegal administration of high colonics in her basement. Is that correct? I mean, didn't you think that it was unusual for her to volunteer this information with you?"

"You'd be surprised what people tell you when they're investing." Wood changed his expression to one of amusement. "Let's not get into it, because we'll spend a week here."

"On what investors told you?" Hollinger asked.

"On investor tales, yes."

"We could probably spend a month on what you told investors?" Hollinger shot back.

"I don't think so," Wood replied, suddenly on the defensive. "I think they told me more tales than I did them. I told the same tale over and over again."

"All right, Mr. Wood," Hollinger said smoothly, "let's move on. The loan that was ultimately obtained from Mary Smith, the $200,000 loan, was necessitated because Heartland Bank and Trust was requesting a payment of money from the Wood-Durkee partners before they would release certain funds under the loan. Is that correct?"

"That is correct, yes," Wood answered.

With all my willpower, I refrained from screaming, "No!" Hollinger had it wrong. Heartland Bank and Trust wanted the cash because we were overdrawn, because Wood's $1 million wire never arrived. I forced myself to sit tight until Jason had the chance to present the facts during his questioning.

"So," Hollinger continued, "you were the one that identified to Peter and Rose that you had an investor in Knoxville that might be able to provide $200,000?"

"That's correct. I think I had talked to them previously about her, because Mary was a problem, and so, I mean, she was ... we had gone around and around with Mary, because she was just a difficult person to deal with. She would get hyper about things. I found Mary's antics to be frustrating and amusing at times. We talked about things like that, but I think I did mention it to them earlier than that."

"What did you mention to them, just that she was a wack job?"

"Yeah, basically," Wood responded.

"As I understand your testimony on this transaction, you and your son flew to Tennessee. Is that correct?"

"Yes."

"So, you took your son with you," Hollinger said. "Can you tell me why you would take your son on a business trip of this nature? I mean, what did you tell Jack Jr. about the reason you were going there?"

"I don't think I ... I just told him I had to take care of some business. We never had much time to hang out together, so I just asked him to go along with me."

"Did you have a relationship with Hannah Smith?" Hollinger was digging up the dirt now.

"Yes, we had an intimate relationship from time to time."

"Is that while you were married, Mr. Wood?"

There was a long pause before Wood answered. He glanced at Strickland, as if to say, "Help me!" There was nothing Strickland could do for him. The question was within bounds, and Wood was under oath.

"Yes, it was," Wood said quietly.

"Continue with what happened when you brought the money back to Naples from Knoxville."

"It was my understanding to bring it back to Wood-Durkee Development's offices to Rose and Peter. While we were on the way, I talked to Rose, and she said to get in touch with Phillip Durkee. My understanding was to bring the money to Wood-Durkee when I came back, but in the meantime, the plans had changed and she said to get a hold of Phillip, which I did, and Phillip said to take the money to Andrew."

"So did you end up meeting with Peter and Rose when you brought the money back?"

"I don't remember meeting with Peter and Rose at all, no."

"So you just went right to meet with Andrew at his law office. And what did Andrew do?"

"He said something about putting it in his safe deposit box."

"Let me make sure I understand everything you told Rose about this $200,000," Hollinger said. "I'll try to summarize it. You said that there were three possible sources. One was the settlement proceeds from some real estate settlement she had or a divorce settlement. There was the colonics that she was performing in her basement and the business of her refunding scam. Is there anything else you told Rose about the source of the money?"

"I don't remember. I just… I told her that I wanted… I told her and Peter that I wanted them to know the source of those funds because they needed to know that she was problematic, and the source of funds was questionable."

Despite his stuttering, Wood was doing a decent job of keeping his story straight—so far.

"Mr. Wood, did you have any of these conversations with Andrew about Mary Smith and the source of the money?"

"Yeah, I mentioned some of it to him. I'm not sure I went into the kind of detail that I did with Rose and Peter. I think I mentioned the colonics after I brought the money. We were chuckling about the situation. I do remember us laughing a little bit about the whole thing. So I imagine we got to talking about Mary. I was tired after a long day on the road, and I wanted to get going. It was the end of the day, as I remember."

"Mr. Wood," Hollinger continued, "you said earlier when you brought the money back from Knoxville that you took it directly to Andrew's office."

"I think I stopped in at home and did some things, and then I ran over to Andrew's office maybe an hour or two later."

"Where was the money? In a bag or a briefcase?"

A moment of truth had arrived. Wood had told so many conflicting stories about the cash, including its packaging, that I was curious to see how the psycho answered this one.

"You know," he said, his already squinty eyes bunched up as if trying to visualize the package, "I don't remember exactly what it was in, to be honest with you. Two hundred thousand dollars is not a huge amount of money when it's in stacks or folded up."

Which is it, Jack? Stacks or folded up? I wondered if Peter was feeling the same frustration that I was. I had written down and tagged every contradiction of his last sworn testimony for the Woerners. They could slam him later.

"So, as I understand your testimony, you never showed the money to Peter Durkee or Rose Visconti. Is that correct?"

"No, I did not. Yes, that is correct."

"Mr. Wood, did you ever tell the agents that Rose Visconti got really excited when she saw the money? I ask that as I review your interview with SAO Fred Bare back in November."

"No," Wood said definitively, "I never told the agents she got really excited when she saw the money, but she was gleeful about the transaction. I might have said that, but I obviously never said that she was excited when she saw it, because she didn't see it, that I'm aware of, anyway."

Wood didn't even have the guts to look me in the eye as he continued his lies.

Hollinger clearly wanted to remove me from the web of lies that Wood was spinning around me. "When you say she was gleeful, do you think it was because you had the money and that Heartland Bank and Trust would now release money under the loan? I mean, that was something that was putting a lot of stress on Rose Visconti, don't you think?"

I saw where Hollinger was going. She was trying to get Wood to admit that I wasn't gleeful about seeing his stack of ill-gotten cash. I was gleeful about getting the loan taken care of and clearing up the million-dollar overdraft that Wood's missing wire had caused. I wasn't a participant in the rotten scheme that he had conjured up. This was his chance to lie about anyone involved with him to cut down his sentence; his story was surely entertaining and cast doubt on the entire group of defendants involved in any way with this $200,000.

"I imagine it probably was, yes, more than I realized." Wood's eyes dropped to his lap.

"When she was gleeful, it didn't surprise you that she was very happy that now you had the money, your commitment was fulfilled, at least for the time being."

The sinister Wood regained control. "Yeah, but there was . . . to me, it seemed like, and it could have been totally my perception . . . it seemed like there was an air of glee about it being the way it was—a clandestine cash transaction, you know, kind of thing. It was picking it up in Knoxville from this wacky lady who did high colonics and, you know, refunding and whatever else. I mean, to say that . . . I can understand with the pressure that Rose was under that it would have taken some pressure off of her, but you have to understand that our line with the bank, I believe, was $25 million, so $200,000 was not a lot of money to see."

"So you're just assuming the reason she was gleeful, correct, Mr. Wood?"

"That's correct. I can only come from my perceptions."

"Thank you, Mr. Wood," Hollinger said smoothly, as if Wood had walked into some trap that only she could see. "Now let's get back to you at Andrew's office and Phillip Durkee. Do you know why Phillip Durkee wanted to take the $200,000?"

Wood shrugged. "He just told me he needed some cash. It was neither here nor there to me."

"Did Rose Visconti or Peter Durkee make any comment about accepting the cash?"

"They knew what it was when I explained to them, and, you know, before I went up there we went through extensive discussion about it—source, problems with Mary, the situation I had with her, how flaky she was. I said, you know, she could be a real problem to deal with."

Hollinger leaned in. "Did you think you were committing a crime by bringing that $200,000 back?"

Wood glanced nervously again at Strickland. This wasn't going the way Wood had hoped. Wood had clearly intended to get me in trouble. Instead, he was just digging himself in deeper and deeper as I stood unwaveringly on Psalm 35:8: "May the net they hid entangle them, may they fall into the pit, to their ruin."

"Well," Wood began, looking less and less in control of the situation, "I knew there were several things relating to it that I was an accessory to, yeah. I knew she was ... if she had gained the money fraudulently though a refunding scam that was fraud. I knew there was tax evasion on the money, because she told me that. You know, if we had been directly involved in depositing anything, which I guess we weren't, there would have been reporting requirements. Yeah, I knew there were some liabilities with that, sure I did."

Before our eyes, Wood had transformed into Strickland's puppet, repeating exactly what he had been told. And the puppet master needed to regain control.

"Let's take a lunch break, if that works for everyone," Strickland interrupted.

"That sounds fine," Jason responded, and then turned to Hollinger. "Della, how much longer do you need with the witness?"

"I don't know maybe another hour or two." Hollinger flipped through her questions. "I've got to cover the Hanover loan and, well, I think I'm finished for now with the $200,000. I'm sure you'll pick up on that again when it's your turn."

"Oh, yes, I've got a few questions of my own." As Jason's face split into a mischievous grin, I felt as if Christmas were just around the corner.

Perhaps feeling a twinge of nerves, Strickland jumped in. "We need to decide after lunch how many days you think this is going to take. I've got to make arrangements with the jail in advance to get Jack out, and I didn't think that you'd be into three or four days."

"Oh, you thought that we'd just ask a few questions of the state's key witness, did you? Come on, Martin." Despite the irritation in his voice, Adam was obviously enjoying making Strickland jittery. "We'll get you a schedule after lunch."

The attorneys all seemed happy with the results of the depositions. They had already successfully discredited Wood and clearly pointed out his inability to tell the truth. I don't know that I shared in their feeling of success. I watched a desperate man willing to say anything or make up anything that would benefit the prosecutor in order to cut even one day off of his time in prison. As it stood, he would be in his sixties when he completed his federal sentence. His children would all be grown, and their only memory of him would be his hands pressed against the glass, wishing he could touch them one more time.

He was an effective liar. He had been lying all of his professional life, so successfully that he was able to bilk a hundred million dollars from some very smart people in Naples. My hope was that by the end of these depositions, whether they took one week or two, Jack Wood would be so tainted as a witness that the state would have to reconsider its case against us. Wood was its only witness who was willing to lie.

All of the other state witnesses had told, and would tell, the truth under oath, and no one said we did anything illegal or questionable throughout our career—at least not me or Peter.

As we left the deposition room, the comments I'd withheld during the deposition were ready to burst from my mouth. Jason must have been able to decipher the look on my face, because he put a finger to his lips for us to be quiet until we left the building. The halls were filled with FDLE agents . . . and they were all ears.

Thirty

As soon as we got in the car, I erupted. "What a liar! Can you believe the crap that came out of his mouth? I think he's been lying for so long that he doesn't know who's on first with which story. I marked each of the conflicting statements that he made regarding the $200,000."

I handed my notes to Jason.

"Breathe, Rose." Adam said as he, Jason, and Peter tried to contain their amusement at my reaction. "This is perfect... he's lying under oath! The bulk of our deposition, Rose, is geared to discredit him as a credible witness. Most people will have forgotten about his Ponzi scheme by the time we get to trial, so we have to demonstrate that he's a liar without relying on the whole $150 million theft that he did on his own." Adam was great at laying out the plan of attack.

"You keep doing what you're doing, Rose," Jason coached. "You're going to be the best counterwitness on the stand. You have all of the e-mails and documented lies that Jack told you, and you've done a great job as a legal assistant for the case. Hey, if you're looking for a job when this is all over..."

"I may take you up on that." I took a few breaths and regained my composure. "After this trial, our business will be gone, along with our reputations. And frankly, after all the publicity, I don't think there's any developer that would hire us. What do you think, Peter?" I elbowed him.

"We're definitely snake-bit." Peter said, laughing. "Hey, Adam, do you have a job for me, too?"

Adam glanced back at him in the rearview mirror. "I think you'd better come up with a new line of work. How about just hanging out at the courthouse protesting injustice?"

Adam was right. What Peter really wanted was justice. We had been wrongfully accused, and Peter wanted nothing short of a written letter of apology from the state. Plea deals were out of the question.

"Hey, Jason," I said, "don't forget to ask Wood about his dealings with demons when we get back after lunch. That should make for some entertainment before he heads back to jail tonight." I wanted more than ever to expose Wood as a freaky fraud—on the record.

I was so excited and anxious that I could hardly eat my lunch. We were setting up Wood for the kill, and Strickland would have to stand by and watch his witness fall apart. But I was also anxious because the lies that were flowing out of Wood's mouth were more fodder for the media. The *Collier Enquirer* got copies of every deposition so it could continue to sensationalize our trial for the entertainment of the community.

The lunch hour passed quickly, and we made it back to the conference room with only minutes to spare.

"Before we start," Strickland addressed the room, "we got a fax while we were at lunch from the *Collier Enquirer* requesting access to the transcript of Jack Wood's deposition. Since we had discussions the last time about certain people's depositions, and we'd agreed at one point that the paper could have access to them if it was willing to pay, if we all agree, it can get one. It has to be a unanimous agreement."

"Let's talk about it later," Patrick Wurster said. "They'll just have to wait."

"Let's get rolling then," Strickland said, clearly disappointed. He wanted headlines every day, especially when Wood had some great accusations, which the media would adore. And by the time the trial came, his lies would be all but forgotten. Strickland, defeated for the moment, waved a hand at Hollinger to continue.

Jason had to return to Miami by early evening; his wife was expecting their first child, a son. He feared he would miss the blessed event if he waited for his wife to call. Jason worked out a deal with Della over lunch to allow him to depose Wood following lunch, and Della could resume later in the afternoon or the following day.

"Jack Wood," Strickland said, "you have been previously duly sworn in and we'll continue direct examination."

I sat up straight in my chair as my team came up to bat. "Good afternoon, Mr. Wood. My name is Jason Woerner. I represent Rose Visconti. Do you understand that you're still under oath?"

"Yes, I do."

"I would like to first briefly cover Coliseum Golf with you. Is it your understanding that it was Nicholas Shubert who had already decided before you came into the deal, the Coliseum Golf deal, to cut Eugene Gannon in?"

"Yes, that's correct."

I noticed that Wood was keeping his answers short and to the point.

"Okay," Jason said calmly. "You're not the person who offered Eugene Gannon an interest in the deal, but you were going to be the financial backer of the Coliseum Golf deal. Nobody was going to get paid until you decided, correct?"

"That's correct."

Jason continued. "Eugene Gannon was not going to get paid until you decided, right?"

"That's right."

"And you agreed to pay Nicholas Shubert only after the partnership agreement was signed?"

"That is correct," Wood said warily. He obviously could tell where Jason was leading him, and it was a direction in which he clearly did not want to go.

"And the same goes for Eugene Gannon," Jason said, pressing him. "You only agreed to pay Eugene Gannon his interest in the Coliseum Golf project after the partnership agreement was signed?"

Wood hesitated a moment as if dissecting the sentence. "I believe that's correct, yes."

Wood had now admitted that he was the one who was financially responsible for the Coliseum Golf deal and that paying Gannon, a seated commissioner, in advance of what the proposed document called for was his decision alone. There was no conspiracy to bribe a commissioner here!

It was Wood who had decided to pay Shubert and Gannon as soon as the agreement was signed, although the partnership agreement clearly stated otherwise. Under the terms of the agreement, Shubert and Gannon would be paid at "escrow break," after $100 million dollars in project funding had been raised by selling other investors on the idea. Shubert had gotten Wood so pumped up about the concept that he convinced Wood to release some cash to him in advance. Gannon was not going to be left out of this deal and approached Wood for similar treatment, and got it.

Jason continued his questions. "Now, after the Coliseum Golf partnership agreement was signed in May, the deal blew up. And the reason that it blew up is because of the public outcry, so to speak, as a result of Eugene Gannon's participation in the deal. And you made the decision, and Wood-Durkee received bad publicity as a result. Then you, as one of the principals of Wood-Durkee, decided with your partners that it was not in the best interest of Wood-Durkee to continue with the deal. And so, essentially, you pulled the plug after discussions with your partners on the Coliseum Golf deal. Is that correct?"

"Yes, that was around July 1997," Wood responded.

"Mr. Wood, how much money did you have invested in Coliseum Golf at the point that you decided to pull the plug?"

"Roughly four million dollars."

"Thanks." Jason seemed satisfied with the questioning thus far.

"Now I'd like to turn to the SmartKids loan to Commissioner Evan Hanover. Did you have any communication with Evan Hanover about the loan before the date of the closing on the loan?"

Wood answered as if he'd memorized a script. "I don't remember having a meeting with Evan Hanover. He said that he had a meeting with us. I don't remember having a meeting with him, or he may have had a meeting with someone else in our office, but it was … it's something I don't remember."

"But you had a meeting with him at the closing of the loan?"

"Of course."

Jason was successfully showing that the only person involved in relationships with commissioners was Wood. First, he'd formed a partnership with Gannon in Coliseum Golf, and then he lent Evan Hanover money for a preschool learning system.

"Mr. Wood, other than Phillip Durkee, Evan Hanover, and Andrew Shanahan, who else did you discuss the SmartKids loan with? Did you ever discuss it with Peter Durkee or Rose Visconti?"

Wood seemed to think long and hard on that one. "I don't recall if I discussed it with … I don't recall. I had some discussions with Peter about Evan Hanover, but I don't remember discussing anything with Rose about it."

"Okay, so as far as you understand," Jason continued, "Rose had no knowledge of the SmartKids loan, and you have a vague recollection of talking with Peter Durkee about Hanover, but you can't state that you talked with him about the SmartKids loan?"

"Correct," Wood replied. "But I do remember one time we were in the Turtle Cove clubhouse doing something, and someone from the kitchen or administration came up and talked to Peter briefly about something that was going on, and Peter turned to me and he said it was about Evan Hanover's wedding reception. Peter said something like 'my father'—something along the lines of 'My father is doing something for Evan Hanover on his reception, and I don't even want to know what Father is doing.' It was kind of a disgusted comment."

What a sick man, I thought to myself. He's doing anything he can to make Peter and his father look like crooks. He is so desperate to get his sentence reduced that he's remembering any conversation, no matter how trite, to aid the prosecutor in his quest to convict a Durkee.

"Tell me, Mr. Wood," Jason continued, "what was your federal sentence again, and are you satisfied with it?"

"Twenty years and, well, I would like for it to have been less, but it is what it is. I had to accept responsibility for what I had done."

The false humility rang like warped wind chimes. Even Strickland had to be repulsed by it.

"Mr. Wood, has Mr. Strickland made you any promises about your sentence in the federal case?"

"No, he simply told me that as part of the agreement, actually, when my public defender in the federal case was working out my plea agreement there, I'm not sure exactly how it came up, whether the feds mentioned it to him, being the U.S. attorneys, or how it came up, I'm not certain, but they offered Rule 35 in the plea for cooperation in this case." Wood was beginning to feel uncomfortable with Jason's line of questioning.

"Has Mr. Strickland made you any promises about your sentence in the federal case? What has he told you he is going to do for you?"

"No," Wood stated firmly, "he has not made any promises. He has mentioned that I needed to testify to my cooperation."

Strickland interrupted. "For the record, a letter was sent by the state attorney's office to the federal U.S. attorney's office saying that pursuant to the agreement, we requested them to file a Rule 35 motion. A motion was filed."

"Is that something that has been disclosed in discovery yet, the actual letter?" Adam asked.

"The letter is not going to be disclosed," Strickland said. "It's under seal."

"It's under seal in the federal case?" Adam challenged.

"Yes, under seal in the federal case." Strickland was beginning to get nervous. "And furthermore, I am not turning it over. My understanding—I haven't seen the order—is that the judge has said he's going to withhold ruling on Rule 35 with something like a sixty or ninety day notice, until this case is resolved."

Adam was not buying Strickland's story. "Your letter is under whose seal?"

"The federal government. My letter went to the federal government. I don't know what they ... they filed that part of it, I believe, under seal.

The letter was sent. Certain things were stated in there as to the cooperation. No time was stated. No expectation is stated. Just that pursuant to the agreement, there is some of the cooperation that has taken place, and please file a motion and have it held."

"So it's not sealed by the federal court," Adam countered, leaning in for emphasis. "You said it was sealed. I don't understand."

"Listen, Adam, they filed the affidavit or used my letter as an affidavit, is my understanding, behind the Rule 35 to be sealed in federal court with the motion as basis."

Strickland realized that Wood was now being backed into a corner.

Patrick jumped into the ring. "The government decided to file it under seal?" he asked incredulously.

"Yes," Strickland replied quickly, holding up his hands. "Not me."

"The court has not ordered it sealed." Patrick was calling Strickland's bluff.

"I don't know," Strickland said as if tiring of this game. "You'd have to ask them."

"Either way, it seems ..." Adam seemed ready to sidestep the issue but instead cut right to the chase. "Are you going to object to the disclosure of that letter?"

"Yes, I am." Strickland dropped his pen on the table. "Ultimately you will get a copy of the letter, but it will be redacted."

"Excuse me just a minute," Patrick interrupted angrily. "For the record, this is Patrick Wurster, and my position on this letter is that it is clearly an offer for assistance to provide favorable treatment to a witness. It is clearly Brady-Giglio material. I would like the court reporter to prepare an expedited transcript of this discussion, because I intend to file a motion asking that it be produced and for sanctions. This is clearly an attempt to assist the witness in receiving a lower treatment. There is no question, and the state, on the record, has stated that they have consciously made a decision not to disclose that information."

"Just for the record," Strickland said snidely, "if Mr. Wurster knew how to read a newspaper, he'd know that the Rule 35 motion had been filed. There was a whole article written about it last week prior to this deposition. And one more thing, for the record, Mr. Wurster and I had this conversation last week. So when he says he didn't know about it, he is not being truthful."

"I know how sensitive you are to being called a liar, Mr. Strickland. Are you calling Mr. Wurster a liar?" Jason gave Strickland a gentle but sarcastic grin.

"I've said what I had to say," Strickland replied.

"Mr. Wood, what prison are you in?" Jason inquired.

"Objection!" Strickland said. "At this point, we would rather not put that on the record."

"Come on," said Jason. "There's an inmate locator on the Web site."

"Then go locate it!" Strickland replied testily.

"I don't have my computer here," Jason said, and I could see he was beginning to get really riled up. He asked Strickland, "Are you instructing him not to answer the question?"

"I am suggesting," Strickland replied, slowly and carefully, "that he doesn't have to answer it."

Jason pressed Strickland again. "Are you instructing him, Mr. Strickland, not to answer the question?"

"If you'll listen to the English language, I said I'm suggesting that he doesn't have to answer. I can't instruct him not to answer unless it becomes something about a pending investigation. He and his lawyer can discuss that." Strickland was sending a clear message to Wood.

"What federal prison are you designated to, Mr. Wood?" Jason said, turning his back to Strickland.

"Give me a minute." Wood looked around as if the bars had already closed in around him. Without looking at Strickland, he said, "I'm in Coleman."

"Thank you." Jason shot a look of disgust at Strickland, who appeared completely unaffected.

"Okay, Mr. Wood, I'd like to ask you a few questions about your fund. How many hours a month would you spend preparing false statements? Well, take a step back. Would you be the only one preparing the false statements for your investors?"

Jason sat back to take in Wood's response.

"Our statements," Wood began, "were set up on a complex computer program that was based in Excel that apportioned to each individual partner based on how much capital they had in at the time. So it was apportioned percentage wise to each investor. What I did was I just gave the total number of return to the person, whoever it was that was putting it in the computer. The number was arbitrary during probably three or four years. Most of the time, when we were flush with the private companies, it wasn't arbitrary. I was calculating based on what I thought the valuation of the private companies was, and there were some months where I gave the actual returns that we had in the fund."

Jack Wood had just changed personalities again before our eyes. Now he was the successful hedge fund manager. Jason's question brought out the business man, the man who believed he could produce a fifty percent return in the market. Jack started his sales pitch as if we were potential investors in his fund! The evil Jack was taking a rest.

Peter and I looked at each other in disbelief. Once again, Wood believed the lie he had lived for nine years. This was better than watching a movie on schizophrenia.

"I noticed, Mr. Wood, that in December of 1999, the last month of the millennium, the fund return came up 6.66 percent. That is the sign of the beast, isn't it?"

"There is no significance to that percent." Wood sat forward in his chair and clenched his jaw.

"Have you ever been possessed by demons, Mr. Wood?" I admired Jason's steadfast demeanor. He never once took his eyes off the witness.

"I don't know how to answer that question," Wood responded.

Strickland spun around in his chair, squinted his eyes and mouthed, "What the heck?" He had not been paying close attention throughout the depositions, but now he pulled up his chair close to the table. You could see by his sudden interest that this line of questions could trash his key witness, and he needed to listen up!

"Well, I know *I* haven't been," Jason replied calmly. "I am asking if you've ever been possessed. Have you ever claimed that you've been possessed by demons?"

Jason would not relent until he got his answer. This was critical in discrediting Wood.

"I may have felt a demonic oppression," Wood said, obviously picking his words carefully. "That is when a demonic force is against you from the outside, not a possession. A possession is like an internal thing."

"And so your life has been one very long demonic oppression. Is that fair to say, Mr. Wood?"

"I wouldn't say that," Wood replied carefully. "I mean, that's not something you can accurately gauge, things that go on in the spiritual realm. It's not like you can register a document or something else."

Jason shifted tactics. "What does a demonic oppression cause in you, Mr. Wood?"

"Demonic oppression is when a demonic force or a force of evil is working against you and you succumb to it, like I did with the fraud."

"Did there come a point when you exorcised those demons?"

"There is no exorcism of demonic oppression," Wood said as if stating the obvious. "I may have rebuked them scripturally."

"And did your exhortation or rebuke of your demonic oppressions cause you to stop the fraud?"

"I don't think that I ever dealt directly with any kind of a demonic oppression directly relating to a fraud, no. I don't know." Wood was just now catching on that Jason was making a joke of this very serious subject.

"Have you ever discussed demons with Mr. Strickland?" Jason asked, smiling.

"No."

"Have you ever told Rose Visconti that you were dealing with demonic oppression?

"Yes, I did tell Rose—well, she experienced it." Wood glanced over at me, sending a chill up my spine as I recalled the incident in the woods. And his look today, the sheer evil in his eyes, was a reminder of that moment. Was he telling me with that look that I should be worried?

"Although you may not have belonged to the same church as Rose, you understood that Rose was and is a spiritual person?" Jason continued.

"Yes. I understood that she was practicing a faith, attending church," Wood responded.

"And did you portray yourself to her as a God-fearing Christian?"

"I believe I did, yeah, inasmuch as I could. I mean I wasn't practicing the way somebody should be. I was committing a fraud. But she did not know about my fraud. No one did." Wood's eyes fell to the floor almost remorsefully.

"I hate to interrupt this line of questioning," Strickland said, his tone sarcastic, "as it has been very entertaining for all of us, but can you please tell me how any of this is relevant?"

Without even bothering to address Strickland's objection, Jason announced, "I'm done. I have nothing else. Thank you, Mr. Wood."

The depositions continued for three more days with no new revelations, just more of Jack's delusional behavior. Wood was content to be out of jail and downing good lunches and hot coffee, even if he was still in shackles. Each attorney took his turn asking the same questions in different ways for their client's benefit. In the end, the depositions shed such an unfavorable light on Wood that I wondered if the prosecutor was beginning to feel that his case was falling apart. His star witness was nuts.

Even if Strickland was discouraged, he had no choice but to press on. A prosecutor in the criminal justice system cannot recant his charges without serious damage to his reputation and credibility. Once he had filed the charges against us, no matter how empty those charges turned out to be, Strickland had to fight to the bitter end.

The only way out for the accused was a jury trial, a plea deal, or the judge dismissing the case.

Thirty-one

After a week of depositions with Wood, my head was swimming. Was there anything that Jack wouldn't say to save his behind? He would be in prison for twenty years. He'd take any reduction to his sentence—days, weeks, or months. He wanted out as soon as possible, and he didn't care who paid the price.

I would occasionally hope for e-mail from eHarmony but was never too disappointed—or surprised—that my soul mate had not yet been found. I had to surrender my passport to the State, so it did not make sense to entertain the idea of an international relationship—not now anyway—so I ended my first eHarmony match.

The month of February began with spiritual renewal. One Sunday morning just a week earlier, an announcement had been made about a new course being offered at church: The Prophetic Significance of the Biblical Feasts. I didn't see what Jewish celebrations had to do with what was going on in my life at the moment, but I felt that taking the course was something I needed to do. And since my work pace had slowed to a near stop, there would be no problem in my attending the classes each Monday evening, so I signed up.

The class was taught by Patricia Hilliard, a petite woman in her fifties with a head full of bouncing blond hair that artfully framed her piercing blue eyes. In the introduction to the course, she explained that the English word "feast" was a translation of the Hebrew word, *moed,* which means "appointed time." We would learn that the seven feasts depicted in the Old Testament were much more than cultural observations of Jewish celebrations. They were, in fact, a detailed rehearsal of God's appointed timetable for mankind.

I wondered if I would discover a clue about God's timetable for my life somewhere in the material. It didn't take long to find out.

The following week we began our study of Passover. In order to lay a foundation for the teaching, Patricia had us open our Bibles to Genesis to read the account of Moses's confrontation of Pharaoh:

> Now the Lord spoke to Moses and Aaron [his brother] about the Israelites and Pharaoh king of Egypt, and he commanded them to bring the Israelites out of Egypt. Now when the Lord spoke to Moses in Egypt, he said to him, "I am the Lord. Tell Pharaoh king of Egypt everything that I tell you." But Moses said to the Lord, "Since I speak with faltering lips, why would Pharaoh listen to me?" Then the Lord said to Moses, "See, I have made you like God to Pharaoh . . . You are to say everything that I command you . . . The Lord said to Moses and Aaron, "When Pharaoh says to you, 'Perform a miracle,' then say to Aaron, 'Take your staff and throw it down before Pharaoh,' and it will become a snake." So Moses and Aaron went to Pharaoh and did just as the Lord commanded. Aaron threw his staff down in front of Pharaoh and his officials, and it became a snake. Pharaoh then summoned the wise men and sorcerers, and the Egyptian magicians also did the same things by their secret arts: Each one threw down his staff and it became a snake. But Aaron's staff swallowed up their staffs.
>
> Exodus 6:13, 28–30; 7:1, 2, 8–12

"Right now," Patricia said with a smile, "you are all probably recalling the scene in the movie *The Ten Commandments*, where Charlton Heston as Moses stood on the marble steps and confronted Yul Brynner as Pharaoh, demanding that the Israelites be set free. I want you to keep that image in mind while we look again at verse one of Exodus 7.

I turned the page in my Bible and read along with her: "Then the Lord said to Moses, 'See, I have made you like God to Pharaoh.'" I had seen the movie a number of times and had read the account in my

Bible, but I didn't remember this part of the story. I wondered where she was going with this.

"Now if the man, Moses, was a picture of God in this confrontation, who, then, did Pharaoh represent in the story?" Patricia asked.

The room was quiet for a moment while we contemplated her question. Then, at the same time, three people exclaimed "Satan!"

"Right!" Patricia nodded. "Now here is what I want you to see as you think about that scene in the movie where the two men faced each other: One man—aided by a group of sorcerers and magicians—is holding God's people captive. And the other man—declaring the word of God and demonstrating his mighty acts—has come to set them free." The room grew quiet again as we each considered the impact of her statement.

"Oh my gosh," I whispered out loud as I realized what she had just said. I covered my face with my hands because I wanted to savor this moment. *I get it, Lord; I understand what you are saying to me.*

The power of one man—Martin Strickland—had held me captive for more than a year now. But his power was no match for the favor of God in my life, which belonged to me through my Savior, Jesus Christ, who said:

> The Spirit of the Lord is on me, because he has anointed me to preach good news to the poor. He has sent me to proclaim freedom for the prisoners and recovery of sight to the blind, to release the oppressed, to proclaim the year of the Lord's favor.
>
> Luke 4:18–19

Although I did not know the exact timetable of the events that would be taking place in my life this year, I was assured of the outcome: Jesus had already delivered me from the power of this one man who was attempting to destroy my life.

Later that night, after Taylor and Lauren were sleeping soundly in their beds, I opened my Bible to read more about God's deliverance of his people:

> For I do not want you to be ignorant of the fact, brothers and sisters, that our ancestors were all under the cloud and that they

> all passed through the sea. They were all baptized into Moses in the cloud and in the sea. They all ate the same spiritual food and drank the same spiritual drink; for they drank from the spiritual rock that accompanied them, and that rock was Christ. These things happened to them as examples and were written down as warnings for us, on whom the fulfillment of the ages has come. No temptation has seized you except what is common among people. And God is faithful; he will not let you be tempted beyond what you can bear. But when you are tempted, he will also provide a way out so that you can stand up under it.
> 1 Corinthians 10: 1–5, 11, 13

I turned out the light and thanked God for his faithfulness; I felt as if I were getting my life back. Within minutes I was sleeping peacefully.

The refueling I had gotten in my feasts class had made me ready to once again face my accuser at another status conference on February 13. Once again, it was nothing more than to reschedule future hearings due to spring breaks, other trials our defense attorneys had, and the like. Judge Heyward was a no-nonsense professional who had little patience for the egotistical crowd of attorneys. Not wanting to waste any more time, he intended to set the trial for the summer.

Despite the assurance I had received from God's word about the outcome of my legal situation, the hearing left me with uneasy feelings about Judge Heyward. He didn't seem interested in listening or asking questions. He'd read everything and was ready to move forward—period. His retirement was being interrupted for this Coliseum Golf case, and he did not want to make a second career out of it.

When I returned home after the hearing, I began planning a special Valentine's Day celebration for the loves of my life, my two beautiful girls. I knew they would appreciate celebrating the day of love together, and the puppies would be celebrating their first birthday. I decided we'd make heart-shaped liverwurst cakes for Tank and Genevieve, topped off with a candle-lit dessert of Frosty Paws, a frozen doggie treat.

Lauren and Taylor were thrilled to have a "date" for the night, even if it was Mom and the dogs. I sent each of them a dozen red roses and a sappy love note. Lauren, I knew, held on to every act of love and kindness and would save her dried flowers for years to come.

The rest of February flew by with no news on the legal front. There were, of course, more depositions and legal bills, but no tangible progress.

As far as work was concerned, I was spending my final days at The Preserve. I decided that I would retire at the end of March. It was somehow funny that I was ending my real estate career right where it began, and in the project that was now the subject of some of these questionable votes by the accused county commissioners Gannon and Hanover.

Peter left The Preserve without a fight at the end of the year. He hadn't really performed any day-to-day operational activities, and he was happy to relinquish his management fee and avoid the insult of working with the club's new manager, Gregory Ashmore, appropriately dubbed "Greg Almighty." After the final refinance with our lender, Charles Jankowski hired Ashmore as The Preserve Club general manager based upon his promise to have the club sold to the members for big returns within ninety days. Gregory knew that he had to get rid of Peter and me. With Charles Jankowski living in Pittsburg, we were the only ones who could challenge his incompetence. He was successful in pushing Peter out the door, but true to my personality profile, I was up for the challenge.

In his late sixties, Gregory Ashmore was a self-proclaimed expert in everything—just ask him! His everyday wardrobe consisted of expensive trousers and collared shirts with a sweater draped around his shoulders. Although his intention was to make a fashion statement, he came off as a little swishy. He wore his wavy, all-white hair slicked back with gel, and his Old Spice cologne arrived in a room well before he did. But after a few weeks with this guy, even I changed my mind. Life suddenly seemed too short to deal with jerks, and this guy was the biggest one I'd ever met, which was saying a lot considering the prosecutors I was dealing with.

Ashmore was not a pathological liar like Wood, but he certainly used the multiple personality approach to accomplish his goal of driving me out, selling the club, and padding his pockets with the profit that otherwise would have belonged to me and Peter. He tried the "let's be friends" maneuver with me in an attempt to use me with the members as a decoy. You know, "If Rose likes him, then he must be okay."

I could see right through his smarmy tricks and decided to leave him to his own fate with The Preserve members. The members could smell a thief a mile away; after all, they'd been exposed to Wood. They would not be taken advantage of by some Boca Raton city slicker in expensive Italian garb. Most of our residents were Midwesterners and did not fancy this kind of man.

I decided to stay through March 31 so the members would have a smooth transition. Most of them returned to their summer homes up north around Easter, so the schedule would work nicely for everyone. I reduced my operational performance to running karaoke nights each Tuesday and Thursday evening from 5:30 to 7:30. We packed the place, sold lots of drinks and food, and the members loved it. True to my profile, I needed an audience to perform to and to be appreciated for what I did. I got both.

Our debut karaoke night was March 4. To ensure a fun-filled night of entertainment, I had worked hard to recruit some "plants" in the audience, which would also help ensure success for the next performances. The plants included my father, from whom I inherited my desire for an audience. He was happy to perform and would do so for free dinner and drinks. My mother came along and was thrilled to see Dad belting out Frank Sinatra tunes, just like the good old days. My father sang in a band when they first met back in 1948, and he was just as good now as he was then. I watched my mother's eyes as she fell in love with him all over again with each song he performed. After fifty-five years of marriage, my parents were a testimony to true love and commitment.

The first Tuesday evening went off just as I'd hoped. We even had members signing up in advance for Thursday night to guarantee their moment in the spotlight. As I drove home I felt a surge of happiness, one emotion that I had not felt in a long time. I was getting kudos from the membership, and I had my platform on which to perform.

For tonight, at least, I was happy.

When I pulled into the garage and saw that the house was dark, my mood suddenly darkened. I was alone. Taylor was with her father for the next few days, and Lauren was out with her friends. I walked into the empty house, turning on lights as I went from room to room. I headed straight for my computer. Since it was quiet on the home front, I had a chance to check into eHarmony, hoping for some good news.

As I removed my entertainer clothes and slipped into an oversized T-shirt, I sang my signature song, Gloria Gaynor's "I Will Survive." I sat down in my suede office chair, turned on my computer, and clicked a button to check my e-mail.

Bing!

My heart skipped a beat. I had a match on eHarmony. Someone had passed all twenty-nine dimensions of my personality profile and survived. Before I even looked at the profile, I began to wonder what he looked like, and then chided myself for my shallow mentality. *The heart and soul are what matters,* I reminded myself as I stopped for a moment of prayer, and then opened the e-mail.

"Brad, 42, from Kansas, a marketing executive."

I sat stunned. Kansas? I leaned back in the chair to look at my globe. *Good grief! Smack dab in the middle of the country. What on earth do you market in Kansas? Corn?* I signed onto the system to see what I could find out about this Mr. Kansas.

I was smiling ear to ear as I reviewed the next step in the matching system. He had selected my first question, "What is the most adventuresome thing you've done in the past year?"

Now there's a question for you. I didn't think I'd get very far if I answered that I'd trekked through the bowels of the criminal justice system as an accused RICO conspirator. I chose a different approach.

"Every day is an adventure in my life!" I wrote enthusiastically. *If only he knew what kind of adventure. He'd probably never e-mail me again!* "In the last year, my company has built its third golf course and country club community. Watching and creating the dream from a blueprint to reality is an adventure."

The reply space was small, so I had to keep it brief. Then I picked a question to send back to Brad with my response. If he was intrigued by my answer, he could respond to the question I had chosen for him, "What is the one dream for your life you most look forward to having come true?"

Then the waiting began again. I had no idea how long the process would take, so I decided to fool around on the computer for a few hours. If anything came through, great. If not, I reminded myself, I was just in it for the fun. At eleven, with no reply, I decided to call it a night.

I had difficulty sleeping, however. I dreamed of Kansas, tornadoes, and the yellow brick road—even the witch and "Toto, too!" I was thankful when the alarm woke me at 6:00 a.m. I was up without hitting the snooze once. It was Wednesday, and all I was doing at the club was putting our files in order, cleaning out my desk, and preparing for Thursday's karaoke. I decided to check my e-mail before jumping in the shower.

There was a response from Brad. *Woo-hoo! He replied to my question.*

"More than anything else," he wrote, "I would like to see my children grow up to be healthy, happy, and to have faith in the Lord. For myself, I dream (pray) that I will be able to share my faith through the rest of my life with a special partner."

I sat back in my chair, warmly satisfied at his sensitivity. As I contemplated his words, I found myself reflecting on the circumstances that had brought about our exchange. I had set out on a quest to find out about myself and to correct anything in my personality that needed to be corrected. I now had a better idea of my strengths and weaknesses, but was I really ready to be involved in a godly relationship? My life was committed to God, and I trusted that at the right time he would send just the right man for me. One of the scriptures I was standing on was Jeremiah 29:11: "For I know the plans I have for you," declares the Lord, "plans to prosper you and not to harm you, plans to give you hope and a future."

I reread Brad's response and then it hit me, *Children?* I imagined that someone from Kansas would probably have a herd. I wanted answers right away, but I was at the mercy of eHarmony's formalized process. The only option I had was to pick questions from a predetermined list. Open communication didn't begin until level five.

The way that eHarmony worked was through a series of questions and answers. They started out on level one as multiple-choice answers, then progressed to one-line answers, paragraph type answers, and then finally at the final level, open communication. Then you were free to ask and answer anything you wanted, no longer relying on the system's questions to guide you.

It took about a week for Brad and me to get to level five. We were both enamored with each other's responses and eager to get into some deeper e-mail conversation. On March 14, our day finally arrived. Our first e-mail included all of the questions we were both dying to ask. We found ourselves spending countless hours e-mailing back and forth, growing closer with each passing day. I felt like a teenager again. My heart would pound every time I checked my e-mail. I was even having difficulty concentrating at work, so it was a good thing that all I had to do was sing from the karaoke teleprompter.

I was happy and joyful and had all but forgotten about my case. This was just the distraction I needed. I was enjoying adult conversation with someone who had no idea that I was currently under $10,000 bail and was in and out of criminal court a few times a month. I decided not to bore him with such details. It would be too difficult to explain via e-mail, and I had no idea where I'd even start.

Brad and I enjoyed each other's company as friends and so decided to move on to the next step, sharing our personal e-mail addresses. Not wanting us to get into a rut with questions about work and the weather, he prepared a list of fifteen questions broken into three categories with five questions in each. We would each pick two questions for the other to answer. As I reviewed the questions, I wondered why he had chosen some of them. "Tell me about the time that you were almost arrested and for what?"

Lord, are you working through him to get me to be honest about my case, or does Brad have some dark past that he's dying to tell me about? I just hoped that wouldn't be the first question he asked. I breathed a sigh of relief when I saw Brad's first two questions for me, "How do you figure out what God's path is for you day to day?" and "What is the biggest shocker that you gave your parents when you were a teen or that your teen gave to you as a parent?"

I couldn't stand the stress of him not knowing the truth about my current situation. I had seen those television commercials with real-life happy couples that had met through eHarmony, and now it was happening to me. I had never in a million years thought that this Internet personality profile would have produced the man of my dreams, a miracle sent directly from God. But it had, and I now had to be completely honest. It wouldn't be fair to Brad if he didn't know that the woman that he was communicating with could, if convicted, spend the next thirty years in jail, according to the *Collier Enquirer*.

I sat in front of the computer, reciting the prayer that Jesus prayed in the garden. "Father, if this cup could pass . . . if there is any other way . . ."

I knew that I had to tell the truth and that God would prepare Brad for my answer.

In four pages of e-mail, I poured my heart out to Brad, telling him all about what I had endured over the previous year, even including a link to the Web site for the *Collier Enquirer* so he could read the accounts himself. I closed my e-mail with some hopeful words:

> I think that I've given you much to think and pray about. Here's the deal: Follow the Lord's leading. He led me to do this very uncomfortable thing, but he knows what you can handle and will give you the wisdom to either stop communications but offer to pray for me, or will give you the supernatural strength to become my prayer partner and the much-needed ear and compassion I need on days when my hug quotient is low. I hope that you will find the joy of the Lord in my testimony. Sorry for the dump. Jesus made me do it!"

I pressed the send button before I could change my mind. Brad needed to know the severity of the situation and the truth about my life. If God truly had used the Internet to answer my prayers for healing of my broken heart and Brad was his answer, then I'd have a wonderful response when I logged on in the morning. On the other hand ... my eyes filled with tears. For all I knew, Brad could have been reading my response just then and looking for a way to change his e-mail address. I went to bed trying not to think the worst.

The next morning there was an e-mail from Brad, sent at 2:00 a.m. Kansas time. My heart thumped as I tried to anticipate what his response would be.

> Dear Rose,
>
> Wow, you have really been though a lot. I had to stop in the middle to pray for the Lord to hold you and your daughter in his all-powerful hands to nurture and protect you both. Psalm 35 was written for you ... 2000 years ago!
>
> If you were afraid that after saying a prayer for you that I would somehow see you as damaged goods and want to run for the exit ... YOU WERE WRONG! In all seriousness, my biggest fear in life is boredom. To truly be happy I need life on all fronts to be stimulating—intellectually, creatively, mentally, physically, and spiritually.
>
> In the final analysis, whatever happens is God's plan. Maybe I have been sent to comfort you and give you a boost as you rebound from the lows that you've experienced. Maybe I am God's instrument of love and compassion to remind you that you are a beautiful and special person created by God and deserving of love and hugs. And maybe, just maybe we are each in search of that one specific person that God wants us to spend the rest of our life on this earth with.

I cried as I read Brad's response. He truly was a miracle sent directly by God. For the first time in years, I felt love, true love. I sang praise and worship songs in the shower thanking God for his guidance and for what might be the love of my life, my soul mate.

Just a few days after my outpouring of emotion, we decided to break our verbal chastity and plan a phone call for March 16. I didn't think it was coincidence that the date recalled John 3:16: "For God so loved the world…"

Because we both had children and a time zone issue to deal with, we chose 4:00 p.m. As the appointed time approached, I became increasingly nervous. I had revealed the deepest parts of my heart and soul to a man that I had never even seen, and now, for the first time, I would hear the voice of the man I was falling in love with.

That magical phone call lasted four hours. I don't think I have ever talked to anyone that long. Our four-hour calls became a nightly routine, as did our regular e-mails. Brad had such a way of filling my heretofore "love tank" with words of affirmation. Our conversations were wonderful, but each morning I would look forward to the special words that he'd composed following the previous night's long talk on the phone.

It didn't take long for Lauren to become suspicious of my long phone calls on the porch. I told a little white lie, that Brad and I met at Universal Studios years ago and had recently started talking again, after the divorce. However, the little white lie grew to huge proportions. I needed a story and quick.

I told Brad that I didn't want anyone to know that we had met on the Internet because I was afraid they'd think we were crazy. He tried to assuage my fears by reminding me that online dating was quite common, that the whole modern world revolves around the Internet. Then he asked if I could travel. I almost forgot my legal restrictions but remembered that I could as long as I provided my travel details.

"I'll set up a meeting for us," Brad said. "I think it's time, don't you?" He was as anxious as I was to see, to touch, and to know each other more.

I almost couldn't believe I was saying the words as they poured out. "I can't wait to look into your eyes, to hold your hand, to finally hug you. Just say the word and I'll be there." *Oh my gosh! What am I doing?*

"How about next weekend? I'll plan the whole trip and send you an itinerary that you can forward to your bail bondsman." Brad's sense of humor was one of the things I found most attractive. "And then you'll have your story."

I wasn't following. What story?"

"You don't want to admit that you're an Internet dating junkie, so I'm giving you a story of how you met me. You can decide what you're doing in New York City and how we meet. That should give you your cover!"

I was amazed at his thoughtfulness.

"And, so you don't have to ask," he added, "I'll make sure there are two hotel rooms."

His voice sent goose bumps all over my body. The thought of finally seeing him was overwhelming.

"I love you." The words came out of my mouth before I could stop them. I wondered how Brad would respond.

"I love you, too," Brad replied.

It was hard to believe that our first e-mail was on March 4. God truly works in miraculous ways. I was amazed at what he had done in just twenty-three days: he had taken two broken hearts and, using one of his modern day inventions, the Internet, he healed his faithful servants and was creating a union that would serve him and testify to his truth. Now, on March 27, Brad and I would be looking onto each other's eyes for the first time.

God is amazingly awesome and true to his word—he promised beauty for ashes.

I packed carefully for my weekend in New York. Brad had planned a perfect weekend and had instructed me to bring two nice outfits, one evening dress, and some city tour clothes. Because it was March in New York, my Naples attire would require some retrofitting for temperatures below a balmy eighty degrees.

It was time for me to tell someone about my Internet love affair. Thus far, I had kept my secret, but I just had to tell Aly. Besides, there was the off-chance that I was about to flit off to New York with a murderer, and no one would know where I was. The last thing I wanted was to end up a footnote on *Unsolved Mysteries*.

"Hi, Aly. Got a minute?" I strolled into her office at The Preserve and pulled up a chair. My facial expression must have said it all.

"What are you up to? You look like the cat that ate the mouse," Aly said as I tried to stifle a smile.

As I erupted with the story of my Internet romance, she sat staring in disbelief.

"Are you crazy?" she asked. "What if he's the Kansas barrel murderer?"

Despite her protests, my gut told me I was doing the right thing, and when she realized I couldn't be dissuaded, Aly allowed herself to be pulled into the intrigue.

"I want to know every detail about your travel: airline flight numbers, hotel—you *are* getting a separate room, right?" Aly narrowed her eyes in a perfect imitation of our mother.

"Of course," I said. I'm sure my face glowed with excitement. "And I didn't even have to suggest that. Brad did."

"You just be careful! Call me as soon as you get there and give me his cell phone number. I want all of the facts before you leave town, missy. Do you understand me? If anything goes wrong, I'm calling the NYPD."

I flew direct to New York and was greeted by a limo driver holding a sign that had my name on it. *Nice touch.* I could feel that fluttering of fear beginning to brew in my stomach. After a twenty-minute ride, the driver pulled up to the Stanhope Hyatt and escorted me to the front desk. When I checked in, the front desk clerk handed me a package and a single red rose.

As I rode the elevator to my hotel room, I opened the package and read a letter from Brad, in which told me to catch a cab at five o'clock to the Empire State Building. There were three additional envelopes in the package. One contained the prepaid ticket to the Empire State Building's observation deck and a note warning me "not to rush"—he would wait for me. The second envelope contained cab fare. *What a gentleman!* The final envelope contained a love letter from Brad that I was to read on the way to our rendezvous.

I looked back at my watch. I had fifteen minutes to shake the airplane look and switch into an appropriate outfit.

As a resident of Naples, Florida, I was unaccustomed to the ways of a big city and called the concierge to have a cab waiting. I wasn't laughed at, but he explained that the cab would be taken care of once I was downstairs. Then I shifted into high gear and somehow managed to get ready quickly and make it to the hotel lobby. It was five o'clock Friday evening in New York City, and there were already three or four couples in line ahead of me waiting for a taxi. The bellman watched me, alone in a beautiful off-the-shoulder black fitted shirt, holding a single rose and some papers.

"Sir," I called to him in a pitiful plea. "I'm meeting the man of my dreams in thirty minutes at the Empire State Building. I've never met him. We've only corresponded by e-mail and phone. If I'm late . . ." The two couples ahead of me, unable to deny the romance of the situation, heard my story and stepped aside. The bellman practically threw himself into traffic to hail a cab for me.

"Get this beautiful lady to the Empire State Building . . . fast! She's meeting the man of her dreams." He slammed the door behind me, blew his whistle, and gave me the thumbs-up.

My stomach was now in a full-fledged stir. As I opened the third envelope, my hands began to shake. Was it the March cold that had blown through my Naples skin, or was it my nerves finally giving in because of what I was about to do?

> My Dearest Rose,
>
> I am so in love with you that it aches. My whole mind, body, and spirit are enveloped in a new reality. I feel like I have loved you forever. These days have engulfed me in a tidal wave of emotions unlike anything that I can remember.
>
> God's unbelievable, unimaginable, unprecedented blessing is

upon me; it is like the feeding of the five thousand, I pass you love, and receive back more than I sent.

The Lord blessed us with our very first live contact on Sunday, March 16 ... We first spoke of our love on the phone exactly four hours ... Sunday 3–16; John 3:16 interesting coincidence? "Whosoever believes in him shall not perish but have eternal life." Traditionally the focus is on "eternal" being forever. But recently my heart has been focused on having "life" ... Life is so much more full and rich and holy now with you, Rose, as my partner in the love of the Lord.

I always believed that I had been blessed with a good life. Only now am I witnessing the true magnitude of the Lord's blessing through your presence in my life, Rose.

My heart is yours and yours alone!

I love you ... Brad

As I read the letter, tears ran down my cheeks. I needed to repair my makeup before the final moment arrived.

We pulled up ten minutes past my expected time of arrival. After I cleared security and rode the first elevator up to the eightieth floor, my nerves broke loose. There was a mile-long line of tourists at the second elevator to the observation deck. I began to panic, and then I remembered Brad's words that he'd wait for me. Lost amid the sweatpants-clad tourists, I looked out of place in my evening outfit—and the rose didn't help matters.

I looked at Brad's note again. "If you have a hard time finding me, I'll be the man with the other eleven roses." Brad had scanned three photos of himself to send to me. Each looked like a different person. In one, with his eight-year-old daughter on his lap, he looked buff, young, and handsome. When I told him that photo was my favorite, he had laughed and joked that the photo was of him and his oldest daughter, who was now twenty.

As I daydreamed about who I should be searching for, two college girls in line finally mustered up the guts to ask me if this was, "like, a *Sleepless in Seattle* thing." I told them it was, and they nearly swooned.

"Oh, can we watch? This is, like, so romantic."

Then it hit me—they could provide the perfect screening opportunity by being the first through the door and giving me a chance to see him before he could see me.

The line had advanced and we, my two new girlfriends and I, were headed to the observation deck. I could feel my heart pounding. *Breathe, Rose, breathe.*

As the elevator opened on the eighty-sixth floor, I stepped off into the gift shop and spotted Brad, who was frozen from circling the observation deck in search of a woman wearing a black top. I knew it was the right man because he was carrying those eleven roses.

He looked up and then ... our eyes met. We each took a step into the other's arms. He was an angel sent straight from heaven—handsome, tall, fit, handsome, emerald green eyes, tall, dark ... did I say handsome? And young. First our eyes met, then our lips met, and then our bodies melted together as one.

We were totally unaware of our surroundings. At that moment the Empire State Building was, for us, the closest place to heaven as our hearts seemed to beat as one. When we finally let go, neither one of us spoke as we stepped back and looked deeply into each other's eyes, confirming that this was not a dream. We were startled back into the moment as the girls clapped with excitement and told our story to bystanders. We had just received our first standing ovation ... atop the Empire State Building. We walked to Times Square, where Brad had planned a romantic bottle of pink champagne at a restaurant overlooking the city. We held hands the entire walk and enjoyed absorbing each other's presence. Although we'd spent countless nights on the phone for hours at a time, on that night no words were necessary. We were recording senses, features, smells, and feelings. We arrived at the top of the Marriott Marquis, and Brad and I sat at a very small table for two, never once letting our hands drop. Our relationship had been intensified beyond belief.

It took about half an hour before we realized that the restaurant was revolving. We were so engrossed with each other that we thought the entire world was revolving around us.

It was a glorious weekend. Brad had prepared a wonderful tourist agenda for me. We visited the Statue of Liberty, walking all the way, I might add. At this point, I could see how he ran in the Boston Marathon, but I was not about to whine or complain about all the walking, I didn't even feel my feet touching the ground when I was with him. We enjoyed walking out to the Brooklyn Bridge to the spot where in the movie *Kate and Leopold* Meg Ryan jumped through the fabric of time to be with her love! Then we stopped at the horrific scene where the World Trade Center once stood. It was very emotional for us, we shared the sorrow and the tears for all of those people who lost a loved one that day.

We both loved sushi and enjoyed an early evening snack of tuna and some really potent wasabi! Brad had third row center tickets to *Nine* with Antonio Banderas, who was of no interest to me. I'd rather look at my love, my soul mate, my Brad.

As Sunday approached, I found it difficult to imagine that we would be leaving each other's side, returning to reality. Brad would be heading to Kansas, and I would be going back to Naples, to my case, to what would now be my new life. I was filled with excitement, joy, and hope—hope for the future, for my life, for my freedom from this horrible trial that lurked in the darkness of every happy moment.

Brad and I sat in the hotel lobby while we waited for the car to take me to the airport. I was overwhelmed with sorrow, and I didn't fight the tears that were now streaming down my face. The hard shell that I'd used to protect me from feeling anything over the past five years had shattered.

I had finally met my perfect match, my soul mate. I had spent an entire weekend hugging him, touching him, looking into his emerald green eyes and seeing a beautiful, compassionate heart and soul. I felt that it was vital to record his image, his smell, his hug into my very being so that I could survive without his physical touch until our next encounter. When would that be?

The tears continued to rush from my eyes. I wanted to be strong, but Brad's strength and love allowed me the moment that I had needed for the last eighteen months. His arms wrapped around me to provide comfort in my time of need. He would protect me; he would love me because of my weakness.

The moment finally arrived when the car service driver entered the lobby where we were lost in each other's arms. Brad walked me out to the car and hugged me so tight I thought we'd melt together. Holding my face in his strong hands he kissed me gently on the lips and promised that we would be together in two weeks and that we would talk on the phone for endless hours about our new lives. He gently closed the car door, signaled the driver to go, and stood waving until I could no longer see him. Though I sobbed all the way to the airport, I thanked God for giving me beauty for ashes, peace for despair, joy for sorrow, and then wondered, *Why do I feel so sad?*

Once we were in the air, I pulled my Bible out of my carry-on bag and opened it to the book of Isaiah. One of the scriptures that kept me strong during my trial was Isaiah 61:1–3: "The Spirit of the Sovereign Lord is on me ... He has sent me to bind up the brokenhearted ... to comfort all who mourn ... to bestow on them a crown of beauty instead of ashes, the oil of gladness instead of mourning, and a garment of praise instead of a spirit of despair."

If we had none other, this one Bible reference would suffice to tell us that we have a loving God who will light our way through the darkest night. He had provided the light I needed so that my broken heart could love again and that I could rest on the promise of his word that he was my Jehovah Jira, my provider, who had given me beauty for the ashes of my former life.

I thought about how I had wanted to do something positive for my community, so I had set up a corporation that would focus on education, communication, and believing that one's dreams could come true. It was aptly name Dreams Realized. Aly agreed to join me in my new adventure that we would kick off with a speaker series in Naples. My personal dream was to write a book—a book about all that my faith had brought me through. I had survived. No, I had thrived, and God had given me more than I could have ever dreamed.

I arrived back in Naples still spinning with joy from the surge of life that two romance-filled days had deposited. Brad was real. The moment I walked in the door, I booted up the computer and checked the answering machine.

"Hi, Rose, it's Jason." All the emotions I'd felt in New York raced back. "Woerner," the message continued. Hearing my attorney's name was like getting a slap in the face.

"Listen," he was saying, "I spoke to the prosecutor. Call me as soon as you get this message. It's time-sensitive."

The last thing I wanted to do was call him from home. I wanted some time to savor the feelings of being with Brad, my soul mate; feelings that had insulated me from the reality of my legal problems. But as much as I didn't want to think about my case, the worry of not knowing what Woerner had to say was robbing me of my joy. It only took five minutes before I had him on his cell phone.

"Where have you been all weekend?" He chided me as if I was a teenager and he'd caught me sneaking in after curfew. "I left you a time-sensitive message, and it takes you all weekend to return my call? Whoever he is, he must be pretty special for you to ignore someone who's busting his butt to keep yours out of jail."

I couldn't tell if Jason was snooping or simply poking fun. "I was out of town. I just got back. What's up?" The tone in his voice and the weekend call did not bode well and my stomach was beginning to turn from anxiety.

"On Friday I ran into Strickland having drinks here in Miami. We chatted for a while, and he knows he doesn't have any evidence that you've committed any crime. He's willing to work out a plea agreement if you're interested. I know that until now you and Peter have been fighting hard, and I agree with your stance. You're innocent and should never have been dragged into this mess. I think this is a great way out for you, Rose. There's still a ninety to ninety-five percent chance that if we go to trial, you'll have all of these charges against you dropped, but a trial is hundreds of thousands of dollars away. On the downside, that leaves a five to ten percent chance that a jury will convict you, and jail is not the right place for you, Rose."

"You got that right," I shrieked.

"I like you, Rose, and I appreciate your tenacity, your fight, and your belief that the justice system will work this out fairly, but there are just no guarantees on that. And I don't want all of your retirement money from selling your real estate ventures to be my son's college fund. You deserve so much more than you've been dealt—this trial, losing your business and your marriage, and everything. You are an inspiration, Rose, a pillar of strength. I want you to consider this deal."

I could hear the sound of the wind in his cell phone as I rubbed my temples and considered his words.

"Do you have any details?" I asked. "I'm not pleading guilty to a damn thing. I did not commit any crimes, and I'm not going to say I did so I can save money. My reputation has already been beaten to a pulp. I want to exit this case with my personal pride, my sense of honor, and truth."

"Here's the deal so far," Jason said, breathing a sigh of relief, as he must have realized that I was now open to discussing a plea bargain.

"You come to Miami on Tuesday, which oddly enough is April Fool's Day, and give an interview to Strickland and Ericka Haack. They know that you are their only hope. We tore Wood apart during the depositions. If he had a shred of credibility before the depositions, we stripped him of that. In discovery, the prosecutor provided some handwritten letters from Wood over the past six or eight months that describe 'prayer meetings' he holds in jail to get the inmates to confess their sins to him. Then he turns their confessions over to the prosecutor. He's working hard to get a reduced sentence, and anybody he can turn on he's doing it. One of the documents actually had a prisoner's name on it. They failed to redact it, and Wood is now scared to death. If that prisoner finds out that Wood ratted on him, he's a dead man. Wood was furious with Strickland over this exposure, and I'm sure he is being less than cooperative now."

I pictured Wood walking around prison constantly having to glance over his shoulder, and I actually felt pity for him.

But only for a second.

"Anyway," Jason continued, "their case is falling apart and they need someone with credibility, someone that they have only very little circumstantial evidence against, that can become a state witness. You're it. Listen, you think about this tonight, and I'll tell Strickland tomorrow that you will plead no contest to the money laundering. We'll word it exactly as it occurred. You did not receive the funds, and you did not deposit the funds; however, you were aware that Phillip Durkee received the funds in cash, and you failed to report his transaction to the government."

I nearly flew into a rage. "How is that my responsibility?" I demanded. "I mean, if you knew that your brother sold his house for cash, is it your responsibility as an American citizen to report a cash transaction that did not involve you? Give me a break!"

"Rose," Jason said, his voice taking on a more somber tone, "you need to get off the soap box for a minute and think about this. You will never get anyone who has ever read the *Collier Enquirer* to believe that you are not a scumbag developer who bribed the commissioners to get her projects approved. Who in Naples do you care about, anyway? Your friends know you're innocent, your family knows you're innocent, so screw anyone who says otherwise. This plea bargain will allow you to take a $20,000 vacation every month instead of paying me to fight with a crazy prosecutor who doesn't give two hoots about you. He'd just as soon put you in jail for thirty years and call it a win."

I had to admit that Jason was making sense. "Well, since you've put it that way," I said and managed a little laugh. "I'll give it some thought tonight. Call me tomorrow once you've negotiated with the devil. Be careful. His contracts are for eternity in hell. I'm expecting you to read between the lines for me."

After we hung up, I held the phone for a few minutes and thought about what I'd been offered. I could put this whole thing behind me in one day. Since I'd only be telling the truth, my testimony could benefit Peter and Andrew at their trial. But would I be giving in or giving up? Before I made any decisions, I wanted to let Peter know what I was considering. After all, we'd agreed to stick together until the end. I knew in my heart that Peter would never agree to anything short of a trial or a written and published apology from the prosecutor and the newspaper.

One very special gift that Brad gave me during our trip to New York was a new cell phone to "test." As the senior vice president of marketing for his company, he tested the new handsets before they were on the market, and I was to be his Florida market tester. I was thrilled, not only for the new gift, but because he still wanted to be connected after seeing me for the first time. The fact that he valued my opinion was a new experience for me too. This cell phone had the new picture feature; you know "Share it when it happens." It proved to be lots of fun and another way that Brad and I could share our daily lives.

Just then my new cell phone rang. It was Brad making sure that his new love had made it home safely and that she'd stopped crying. We talked for hours, mostly about the thrill of our weekend, the intensity of looking into each other's eyes when we talked. It was like being teenagers again, in love for the first time.

I decided to tell Brad about the plea bargain that had been put on the table, but I wanted to ease him into it.

"You believe that God miraculously matched us on eHarmony, right?" I asked.

"Of course, Rose. You are my angel."

I smiled and felt my face flush. "Thank you. And we both believe that he answered our prayers to heal our broken hearts. God has gone above and beyond the request with our relationship. He has wiped away the pain of divorce and replaced it with loyalty and trust. He's wiped away loneliness and replaced it with a caring and kindness. And I know you're not going to believe this one, but I think God is providing a way for me to exit the trial." I sighed with relief, unable to believe that so much good was happening for me—for us—at once.

"That's great! How?" Brad was as excited as I was. He had half-joked that he would be prepared to visit me in jail if it came to that, but this way, God's way, was so much better.

"I have to plead no contest to not receiving or depositing that $200,000. Doesn't that sound ridiculous?"

"It is," Brad sighed, knowing I wasn't going to get away without a scratch. "But let's not look a gift horse in the mouth. What else?"

"I have to let the prosecutor and his sidekicks interview me. They need me as a witness against Peter and Andrew on this transaction. The beauty is that I have no first-hand knowledge on what or how Andrew was involved with Wood or Durkee Senior except what I've heard at the depositions. So I can't help with that. As far as Peter is concerned, he's in my boat. Neither of us ever saw the money or deposited it."

"I think you've got to be very careful with Strickland. Don't trust him and don't go without your attorney. He only has one thing in his sights and its multiple convictions. What did you call it that he did to Hanover after his plea agreement? 'Violate' him? And he's now sleeping at the Collier County Jail every night for the next three hundred sixty-five days. Only answer the questions that he asks and only tell what you know personally, not from depositions or the newspaper."

Brad's voice remained firm. He wanted only to protect his little angel. I was amazed how quickly Brad had gotten up to speed on my case. He really cared about me, and although he was willing to succumb to weekend visits looking at me through bulletproof glass at the county jail, his real goal was to support me emotionally and help me make some really tough decisions.

"I know," I replied. "I'll listen carefully, don't you worry. I've seen Strickland try to trip witnesses up before." I was glowing with the love and support I was receiving from my soul mate. It was as if he were at my side, holding my hand, feeling my fears, and supporting my decisions and me.

I could hear Brad's voice strain with emotion as he continued. "I love you, Rose, and I would love for this whole mess to be behind you, behind us. I want you to be free from the burdens that this case is causing. But I understand that you don't want to give up the fight against injustice. This false accusation has cost you and Peter over a million dollars. You've got to think about you now, Rose—you, Taylor, Lauren, your family. They've been through a lot with you. You know that I'll stand beside you through it all, no matter what you decide. Do you want me to fly down there tomorrow to drive to Miami with you?" Brad's compassion and thoughtfulness was like a breath of fresh air.

"Don't be silly," I said, although I secretly hoped he wouldn't listen. "If you're flying anywhere to meet me, it's not going to involve a prosecutor and some attorneys."

"Speaking of our next meeting," he said, his voice changing to a more playful tone, "what are you doing Friday after next?"

I snuggled further down into my chair and adopted a similar tone. "Seeing you, I hope. Since you planned such a wonderful first trip, will you let me plan the next one?" I wanted to share the cost of our long-distance romance. We had decided in our early e-mails that a manageable long-distance relationship would include seeing each other every other weekend for at least a year. I glanced over at my calendar and began counting down the days until I could be held in Brad's arms again.

Thirty-two

My appointment for April 1 was set, and Aly, as she had every other time, insisted on being with me. We drove anxiously to Miami and arrived at the courthouse downtown where the prosecutor maintained his office.

"We're not in Kansas anymore, Dorothy," I quipped as I eyed our seedy environs. The courthouse in Miami is a place that tourists rarely see. Miami was recently awarded the dubious honor of being the poorest major city in America. The penthouse hotel suites and the contrasting rat infested slums are only a couple miles apart. For a tourist, one wrong turn on the way back to the airport could shatter all the beautiful images of Miami forever.

Aly and I felt our palms begin to sweat as we weaved through the maze of blighted downtown streets to the office of the prosecutor. It appeared that urban renewal had bypassed these parts of town. As Naples residents, we were highly overdressed for the occasion and looked grossly out of place.

My palms continued to sweat as we headed through building security, which was even more stringent than at the airport. Jason Woerner greeted us with a hug.

"This is off the record, Rose," Jason said as he gave me a pat of confidence. "The only way I agreed to this interview is by allowing them to ask questions and take notes, but not with you under oath. You will, of course, tell the truth, but I don't trust him. I think if he had you under oath he'd find a way to say you committed perjury and then violate your agreement. Once they've completed their interview, we'll compile a statement for you to write that will include their questions and your answers. You will only have to testify to that statement as a state's witness. My goal is to have you out by April 10. I don't mean to push you out, but I've got another trial coming up, and if I can settle your case, I can get on to saving my next innocent client."

Jason told Aly she would have to wait outside the meeting room. She hugged me and whispered, "I love you" in my ear. Tears rolled down her cheeks. She knew how hard this was for me.

It was amazing how different Strickland and Haack were when you were in their office and not on stage in front of a judge. It was like we were old pals. I remembered what Brad had said about Strickland, "He's the devil and is trying to lure you into believing that he is your friend." He only wants one thing: to see at least one Durkee and, of course, his original victim, Eugene Gannon, behind bars.

"Can we get you a drink, Rose? I know you like Mountain Dew." Strickland held up his empty bottle.

"Sure," I replied, keeping my guard up, "if you have diet. I can't afford the sugar."

"Can't help you there. We only have full strength. Hey, we also have some great Cuban coffee. Do you like that?" With a glance, Strickland got Haack to jump to attention and pour the coffee.

"I'll be right back," Strickland said cheerily. "Make yourself comfortable."

As Strickland and his minion left the room, Jason rested his hand on my shoulder and reminded me to relax and listen to the questions.

"I'll behave myself," I promised.

The hearing was filled with questions that I'd already heard a thousand times, everything from the cash transaction to the initial meeting of the "boys' club" on Coliseum Golf. My story—the truth—had not changed since the first time I'd met this prosecutor eighteen months earlier.

Finally, Jason looked at his watch. "We've been at this for eight hours. You've asked her everything about the case more than once, and she's provided you with truthful answers. She's got to drive back to Naples, and the traffic is going to be horrible. Do you have any more questions?"

"Nope, you've been very helpful, Rose," Strickland said, and he smirked as if I'd dropped some new tidbit of information that would have me or someone else behind bars before the evening news. But I'd witnessed him in action enough times to know that was just his style and that I hadn't put Peter or Andrew in any more danger than they already were.

Jason said to Ericka, "When you've written up the questions, just e-mail them to me. Rose will put her answers into a statement form. We'll review it and hopefully have it turned around and the deal ready by the end of the week." He stopped to look at his calendar. "Have you spoken to Judge Heyward about this yet?" Jason asked Strickland.

"Of course, and he would prefer that we do this plea in Sarasota. That way he doesn't have to come to Naples just for this. It may work to your benefit, Rose, that the media may not want to make the two-hour drive to catch you one more time—before the trial, that is." Strickland wanted to remind me that I was his after this plea agreement.

"How does the tenth look for you guys?" Jason said, keeping us on track.

"We'll have to check with the judge," Haack said, "but as far as our schedule goes, we can do it, no problem. I'll call Heyward's office tomorrow and see what we can do to accommodate your request."

Ericka thanked Jason and me and quickly excused herself, leaving just the three of us in the room.

"Does your client understand that once she's out of this case, she should not be talking to the other defendants?" Strickland wanted to keep Peter feeling like I'd flipped. Before I could answer, Jason did.

"They are neighbors and business partners, for God's sake," Jason snapped. "Your request is ridiculous. They've been living and breathing this crap for almost two years. No deal. You'll just have to know that Rose is honest and truthful and will testify to her statement under oath in the courtroom. Nothing more!"

Jason stood up and pulled me quickly from the room.

"Drive safe, Rose," Strickland replied. "Tell Peter we said hello."

Yeah, and I've got a few things I'd like to tell you, I thought.

Strickland had returned to his sarcastic self so quickly you'd have thought someone flipped a switch.

Once we were out of hearing range, Jason slipped an arm around my shoulders and gave me a congratulatory hug. "You did great, Rose, really. They tried to trip you up, but you know the truth and that truth is about to set you free. Drive carefully. I'll e-mail you the questions as soon as I get them. See you in Sarasota." I hugged Jason and thanked him once again for being such a great attorney and trusted friend.

Aly and I said good-bye to Jason, and as I slipped behind the wheel of my car, I felt a great weight lifted from my shoulders. This horrible trial was soon to be over, at least for me. The only thing I'd have to worry about was being on the witness stand for the Durkee, Gannon, and Shanahan trial.

I got some e-mails from Adam Woerner calling me a "traitor" and "weak." He was just kidding, of course. I think he secretly wished that Peter would do what I had done, but that deal was not on the table for him, not yet anyway. Peter was determined to go to trial and regain his reputation—no matter what it cost.

Jason Woerner had my statement and the agreement tied up in a beautiful bow by the time it came for me to plea in front of Judge Heyward. Knowing that the *Collier Enquirer* would probably follow me all the way to Sarasota for this new development in my saga, I decided to send off an e-mail to my friends and family before the paper distorted the facts yet again.

Dear family and friends,

First, I would like for each of you to know how much I love you. You have all stood by my side during very difficult times, most importantly over the last eighteen months. I cannot begin to find the words that can tell you how much your investment of time, words, standing by my side, or simply praying for God's end to this trial has meant to me. I have stood firm on God's promise that no weapon formed against me would prosper (Isaiah 54:17) and that my God would awaken and plead my case (Psalm 35). He has.

When I was arrested, the thought of fighting with all that I had emotionally, financially, and ethically to prove my innocence and to be vindicated was all that mattered to me. Many of you suggested that if there were a way out, to take it. During the last eighteen months I could not consider that.

With the new judge and our first introductory hearing behind us, my lawyer offered the following. He is sure that we can win this case—all witnesses provide testimony that I am innocent of the charges—although it might take another $200,000, not including the time, energy, emotional distress, and possibility of an appeal. He also offered, based on the discovery and testimony of all state witnesses, that now would be a good time to approach the prosecutor with a plea.

We have reached an agreement. I will plea Nolo Contendere (no contest) to a misdemeanor on count fourteen, which is the financial transaction count. Adjudication will be withheld (no record of the misdemeanor), and I will happily serve three hundred hours of community service at the Harry Chapin Food Bank for children in Collier County.

I provided a truthful statement to the prosecutor last week, which may or may not assist him in his case. It is important to remember that it is my truthful testimony that would have been and will be provided at a trial. All charges in the Coliseum Golf case against me are dropped; count fourteen did not involve Coliseum, so as you read the regurgitation of the Collier Enquirer, it is important that my friends and family understand that all charges against me are dropped in that case. I have pled Nolo Contendere (no contest) to a regulatory reporting misdemeanor offense. I have not admitted guilt to anything, and adjudication is withheld. This means that in the eyes of the law, I am not even a convicted misdemeanant. I am also entitled to have my record sealed when *the proceedings are complete. I will not be placed on probation. I simply must do the community service, and as you all know, serving our less fortunate children in Collier County is what Rose and Dreams Realized is all about!*

To boil this down to a simple example, if I had been given a ticket for speeding, I have decided not to go to the courthouse and instead contest the ticket (as you know I don't speed). However, I will go to driving school to avoid the points on my driving record.

On Thursday, as I drive to Sarasota where the judge will accept my plea, I ask that you pray for my supernatural protection that the Collier Enquirer will report the truth (stretch goals prayer warriors!) and know that this decision was prayerfully considered and acceptable to my heavenly Father.

"For this reason I am telling you, whatever you ask for in prayer, believe (trust and be confident) that it is granted to you, and you will get it" /Mark 11:24.

All of my love and appreciation for your prayers, support, and love,

Rose

After sending the e-mail, I could sleep soundly knowing that the next day everyone who knew and loved me would understand. Now all I had to do was find the right way to tell them about Brad.

Thirty-three

On the morning of April 10, I awoke feeling renewed. Today I would finally be free from the life-sucking energy of the one man whose accusations had damaged so many lives. Yet despite my high hopes about the promises I had received, I still felt a small itch of worry about Martin Strickland. To quote his words in that day's paper, "My only answer is, nothing is finalized until it is finalized." Until I was standing in front of the judge in Sarasota, I wasn't popping any bottles of champagne.

I tried not to let even the thought of that devil with a JD degree get me down. Instead, I concentrated on the positive impact on my life, the most significant of which was my finances. I'd no longer have to budget, scrap, and borrow to pay Woerner $20,000 every month. The thought of all those extra zeroes in my bank account filled me with elation, and I did a little money dance. Once that was out of my system, I headed to the shower to prepare for my 1:00 p.m. appointment in Sarasota. There was no way I was going to be late.

To save me the $350-per-hour drive, Jason was flying from Miami to Sarasota, where I would pick him up at the airport. We had an hour before the hearing, and we stopped at a diner directly across the street from the courthouse for a quick bite. Although eating was the last thing on my mind, Jason needed his strength for the hearing.

"Strickland is eager to get your matter behind him before the hearings start next week," Jason said between bites of his Cuban sandwich. "Judge Heyward is expected to decide the location of the trial and determine whether Strickland improperly used evidence from your immunized statements that you all gave in the first Coliseum Golf investigation to charge the defendants in the second investigation. He needs you more on the witness stand than he does at the defendant's table." He glanced at my barely touched chef's salad and then at my furrowed brow. "Rose, you're doing the right thing. I know that it was a hard decision to make, but it's the right one. The deal that you got, it's like a speeding ticket. You'll have no record." Jason hesitated only to take another bite.

"Oh, I have a record all right," I joked. "Maybe not a felony, but a record of losses that this crazy case has cost me, many of which I'm better off without."

I didn't have to mention any details. Jason got my drift and gave me a compassionate smile. I used that as a chance to segue into my new romance. "You know, Jason, I've met a wonderful man."

Jason dropped his sandwich to the plate in surprise then quickly changed his expression to one of joy.

"I guess that explains the tan and your relaxed look!" he exclaimed, clearly delighted for me. "Come on, Rose, confession time!"

I could feel my face glow as the words spilled out of me. "Meeting him," I began, "and feeling so deeply loved and supported has made this decision an easy one. You'll never believe how we met, but I don't have time for that story now. His name is Brad, and he is honest, loyal, and caring."

I gave Woerner a playful wink. "We met for the first time," I continued, "on the observation deck of the Empire State Building."

"In New York City?" he asked, surprised.

"Can you believe it? Our next meeting is tomorrow. We'll meet in the Atlanta airport and then fly to Amelia Island to enjoy my newfound freedom." I was wasting no time in putting this plea deal behind me and moving on with my life.

"Well now, missy, you've been doing more than legal research on your case, haven't you?" Jason flashed an impish grin before shoving the last bite into his mouth. He stood up, looking at his watch. "Let's get this over with so that you can sail away into the sunset."

As we left the diner, I tried to catch a glimpse of the scene outside the courthouse. "Do you think that there will be any media mongers there today?"

"Of course, Rose. You're the biggest news in Naples. Don't think for a minute that the cameras and the paper won't be lurking at the steps of the courthouse. You should consider making a statement. This is your last chance, and you finally have my permission." Jason hugged me playful around the shoulder as we marched across the street to my destiny.

I began to rehearse my statement as we approached the stairs to the Sarasota Courthouse. As Jason had anticipated, both the news channel reporters and the *Collier Enquirer* were present and awaiting my arrival. Jason and I walked right past them and into the building, where for the first time in the last eighteen months I joined him at the defense table. I had always been seated in the galley with the jury box to my right. But this time I was crossing through that swinging gate. My heart began to pound, and I fought to keep the confident smile on my face that I'd become famous for. "The nonstop smile of Rose Visconti" started many a sentence in the *Collier Enquirer*, so much so that you would have thought they had a quota to meet.

I maintained my smile as I remembered the words of James: "... count it all joy when ye fall into various trials, knowing this, that the testing of your faith worketh patience. But let patience have her perfect work, that ye may be perfect and entire, lacking nothing" (James 1:2, KJV). I was now free, in love, and happy. I was no longer worried about the financial issues of running a company, its three hundred employees, or the one thousand residents with their myriad needs and desires. I now had time to be a good and loving mother to my girls. I knew who I was and what my purpose on this earth was. It was a horrible ordeal, one I would never wish on anyone, but it was a valuable lesson. I had relied on my business to make me happy. I needed the accolades of the employees, the residents of each community, and my peers to feel fulfilled. That role should have been filled through my faith and my family.

I was a certifiable workaholic. I had sacrificed time with my family for the love of strangers who had disappeared from my life because of the trial. But God is all about second chances, and he delivered! I was ready to start anew the very next day.

I smiled as the court clerk instructed, "All rise. The Honorable Judge Steven Heyward presiding."

The only sound I could hear over the pounding of my heart was the clicking of cameras. I took a deep breath, thanked God for seeing me through to this victorious point, and waited for instructions.

"Please be seated," Judge Heyward said as he shuffled papers. "It looks as if Rose Visconti is here to enter into a plea agreement with the state. Is that correct?" Judge Heyward looked over his glasses at Strickland, who jumped obediently to his feet.

"Yes, Judge, that is correct," Strickland replied in his usual obsequious manner. "Ms. Visconti is here and we have an agreement." Strickland stretched his neck and pulled at his shirt, which was too tight and obviously uncomfortable.

"Mr. Woerner," Judge Heyward said, turning to my lawyer. "I am disappointed to hear that Ms. Visconti is pleading out. I was looking forward to some real lawyering from you in this case."

"You still have one Woerner left," said Jason, referring to his brother Adam's representation of Peter. "We try to have one Woerner on every case."

The judge laughed. "I suppose Adam will have to do," he said, "but don't tell him I said that."

I began to feel a little more comfortable. That was the first time Judge Heyward had displayed a sense of humor. "Mr. Woerner, have you fully advised your client on the terms of this agreement?"

Jason stood as he addressed Judge Heyward. "Yes, Your Honor, I have."

"Please have your client stand to be sworn in."

My knees temporarily weakened as I remembered my previous experience of being sworn in at the Collier County Courthouse, after which I had been processed like a common criminal.

"Please state your name for the record," the judge said, his tone matter-of-fact.

"Rose Visconti."

Judge Heyward first asked a series of questions about my mental state to be sure that I was not under duress, and we then moved to the actual sentencing.

"There will be no finding of guilt on the misdemeanor charge, and you will not serve any probation. You have agreed to two hundred fifty hours of community service at the Harry Chapin Food Bank in Naples, and either another fifty hours of community service to the food bank or a check of $2,500 donation to the charity. You will also pay a fine of $2,500 to the Florida Department of Law Enforcement and a $2,500 fine to the State Attorney's Office of the 11th Judicial Circuit. If you willfully fail to perform the community service within one year, you will be sentenced to six months in the Collier County Jail. Do you understand all of this, Ms. Visconti?"

"I do," I responded with my famous smile.

And that was it. We were done.

I had to sign my sworn statement and some other administrative papers, and then I was truly free. Once that was done, I returned to the defense table for the last time to write out the three required checks. The cameras were snapping away, and for the first time, I felt more like a movie star than an accused felon. I smiled straight into the cameras. The photographers looked shocked.

Lila Croxton, the reporter for the *Collier Enquirer*, had waited patiently for us to emerge from the courtroom before asking Jason for a comment.

"Rose Visconti," Jason declared in a proud, booming voice, "would not enter a plea of guilty because she isn't guilty. We tried to delay the plea deal to avoid traveling to Sarasota, but the prosecutor wanted this matter behind him before the series of hearings begin on April 21."

Strickland was close behind and offered his own statement.

"Because of the state sentencing guidelines," the prosecutor began, officious as ever, "and the fact that Visconti would be a first-time offender, she likely would not have faced jail time even if convicted of all charges. I agreed to Visconti's plea because the state's case against her was the weakest of the now remaining three defendants, Durkee, Shanahan, and Gannon. Visconti's testimony could have influenced the jury and weakened the state's case. We could have convicted her of all of the charges, and under Florida guidelines, she still may not have gone to jail. The plea was in the best interest of the state."

I was right behind Strickland to sing my final song.

"Would you like to make a statement, Ms. Visconti?" Croxton smiled gently.

"I thank God for the patience, perseverance, and strength for this personal trial. I have no further comment. Thank you."

Just as I made it around the corner, I ran into a news anchor waiting at the front door.

"Come on, Rose," he said as if we were old friends. "This is your last hurrah! Tell Collier County how you feel."

I took a deep breath and realized he was right. They had had more than their fair say. I deserved a word in my hour of triumph. I looked straight into the lens and let it roll.

"I am thankful that this nightmare is finally behind me. I also know that no matter what I say right now on these courthouse steps, you, the residents of Collier County, have already made up your minds and that I cannot in a short time change how you feel. You have believed what you've read in the paper without question and have already tried and convicted us.

"I thank God for the strength and courage to have survived the false accusations that have been brought against me.

"Today, all of those charges have been dropped by the state.

"To my family and friends, thank you for all of your support and love."

I smiled and continued my descent of the courthouse steps, hearing the cameras snapping all the way. I couldn't wait for the first time to see the paper tomorrow, to see if Croxton would report the story truthfully.

"You did it!" Jason said, beaming like a proud parent. "And you looked great on camera." He hugged me for what would be the last time.

"Thank you so much for all that you have done," I said, trying to keep from crying. "You've been so much more than an attorney. You've become my friend, my defender. Thank you for believing in me and for doing such a great job defending me."

He patted my shoulder. "Come on, I've got a flight to catch—and I guess you do, too."

I could hardly wait to call Brad and tell him the great news. His girlfriend was free! The drive from Sarasota to Naples was filled with phone calls to my family thanking them for their unwavering support.

Tomorrow I'd be on a plane to see my love, and I wouldn't need the permission of a bondsman to go. I was truly free.

That evening was filled with family celebration. Peter even joined in, teasing me about being a traitor. He was filled with even more fire to fight the good fight.

"Somebody has to have some principles around here," Peter roared.

"My principal is earning interest in the bank, thank you," I responded with a grin.

"I may need to borrow some of that to keep up the fight!"

I needed to do some final packing for my early departure to Amelia Island and was anxious to move this party to a successful end. Only Aly knew where I was going for my real celebration, and she gave me a wink as she headed out the door.

"Have a restful weekend," she told me.

I tuned into the nightly news and was pleasantly surprised by the clip that they showed on my case.

"Rose Visconti had all of the Coliseum Golf charges dropped today in a plea deal with the state," the perky news anchor reported. "She pleads no contest to a misdemeanor for not reporting the cash that she did not receive. Ms. Visconti agreed to an on-camera interview following her meeting with Judge Heyward."

Although my hair was blowing and the sun was making me squint, I looked okay for a forty-something woman who'd been put through the wringer the past two years. I taped the interview so that Brad could celebrate properly with me the next day.

As soon as I woke up the next morning, I raced to the end of the driveway to see how the paper had portrayed the plea deal.

Just as I had suspected, it was front-page news and in living color. They had captured a wonderful picture of me smiling, of course, and talking to my attorney. The headline read "Coliseum Golf; Visconti enters plea to misdemeanor charge," and continued by saying, "Visconti, looking tanned and relieved, entered her plea to Judge Heyward and said her faith in God is what has gotten her through the eighteen-month-long nightmare, which she wants to put behind her."

"I don't believe it. They printed my quote!" I said out loud. I thought I was alone, but then spotted Peter at the end of his driveway.

"Nice picture, Ms. Visconti," he said, smiling. "Where are you off to today?"

"A writer's conference," I heard myself say. "I can finally get started writing our story."

Oh, that little white lie came out way too easily. I'll have to find a writers conference to attend, and soon! I continued reading my paper as I walked back to my house.

"Have fun, Ms. Visconti. And remember—you're on our side, right?" Peter snickered.

"Of course, I am. I'm on our side, the side of truth, and the truth will set you free, Peter. If you're willing to take a plea deal, you could save yourself a couple hundred thousand bucks." Of course, I knew he was too stubborn and proud to accept.

"I'm fighting till the end!" he declared. He was obsessed with his case. Next week, the judge would be deciding if it would be in Naples or Sarasota.

Thirty-four

I began attending the hearings as a spectator. For the first time in two years, I entered the courtroom as a free citizen. But I was still haunted by the feeling that I'd had while my trial was continuing, that as quickly as my freedom returned, it could be taken away by Strickland. Part of me wanted to stay far away from the court scene, but I knew I needed to show support for Peter and Andrew and to gather all of the facts that were being presented in the final weeks.

The purpose of today's hearing was for Judge Heyward to decide if charges should be dropped against Peter Durkee and Andrew Shanahan. This issue was whether Strickland had illegally used evidence from the immunized sworn statements they made to the first state prosecutor. If so, it would deprive them of their Fifth Amendment rights against self-incrimination.

Adam Woerner was first to address Judge Heyward.

"Your Honor," he began, "the *Collier Enquirer* has polluted the jury pool by publishing my client's sworn immunized statement and other evidence not likely to be submitted as evidence in the trial. The newspaper has called for the conviction of my client before the trail has even begun. Your Honor, potential jurors would know that a failure to convict Durkee, Shanahan, and Gannon would subject them to the extreme abuse of the *Collier Enquirer*." He paced the length of the jury box as if it were occupied.

Strickland jumped up from his chair in protest. "Your Honor, if I may," he objected. "Trials of some high-profile serial killers in Florida, such as Ted Bundy and Danny Rolling, have been held in the towns in which the murders occurred."

"The difference, Mr. Strickland," Adam immediately shot back, "is that the victims' families weren't seated as jurors. The Collier County citizens are the alleged victims in the Coliseum Golf case. Using your argument, Mr. Strickland, the trial should be moved because of the effect this case has had on the population of Naples."

"I agree with Mr. Woerner." Judge Heyward's voice rang strongly throughout the courtroom. "The publicity surrounding the case has been so prolific and far-reaching that it would be next to impossible to seat a fair and impartial jury in Collier County."

Strickland looked defeated. Adam asked the judge for permission to continue. "Your Honor, it is clear that the charges against Peter Durkee for racketeering conspiracy and conspiracy to launder money trace back to Gannon's statement to the Ethics Commission. Further, Your Honor, FDLE investigator Ben Thistle used evidence from Peter Durkee's sworn statement in a chronology of the investigation and in a statement that he wrote when he closed the case back in 1998. Mr. Strickland used those documents to charge Mr. Durkee."

Judge Heyward addressed the attorneys. "I have listened for hours to what was painfully tedious testimony, and I'm going to set some deadlines. The prosecution has until May 16 to submit final arguments. The defense team has thirty days thereafter to respond. A final response for the prosecution is set for June 16. After I have reviewed the submissions, I will decide whether the defense attorneys were right when they claimed evidence used to charge Durkee and Shanahan was derived from their sworn immunized statements." The judge pushed back his chair.

The court administrator instructed the room to rise as the judge left.

"Why are they making such a big deal over these old immunized statements?" Peter asked Adam.

"Because the Fifth Amendment protects individuals against self-incrimination. Evidence derived from immunized statements cannot be used to charge suspects. They absolutely, without any doubt, used your statements to charge you. Now the burden of proof that such evidence was not used is on Strickland." Adam gathered his papers and shoved them into his briefcase. "Let's get out of here."

Just two days following the hearing, the *Collier Enquirer* begrudgingly reported that Judge Heyward agreed to a change of venue for the racketeering conspiracy trial of two of the remaining three defendants, citing prolific and far-reaching media coverage, which Judge Heyward was quoted as describing as "intense, consistent, and chronic."

Andrew was adamant about his trial being in Naples. Although he knew that the *Collier Enquirer* had biased the majority of the town's residents, Andrew had grown up here and wanted to be tried by his peers. He was finally granted his wish to be tried in Collier County.

Legal motions on whether to throw out the conspiracy-to-launder charges against Durkee and Shanahan worked their way to the Second District Court of Appeals, while the defense team pulled out all the stops to get the charges dropped before a trial.

Here is the editorial that followed the ruling on the money laundering:

> **Money Laundering Within Scope of Corruption Case (May 22, 2003)**
> Down but not out. That covers the prosecution's posture on money-laundering charges against two of the three remaining Coliseum Golf defendants.
>
> Hurrah for special prosecutor Martin Strickland's inclination to fight an appeal court's set-aside of the charges because, incredibly, judges could not see the connection between cash and what was going on with Coliseum Golf. The court said the fundamental charges against developer Peter Durkee and his attorney, Andrew Shanahan, that they arranged the delivery of a suitcase crammed with $200,000 in cash, out of the view of the IRS and a development investor's spouse, from Tennessee to Naples, somehow exceeded Gov. Jeb Bush's executive order for Strickland to prosecute "all matters pertaining to or arising from allegations of public corruption and racketeering pending against

> Eugene Gannon, Evan Hanover, Phillip Durkee, and any and all additional individuals that were involved in these matters."
>
> Money is at the heart of this criminal corruption case and Gov. Bush's directive to the special prosecutor, which the governor himself has reiterated twice, seems to include following the money.

Since the charges were now expanded, Judge Heyward moved Andrew's trial from August 4 to November 3, and Durkee and Gannon's trial from November 3 to January 5. The delay meant more legal fees for Peter and Andrew, and I continued to be thankful that I was no longer donating to the Woerner college fund.

I took advantage of being "retired" and enjoyed traveling with Brad. I had been a prisoner of the legal process for too long and was ready to be free to travel without notifying a bondsman. Brad had banked a lot of vacation time and was happy to finally enjoy some time off from the Kansas heat. Seeing it fit to take our relationship to the next level, he took me to California to meet his children, his parents, and his brother and sister. We had a wonderful weekend visit with his family before taking off in a convertible to see the California coastline.

We finished our tour with a weekend in the romantic rolling hills of wine country. It was there that Brad told me he had already planned a trip to Paris for us the following month. I was elated to be realizing my lifelong dream of visiting the City of Love with my soul mate.

We arrived in Paris on July 12, dropped our bags at the Hotel San Regis and were off to the Louvre and the Arc de Triomphe. The concierge confirmed our dinner reservations at Jules Verne, the restaurant atop the Eiffel Tower, where we would have a stunning view of the city we had toured all day. When we arrived at the Eiffel Tower, there was a huge crowd waiting to go to the top, owing to the fact that it was the weekend leading up to Bastille Day.

"Let's just go to the restaurant," I suggested. "They have a private elevator, and then after dinner we can go to the top." I was hungry and did not want to chance missing dinner at this famed restaurant.

"Great idea." Brad smiled warmly as he grabbed my hand. "But there's no need to worry, Rose. In Europe, dinner is usually after nine. Even if we take the private lift to Jules Vern, we will still need a ticket to the top of the Eiffel Tower. You stay here, and I'll be right back with the tickets."

Brad returned to the elevator line with our tickets just as it was my turn to step on. "You just made it," I said as I hugged him the entire ride to the top. When the doors opened, the sights before us were breathtaking. Brad had a particular sight he wanted me to see, and no crowd was getting in his way. We worked our way to a secluded corner that showcased the Louvre.

"See," Brad stood behind me. I could feel his strong body pressing into mine, and I could smell his skin and feel the beat of his heart against my back. "That is how much ground we covered today—The Louvre, Arc de Triomphe. Hand me your camera so I can take a picture." Brad gently turned me around to face him so that I could hand him the camera in the tight space.

The wind whipped across the platform through the grate floor and sides of the tower. As I began to shrug off the camera case, Brad reached for it, but it dropped to the floor. A second later, he was crouched down on the grate flooring.

"Are you all right?" I looked down at him with concern when suddenly he gazed up with tears in his eyes. He grabbed both of my hands but did not stand up. *What is he doing?* For a split second, I thought I was only imagining what was happening. "Rose," Brad began, his voice so strong and warm that it seemed to calm the winds that gusted about us. "You have made all of my dreams come true. Will you marry me?"

"Yes." I didn't have to give it a moment's thought. I knew that God had sent him and that I loved him.

Brad reached into his pocket and pulled out a diamond engagement ring. As I looked down at him perched on the grate flooring, all I could think was, *Don't drop it!*

"I will love you forever," Brad whispered as he slipped the ring on my finger. "I will be faithful to you and you alone. Thank you for saying yes."

The next day we drove to Normandy and planned our entire wedding along the way, choosing New Year's Eve for our pink-champagne celebration. We decided that the best way to blend our families would be to spend more than one or two days with all of us together. Brad and I opted for a Union Cruise, a weeklong cruise right after Christmas.

The only thing clouding our joy was the two trials. I would have to take the stand in both, one before our wedding and one the day after we arrived home from our cruise.

Thirty-five

October opened with some favorable rulings for our former attorney, Andrew Shanahan. Judge Heyward declared that the statute of limitations had run out on four of the seven charges against him.

It seemed like so much time had passed between my plea deal, and now I was about to testify on behalf of the state at the trial of my lawyer, my friend. I did not want to testify again my friend. Before facing Strickland again, I would need God's protection over me.

My Biblical Feast classes were building up my faith and preparing me for any situation I would encounter. When Andrew's trial date was only a day away, I asked my class to pray with me. By now everyone in the class had grown close, and we routinely prayed for each other's needs. Patricia Hilliard led us in a mighty prayer of protection as the others stood in agreement. She closed the prayer with one final request, "Lord, if it be at all possible, we pray that Rose will not have to testify as a witness for the state." I left the church knowing that I was ready for whatever lay before me.

That evening, I received a call at home from Martin Strickland. "Hi, Rose. It's Martin. How are you?"

Chills ran up my spine at the mere sound of his voice, however innocuous the words. "I'm fine, thanks."

"Listen, I just want to go over your statement with you before tomorrow, okay?"

I steeled myself. "I have been over my statement, Mr. Strickland, and I will testify to that statement under oath tomorrow." I did not want to get into any extended conversations with him.

"Let me just review the line of questioning so that you're prepared. I don't want to catch you off-guard. This is for your benefit, Rose." His voice rang of evil, yet as I recalled the prayers of my friends earlier in the evening a sense of peace settled over me.

I reluctantly listened to what he had to say for over an hour. It was almost 11:00 p.m.

"Hold on, Rose." I could hear Strickland's muffled voice talking to Ericka Haack. "I've got to go. We've got Shanahan's lawyers on the phone in the other room. Do you have any questions?"

"Where do I meet you?" As a state witness, I wasn't sure if there was a pre-meeting room.

"Come to our offices on the eighth floor. That way we can go over any last-minute details before we go to the courtroom. We'll see you in the morning." Strickland tried to sound friendly, but I needed to remember he was still the enemy.

I was up with the first light, unable to sleep. I showered and dressed, praying all the while that it would end before it began. I pulled into the parking lot I decided to call Peter to make sure he wasn't late.

"Good morning, Ms. Visconti. Where are you?" Peter's voice was gloomy.

"Sitting in the parking lot at the courthouse. Are you on your way?" My heart was beating rapidly.

"Don't bother. Andrew has joined your club," Peter snapped, his disappointment evident. "He made a deal with the devil last night after midnight. The only thing the judge will be doing this morning is reading him the riot act for seating a jury and then wasting everyone's time."

"Are you next, Peter?"

"Heck, no!" I could almost picture steam escaping his nostrils. "I'm going to the mat with that SOB. Strickland. There is no way in hell that he'll get me to admit to anything—not even a speeding ticket. Mark my words. I guess you can go on home."

"What did Andrew plead to? Do you know?" I wanted to have some information before I checked in with Strickland. I did not trust him and did not want to go into his office completely ignorant.

Peter seemed to calm a bit. "He pleaded guilty to two misdemeanor charges of failing to report a cash transaction. They dropped all felony charges of racketeering, racketeering conspiracy, and unlawful compensation. See, their case is so stinking weak that the only thing they have been able to get you and Andrew to do is plea to seeing some cash. If the two of you could have just stuck it out a little longer we could have beaten this guy at his game. You two are just…"

As his voice trailed off, I wondered about the words that had gone unspoken. "Anyway," he concluded, "I'm fighting until the end. If you see Andrew, pat him on the back and tell him we love him."

"Okay, I'm going in to see your favorite person now. I'll call if he wants to talk to you!" I laughed and was happy to hear Peter do so too.

"No, thanks. Hey, you can tell him I said to shove—"

"Be nice. Your phone is probably bugged! You don't want to be all alone as a target and calling Strickland ugly names, do you?"

After saying good-bye to Peter, I walked up to the Special Prosecutor's Office as if I did not know about the deal.

"Good morning," I said, opening the door to a large room sparsely furnished with folding tables and banker boxes. Our pictures were now plastered onto a giant white board as "Exhibit One." *I see some things have not changed.*

As I scanned the room, I noticed several other exhibits that were ready to go to trial today. Just as my eyes finished their sweeping, they found Strickland as he scurried from the coffee station to the computer, where Haack was busily typing as her boss barked out orders.

"Have a seat," Strickland ordered as he continued with Haack. "Have you heard that Shanahan pled out last night? He could have saved us all a lot of time and money doing this a long time ago. He knew that the jury trial would land him in jail. I don't know why I'm being so nice to him with this deal. Strickland was so melodramatic.

"We just have to finish typing up the plea agreement so that

Andrew can sign it in front of the judge," Strickland continued. "You know, Rose, you may want to encourage your partner to do the same. Heyward doesn't like wasting his time or a jury's just to have the defendant chicken out the night before. And I may not be in such a good mood when we get to Durkee's trial." Strickland peered at me through his smudged glasses.

"I don't think he's interested, but you should really talk to Adam Woerner, not me." I had no desire to be in the middle. As I sat waiting for my dismissal from Strickland, I thanked God for once again answering my prayers.

The cup had passed. Although I was testifying to the truth, and I knew that no crimes were committed, the very act of being a witness for the prosecution did not sit well with me at all.

Brad and I welcomed December with excitement—only thirty days until we were to be married. Miraculously all of our family members—thirty-nine in all—were available to join us on the Union Cruise. Our ship, the *Costa Atlantica*, would leave from Fort Lauderdale on December 27 and visit Puerto Rico, the Dominican Republic, and finally on New Year's Eve, St. Thomas, where we would have our wedding ceremony. We had planned a beach ceremony, with the blue waters behind us, tropical flowers all about, violins and harps, and, of course, pink champagne.

The final scheduled stop on the cruise was Nassau, after which we would head back to Fort Lauderdale on January 4—just in time for Peter's trial to start. I knew that I had to put it out of my mind. I had to claim the same victory over Peter's situation as I had been given in Andrew's. *Lord, just let this cup pass—one more time.*

In mid-December, Peter filed a motion to separate his trial from Gannon's. The hearing was to be held on December 22.

Judge Heyward listened carefully to Adam's plea for dismissal and ruled immediately. "There will be no dismissal of this case, gentlemen, and there will be no more delays. This trial will begin on January 5, 2004."

The judge left the courtroom. Adam knew that additional motions to dismiss would fall on deaf ears. It was time for the battle. The new year would see Coliseum Golf finally come to trial after six and a half years.

Brad and I had a wonderful Christmas celebration with our family in Naples. Taylor and Lauren opened their presents with the same gleefulness that they had when they were little. Christmas was for every age!

I had received the best Christmas gift ever—my freedom from this case and a wonderful man who was about to be my husband. We would be leaving in just two days for our Union Cruise.

As part of our cruise gift to our families, Brad and I wrote a different love thought for each day and delivered it to their cabins each night so that they—our brothers and sisters, mothers and fathers, and sons and daughters—could experience the love that was overflowing in us. We made sure that each cabin had the book *The Five Love Languages* by Gary Chapman and a romantic CD of love songs for them to snuggle up with at night. Our goal was to share the love that we had been so blessed with, to hope that if any of them had allowed the world to rob them of that special love—that passion, that desire to be together every minute of every day—that those feelings would be renewed on this Union Cruise.

Brad and I had both experienced what divorce does to you and your children. We wanted to nurture any wounds that our family may have suffered. We wanted to bulletproof them from the potential dangers of not focusing on your spouse. We didn't want to see any of our family members suffer as we had. We wanted to cover them in love. Love conquers all!

I did not give the case one thought during our Union Cruise. For the first time in what seemed like an eternity, I concentrated solely on my family—both immediate and newly extended—and the love we were sharing.

New Year's Eve, our wedding day, soon arrived, and it was just as I had pictured. The skies in St. Thomas were clear and blue. Our ship anchored out in the harbor, so we tendered in on a smaller boat. Brad carried my wedding dress as we were transported to the courthouse to pick up our marriage license and head to Blue Beard's Beach for the ceremony.

When we arrived, our family was waiting under the palm trees while the children played with the iguanas. Rose petals carpeted our footsteps and the harpist and violinist played dreamlike melodies as the waves lapped at the sandy beach.

Brad and I joined hands and made our grand entrance.

We had our family facing the ocean as we faced them. Each of our six children read a personally selected scripture about love, commitment, and faith. Brad's son sang "Beauty for Ashes," a song that held a truth in which Brad and I deeply believed. God had granted us a miracle. He had given us beauty for ashes, strength for fear, gladness for mourning, and peace for despair. He had abundantly blessed our lives with a renewed trust, loyalty, faithfulness, and love.

"I now pronounce you husband and wife. Brad, you may kiss your bride," the minister finally announced.

That kiss, that embrace, that moment in time is the reason I believe in love.

We popped bottles of pink champagne and ate carrot cake on the beach. Our family had the rest of the day to shop, after which we held the reception on board as we sailed away from St. Thomas.

As we disembarked the ship in Fort Lauderdale and shuttled most of our family off to the airport, a limo stood ready to take us home.

Across Alligator Alley we went—again. Suddenly, the long silent road reminded me of that dreadful drive that Peter and I had made two years earlier, pondering our arrest. Now only Peter remained caught in Strickland's web. And in just twenty-four hours, his trial would begin.

True to form, the *Collier Enquirer* took the New Year opportunity and the twenty-four hours prior to the jury selection process to regurgitate the entire Coliseum Golf corruption story—from their angle, of course—and to remind the suffering Collier County public that eight of the defendants had already entered plea deals, and only two had ended up in jail.

I called Peter to see how things were going in Sarasota. He and his family had gone up prior to the trial and rented a beach house in which to de-stress after each day in court. Adam Woerner also stayed in the beach house to save Peter some additional expenses and to give them plenty of time to prepare for the trial.

"Hi, Peter! How's the 'temperature' in Sarasota?" I asked, referring to the publicity leading up to the trial.

"Good. Today is the first day of jury selection. Adam opened by telling the court that I rejected a generous plea deal." Peter was baiting me.

"You *what?*" I shouted, shocked.

"Yep, I rejected that SOB's deal. He offered me pretty much what you had, and as I've told you before, I'm not pleading to anything!" In spite of it all, Peter had not softened in the least. I admired his resilience.

"You're nuts! But then again, we've always known that." I tried to lighten the conversation.

"Rose, I have done nothing wrong and the evidence in this case will prove that. I refuse to plead. Someone has to have some principles, and it's going to be me. You know that if I entered a plea agreement with Strickland that everyone would assume I'm guilty. I am not guilty and I will not be weakened!"

"You're a brave soul," I told him, meaning it with all my heart. "I'll pray that this trial ends before it begins and that all of the charges are dropped!"

"I need all the prayers I can get. Today when the judge addressed us, he made it clear that once the trial begins the previous plea offers are no longer an option. I guess he doesn't want another Andrew performance at the last minute. Strickland offered Gannon a deal too, but his attorney wouldn't reveal the details."

"It looks like you're right," I said. "Strickland's case is so weak that he's offering everyone a deal in order to save face."

"Today they interviewed a hundred and thirty-five potential jurors. I heard fifty-two survived the first-round cuts. I think that by tomorrow we'll have our jury, and you better be sitting right behind me in the courtroom." Although he laughed, I knew Peter was dead serious.

"I'll be there with bells on," I replied.

Heyward thought that the jury selection process could be completed by noon, and the trial can begin with opening statements on Wednesday. Pack your bags, Rose. It's show time!"

After I hung up, I gave my new husband the update. He had been standing close by offering support and was anxiously awaiting any news. "We'll pray hard tonight for dismissal and claim victory over this situation. I bet when we pick up the paper at the end of the driveway, we'll see one happy Durkee!" Brad hugged me, and we returned to our newlywed bliss.

I could hardly wait to sprint down to the end of the driveway to see the paper. The next morning I sprinted down the driveway to see the paper. As I pulled it out of the plastic wrapper I screamed with excitement.

"State to drop charges against developer Durkee; Gannon enters plea," the headline read.

"Answered prayers!" Brad and I danced at the end of the driveway. I was completely delivered from this case without ever having to take the stand for the state. God was merciful and was once again my Jehovah Jira, my provider.

"What does the article say?" a fact-hungry Brad said as he tried to read over my shoulder.

I began to read out loud. "It says that a judge's ruling weakened the case against Peter, and that the prosecutor agreed to drop the charges against him completely. It says that Strickland contacted Adam around 11:30 p.m. on Monday offering to drop the charges if Peter would pay $50,000 for investigative costs. Durkee is the only one of the ten defendants to have the charges completely dropped. Gannon will serve a year of house arrest and five years probation in exchange for his guilty plea. Strickland said that dropping the charges against Peter strengthened his case against Gannon."

Then I read him a quote by Peter, the one he'd been waiting to deliver: "I have consistently refused to accept any other resolution of this case because I did not commit any crime. From the beginning, I have maintained my innocence, truthfully cooperated with the investigation, and even passed a lie-detector test." Peter lamented that the other defendants didn't have the resources to fight the charges for as long as he did. "Unfortunately, other innocent defendants in this case did not have the financial resources or the physical and emotional stamina to withstand this prolonged prosecution." That was just like Peter. Not only did he feel the need to exonerate himself but also the rest of us who had been dragged through the muck.

Then there was a Strickland quote: "If I could only go after one, it needed to be Gannon." He also said that the plea talks Monday night did not go exactly as Adam Woerner implied, saying talks began earlier in the evening when Woerner contacted prosecutors and that the late-night call was one of several.

"Can you believe it?" I said to Brad, my eyes still wide with disbelief. "I mean, I believe that God is almighty and hears our prayers, and I never want to doubt that I have the power of prayer at my disposal. However, it is always a wonderful surprise to claim that victory when it happens as answered prayer, not necessarily legal prowess. We know why the charges were dropped!" I burst into tears as the realization hit me that the case was finally closed.

Days later, Strickland had a final quote: "It became clear to me this was going to be the most complicated thing I'd ever done. It turned out to be [just that]."

Strickland had more than thirty years experience in practice as both a defense attorney and a prosecutor, yet he was unable to make his case despite the backing of the state and the support of the local media.

In the end, it turned out that Martin Strickland was just one man who had no idea of the one who he was up against.

Afterword

On Faith

Now that you have read my story, I hope that you will think twice about trusting the justice system's promise of "innocent until proven guilty."

It is also my hope that you will have heard the still small voice of faith that carried me through this entire ordeal and that you will begin to experience a "faith-based life."

There were many life lessons, faith lessons that have changed my life from a mediocre existence on this planet to a life that is full to overflowing with joy, peace, and prosperity.

For those who want to read on into the faith lessons, I have outlined them in hopes that perhaps just one life can be changed through the trials that I experienced. If you learn to depend on God for hope and strength after reading my story, then all that I suffered through these life trials was for God's glory and honor. I ran the good race (see Hebrews 12: 1–3).

Lesson One: Faith and Belief

Believing in something that you cannot see or touch.

I did not understand the power of prayer or the power of the covenant promises in the Bible. God provided a quick study for me through my church, where I attended the nine-month school of ministries (before my arrest). Talk about an awesome God. He knew what trials were ahead for me and he prepared me, he suited me up for the spiritual battle of my life (I was victorious in him)! He is my Jehovah Jira, my provider.

Lesson Two: Forgiveness

Through this sad and terrible time in my life, God truly taught me a lesson on forgiveness. I had to forgive myself and my former spouse in my heart, and not just with my words for our failed marriage. Until I was completely willing to let this human failure go, I was not able to accept the full grace and forgiveness that God had for me. Resentment is like taking a poison pill and waiting for the other person to die—it will only kill you, your joy and your happiness. Forgive today and find freedom beyond anything you can imagine. He is my Jehovah Shalom, my Prince of Peace.

Lesson Three: Pride and Humility

I had a serious pride problem and this lesson was the longest and the hardest to release. My pride in my work became my value as a person. The more I did, the more praise I received. Eventually, I was addicted to praise. This has to be the greatest offense to God. It took me being arrested (humility), losing my marriage (humility), almost losing my daughter. It took me standing completely broken in front of God; sorrowful for having my life focus so far out of balance. Where was he in my life? Now, *he* was the center and from that, he returned beauty for ashes. When God is the center of your life, your life will be filled with all of the fruits of God's unwavering love and attention. He is my Jehovah Nissi, my victory banner.

Lesson Four: Loss and Restoration (Trust)

I lost everything that made me who I thought I was, leaving me with nothing except my faith and my family, my children. What really is important is God and family. Nothing shook that—the world took my business, my worldly reputation, and my worldly marriage and left me with more than I can describe.

He left me with two beautiful girls who love me unconditionally and a God who was excited to rebuild my life in his time and in his way. I had to trust God completely. I had no job, a tarnished reputation in the community and a broken heart. God promises to give you double for your trouble and did he ever! Trust him, trust his word. God does not have a hidden agenda. He has a grand plan for your life, and he wants to bless you and prosper you all the days of your life!

Lesson Five: Beauty for Ashes

I would have never believed after my marriage ended that love would ever cross my path again. I don't even think I wanted to think about it! Marriage is hard. Understanding another human being, the way the other person thinks, speaks, and feels love requires us to focus time and energy on the needs of the other person. It requires a state of selflessness. The only way that you can accomplish this monumental task is by having Jesus Christ as the centerpiece of your marriage, of your life, in your heart.

God did provide me with beauty for ashes. My love life was nothing more than a pile of ash. Hurt, pain, suffering, unforgiveness, all of these emotions needed to be purged from my heart. In obedience, if you will lay all of these feelings at the foot of the cross, God will replace it all with beauty! He did for me!

He used eHarmony to bring together two brokenhearted people who were crying out to God for healing. And in God's great plan, we have found the love of a lifetime. God has given us the ability to see each other though his eyes. God sees us redeemed—through the blood of his precious Son. He does not see the sinner. God loves us unconditionally and he wants us to love each other in the same way.

I have been so abundantly blessed through the trials of my life. I have gladly lost the grip that the world had on me and replaced it with the wonderful loving grip of grace that God had always planned for my life. God loves you; he wants to do a mighty work in your life.

The nearer you draw to God, the nearer he draws to you. Take up your shield; prepare to fight the good fight. We live in a time of spiritual warfare; you must know the truth of God's word to win the battle.

The "accuser" in your life will tell lies to you, about you. He wants to turn you as far from God and the truth as possible.

The voice of truth tells me a different story—step out into God's plan for your life—it is for his glory!

I pray God will bless your life to overflowing with the joys and wonders that he has stored up for you.

e|LIVE

---

listen|imagine|view|experience

AUDIO BOOK DOWNLOAD INCLUDED WITH THIS BOOK!

In your hands you hold a complete digital entertainment package. Besides purchasing the paper version of this book, this book includes a free download of the audio version of this book. Simply use the code listed below when visiting our website. Once downloaded to your computer, you can listen to the book through your computer's speakers, burn it to an audio CD or save the file to your portable music device (such as Apple's popular iPod) and listen on the go!

How to get your free audio book digital download:

1. Visit www.tatepublishing.com and click on the e|LIVE logo on the home page.
2. Enter the following coupon code: 64d0-46c0-58e4-3dcd-8166-1b84-2345-ec62
3. Download the audio book from your e|LIVE digital locker and begin enjoying your new digital entertainment package today!